Strategy, Risk and Personality in Coalition Politics

The Case of India

BRUCE BUENO DE MESQUITA

Assistant Professor of Political Science,
University of Rochester

Cambridge University Press

CAMBRIDGE

LONDON · NEW YORK · MELBOURNE

Published by the Syndics of the Cambridge University Press
The Pitt Building, Trumpington Street, Cambridge CB2 1RP
Bentley House, 200 Euston Road, London NW1 2DB
32 East 57th Street, New York, NY 10022, USA
296 Beaconsfield Parade, Middle Park, Melbourne 3206, Australia

© Cambridge University Press 1975

First published 1975

Composition by Linocomp Ltd., Marcham, Oxfordshire, England

Printed in the United States of America

Library of Congress cataloguing in publication data
Bueno de Mesquita, Bruce, 1946–
  Strategy, risk, and personality in coalition politics.
  Bibliography: p. 184.
  Includes index.
  1. Political parties – India. 2. Coalition governments – India. 3. Coalition governments. I. Title. JQ298.A1B83 329'.00954 75-3853
ISBN 0 521 20874 2

Contents

	page
Acknowledgements	v
Glossary of political party names	vi

1. Introduction — 1
2. A theory of coalition behavior — 3
   - *Conditions encouraging coalition formation* — 4
   - *The episodic condition* — 6
   - *The episodic coalition formation literature* — 11
   - *Strategic behavior in the iterative literature* — 18
   - *The redistributive condition* — 19
   - *The redistributive condition and coalition formation* — 22
   - *The redistributive condition and coalition maintenance* — 26
   - *Strategic behavior in coalitions* — 30
   - *Risk-taking and strategic preferences* — 36
   - *Need for achievement and risk-taking* — 41
   - *Organization and success* — 44
   - *Coalition termination* — 45
   - *Summary* — 47
3. The Indian context: 1967–1971 — 49
   - *Why India?* — 49
   - *The actors* — 50
     - The Bharatiya Jana Sangh — 50
     - The Swatantra Party — 53
     - The Praja Socialist Party — 54
     - The Samyukta Socialist Party — 55
     - The Communist Party of India — 57
     - The Communist Party of India (Marxist) — 58
     - Summary — 59
   - *The coalition environment* — 60
     - Income — 61
     - Number of candidates — 63
     - Other factors — 64
     - Summary — 66
   - *The states* — 66
     - The Punjab — 66
     - Uttar Pradesh — 68
     - Bihar — 72

Contents

West Bengal	76
Orissa	81
Madhya Pradesh	81
Kerala	85
Summary	87

4 Size and coalition politics — 89
The meaning of size — 89
Temporal framework — 91
The meaning of benefits — 92
Size and coalition formation — 93
Ideology and coalition formation — 100
Size and redistributive benefits — 103
Size and All-India parties — 107
Case history: Uttar Pradesh — 108
Summary — 110

5 Strategic behavior and political influence — 112
Elite perceptions — 112
The meaning of strategic preferences — 116
Strategy and coalition benefits — 119
Strategy and electoral success — 120
Case history: the Jana Sangh — 124
Summary — 128

6 Need for achievement, risk and success — 129
Measuring need for achievement — 129
Need for achievement and strategic preferences — 133
Need for achievement and redistributive benefits — 137
Organization, motivation, strategy, and political success — 140
Case history: Bihar — 148
Summary — 150

7 Conclusions — 151
Coalition politics — 151
Implications for India — 153
Political coalitions and political development — 155

Appendix I: Election results — 157
Appendix II: Research design — 161
    The interviews — 162
Appendix III: The questionnaire — 164
Notes — 167
Bibliography — 184
Index — 193

Acknowledgements

This research would not have been possible without the generous support of the American Institute of Indian Studies. They helped make my stay in India during 1969 and 1970 both pleasant and rewarding. Additional financial assistance was given to me by the University of Michigan, Michigan State University, and the University of Rochester.

There are many individuals who have played an important role in the preparation of this volume. While I cannot possibly thank all of them by name, I would like to express my special gratitude at least to some of them.

Three individuals were instrumental in shaping my interest in coalition theory, risk-taking, and Indian politics. They are Donald Stokes, A. F. K. Organski, and Richard Park. I owe each of them a much greater intellectual debt than I can ever repay.

While in India, I benefited greatly from my association with P. Mehendiratta, Marcus Franda, and Rajni Kothari. In the United States I benefited from the critical eye of Alan Lamborn, Subrata Mitra, and Kenneth Shepsle.

My wife and parents provided me with continuous encouragement through many hard times. My wife and daughter also tolerated the eccentricities of a husband and father who must have seemed to be running endlessly to a computer console.

Finally, I wish to thank the many Indian politicians who spent hours answering my peculiar questions. They were kind beyond my greatest expectations. I hope none of them are offended by anything contained in this volume. If any of them benefit from this book then I will certainly feel as if I have succeeded.

Rochester
May, 1975

Glossary of political party names

AD (M): Akali Dal (Master) This Punjabi party was formed when dissident members of the Akali Dal, led by Master Tara Singh, withdrew their support from the parent Akali Dal organization. By 1969 it had virtually ceased to exist.

AD (S): Akali Dal (Sant) This predominantly Sikh party, located in the Punjab, continues to be one of the major political forces in that state. Its primary concern is to promote Sikh culture and to insure adequate political representation for that religious group.

JS: Bharatiya Jana Sangh The Jana Sangh is one of the major All-India parties. Based on a commitment to Hindu culture and Hindi as India's national language, it has secured a great deal of support in northern India. In recent years it has been attempting to spread its influence to southern India. Although it suffered a serious setback in 1971, it continues to be a major political force in several states.

BKD: Bharatiya Kranti Dal The BKD emerged after the 1967 general election in response to dissatisfaction among many Congressmen with the leadership of their party. Under the guidance of Chaudhuri Charan Singh it achieved remarkable success in Uttar Pradesh, while securing a foothold in Madhya Pradesh and Bihar.

BC: Bangla Congress This West Bengali party was formed by dissident members of the Congress Party. It enjoyed a period of great strength and influence, particularly between 1967 and 1970, when its leader, Ajoy Mukherjee, was chief minister of West Bengal. In the 1971 election it lost almost all of its support.

CPI: Communist Party of India The CPI is one of the major All-India parties. Its support is widespread, though it has enjoyed its greatest triumphs in West Bengal and Kerala. The party suffered a split in the early 1960s in response to differences of strategy and differences in attitudes toward the Soviet Union and the People's Republic of China. The CPI, after its division, maintained the support of the more moderate, and more Soviet-oriented of India's communists.

CPI (M): Communist Party of India (Marxist) When the CPI split, the more revolutionary, Chinese-oriented of its members joined the CPI (M). This party has managed to secure an extremely large following in West Bengal, where its base of support seems to be in a state of flux. It has enjoyed a period of great success in Kerala as well. In that state, however, its influence seems to be declining, especially since late 1969, when the CPI (M)-led ministry in Kerala suffered a series of setbacks.

Glossary of political party names

The CPI (M) registered remarkable gains during the 1971 general election.

Congress The Congress Party has controlled the national government of India since independence. In October of 1969 it was split into two factions. One, led by Indira Gandhi, became known as the new Congress, or the Congress (R). The Nijilingappa-led Congress became known as the syndicate, or the Congress (O). The former group is generally considered to be the more progressive, while the latter group is thought of as being composed of the old-guard, conservative members of the Congress. In 1971, the Congress (R) enjoyed an unprecedented electoral success, while the Congress (O) suffered very serious setbacks in virtually every state.

FB: Forward Bloc Although this party maintains an organization in several states, it has really only succeeded in securing a sizable quantity of support in West Bengal. It participated in the coalition governments in that state between 1967 and 1970. As with the other members of those coalitions, it is a progressive, socialist party.

FB (M): Forward Bloc (Marxist) This party is composed of a small group of dissident members of the Forward Bloc in West Bengal.

GL: Gorkha League The Gorkha League is a very small, but stable, political party in West Bengal. Although they win very few seats, they continue to command control of the few constituencies where there are large numbers of Gorkhas. They were members of the Bengali coalition governments.

HMS: Hindu Maha Sabha The Maha Sabha is a very conservative, religiously oriented Hindu party. Until Gandhi's assassination it was the major voice of Hindu conservatism in India. After the formation of the Jana Sangh it lost much of its appeal and support to that party.

HJ: Hul Jharkhand This extremely small Bihari party was composed of dissident members of the Jharkhand. It played a major role in toppling one of the coalition governments that was formed in Bihar. After 1970 it virtually ceased to exist.

INDF: Indian National Democratic Front The INDF was composed of a group of defectors, led by Ashutosh Ghosh, who withdrew their support from the Congress-supported coalition in West Bengal in 1968. This group was unable to form a government and so President's Rule was instituted. The INDF no longer exists.

ISP: Indian Socialist Party The ISP was formed when a group of legislators from the Samyukta Socialist Party refused to follow a directive from the SSP's national office. This Kerala-based party was unable to maintain its legislative strength when forced to contest in the elections. By 1971 it had all but disappeared.

JC: Jan Congress Actually, there were two Jan Congress parties. One,

Glossary of political party names

    located in Madhya Pradesh, was made up of a group of defectors from the Congress Party. It ceased to exist shortly after its formation in 1967. The other, based in Orissa, was a partner in the Swatantra-led coalition government in that state. Although it secured a large number of seats in 1967, it failed to develop a strong base of support. After the 1971 election it lost virtually all of its representation in the state legislative assembly.

JKD: Jana Kranti Dal   This Bihari party existed for only a short while. During that period, however, it provided Bihar with a chief minister, and with the margin of strength to prevent the Congress from returning to power. Many of its members later joined the BKD.

JP: Janata Party   There were actually two Janata Parties in India between 1967 and 1971. One, formed in the Punjab, was composed of defectors from the Akali Dal (Sant)-led coalition government. They formed their own coalition which was soon overthrown. That party no longer exists. The other Janata Party was formed in Bihar by the Raja of Ramgarh. It frequently appeared and disappeared as the Raja shifted political allegiance. With the Raja's death in 1970 the party has lost much of its former influence and strength.

Jharkhand   The Jharkhand Party was a very small Bihari party which participated in several of that state's coalition governments. Although very small to begin with, it was torn by factionalism and eventually split in two. It appears that the Jharkhand Party no longer exists.

KMP: Kisaan Mazdoor Party   This is another very small party. Although at one time it was an important voice of farm laborers, it is now virtually non-existent.

LCD: Loktantric Congress Dal   Many defectors in Bihar banded together after 1967 to form this party. It no longer exists.

LSD: Lok Sevak Dal   The Rajmata of Gwalior formed this party in Madhya Pradesh while a member of that state's coalition government. It was later disbanded when she joined the Jana Sangh.

ML: Muslim League   The Muslim League was once the major voice of Muslims in India. After partition it lost most of its strength. In Kerala, however, it has continued to be a fairly influential, though small, political party. It enjoyed membership in the Kerala government throughout the late 1960s and early 1970s.

PSP: Praja Socialist Party   The PSP was one of India's major parties. The PSP merged with portions of the Samyukta Socialist Party in 1971 forming the Socialist Party.

RPI: Republican Party of India   The late Dr Ambedkar founded this party to be the voice of the Harijans and other downtrodden people. Although it is a small party, it enjoys support in several states and continues to represent the poorer, oppressed classes of Indian society.

Glossary of political party names

RSPI: Revolutionary Socialist Party of India   The RSPI is a Marxist party with support in both Bihar and West Bengal.

RCPI: Revolutionary Communist Party of India   This is a small, revolutionary party composed of dissidents from West Bengal's other Communist parties.

SSP: Samyukta Socialist Party   The SSP is one of the major All-India parties. It was formed in 1964 by a group of dissident members of the PSP. While it continues to enjoy support in most states, it has suffered serious losses in recent elections. The SSP and the PSP have been seriously negotiating toward a merger for quite some time, but especially after the 1971 general election.

SUC: Socialist Unity Conference   The SUC is a small, Marxist, West Bengali party. It participated in both coalition governments in Bengal between 1967 and 1970.

Swatantra Party   Swatantra is one of the major All-India parties. Formed in 1959, it captured much of the conservative vote in 1967. In 1971, however, Swatantra suffered a serious setback in the general election. Nevertheless, it continues to be a very important political force in India.

*In memory of my
grandparents*

1. Introduction

The political process is, to a large extent, the process of making, maintaining, and breaking coalitions. Not surprisingly, therefore, coalitions have attracted considerable attention among students of politics, although most research on coalition behavior is focused on coalition formation, while only scant attention is given to coalition maintenance and coalition termination. I believe this is unfortunate, because the interdependence of these three aspects of coalition behavior makes a complete explanation of any one aspect impossible without reference to the other two. One objective of this study is to contribute to the construction of a complete theory of coalition behavior.

The second, equally important, objective is to present a systematic, rigorous test of the theory using a 'real world' political setting. By doing so, it is possible to evaluate the inadequacies of the theory, while also clarifying the pattern of coalition behavior in an important political system.

Too often these two objectives form the core of competing rather than concurrent approaches to the study of politics. This is unfortunate since neither empiricism nor theory can stand alone. Empiricism, without a guiding theory, offers no means of distinguishing true patterns from spurious relationships. As a result, empirical studies cannot explain behavior, although they may accurately describe and even predict political phenomena. Conversely, a theory without the support of rigorous empirical evidence may constitute an elegant structure, but it tells us nothing about the political behavior of real people. Only by applying rigorously derived theories to rigorously derived data can we begin to judge and understand the patterns of political behavior.

The coalition theory developed here takes as its point of departure the assumption that a participant's behavior in one coalition has a direct bearing on that participant's future influence and future access to new coalitions. As a consequence of this assumption, cooperation with one's coalition partners is not in the best interest of coalition participants who hope to increase their future influence. On the other hand, extreme competitiveness is not in their long-term interest either, although it is the best strategy for coalition members interested in short-term gains. The ideal strategy for those who seek long-term increases in their influence is shown to be a mixture of competition and cooperation.

From the assumptions of the theory it is not only possible to specify the ideal strategies actors should follow to achieve long-term or short-term increases in their political influence, but also to specify why some actors might rationally deviate from the apparently ideal strategy. This is accomplished by linking, in a rational choice model, the research on need for

Introduction

achievement and risk-taking preferences. By doing so, the theory explains both the consequences of particular strategies and the strategic inclinations of individual decision-makers.

In addition to exploring a new approach to coalition politics, this book suggests new interpretations of political behavior in the specific empirical setting that is investigated. That setting is the Indian political party system between 1967 and 1971 – a period of widespread and extremely diverse coalition politics. Because the theory on which this study is based is intended as a general explanation of coalition behavior, I have deviated from the focus of many earlier studies of Indian party politics. While previous studies of coalition politics in India examined either several parties in one state, or one party in several states, this study explores the coalition behavior of six All-India parties in seven states. To a lesser degree, it also investigates the role of regional parties and splinter groups in several coalitions that existed between 1967 and 1971. An exploration of so large a data base makes it possible to distinguish between general patterns of coalition politics and the idiosyncracies of politics in particular locales, or among particular parties and leaders.

More significantly, the theory suggests an explanation of the outcome of several elections in India without exploring the very complex patterns of caste, regional, and linguistic influences on voter preferences. Instead, the exchange of legislative seats is accounted for with considerable precision from knowledge of the strategic preferences of decision-makers, the organizational capabilities of their parties, and differences in the level of need for achievement possessed by the leaders of each party. That is, a very significant proportion of the variance in the success parties have had in Indian elections, at least since 1967, is explained by differences in the political 'styles' of their leaders. This is true even when virtually nothing is known about the characteristics of the constituencies they contest.

This book also attempts to reconcile the apparent inconsistencies that exist between the ideological declarations of such disparate parties as the Jana Sangh and the Communist Party of India with their joint membership in coalition governments. In doing so, evidence is offered to suggest that coalition benefits such as access to the machinery of government, patronage, and exposure in the media were sufficiently appealing to help these parties put aside their ideological differences. In fact, it will be shown that ideology played only a minor role even in the decision of the 'opposition' parties to exclude the Congress Party from their coalitions.

Finally, by linking a general theory of coalition behavior to Indian politics I hope to encourage additional research that applies systematic theories and methods to the study of Indian politics, while also encouraging further explorations of the implications of the specific theory presented here.

2. A theory of coalition behavior

Under what circumstances do political parties join coalitions? Why are coalitions with some parties preferred to coalitions with other parties? What benefits can a political party derive from membership in a coalition?

The answers to these questions are far from clear. They vary from party to party and from time to time, but they do not vary solely in response to the idiosyncracies of each particular political party, or each particular political situation. Instead, systematic relationships among the goals, the strategies, the skills, and the personalities of the leaders of political parties influence their response to these questions. The identification and exploration of those relationships is the principal objective pursued in this chapter.

The search for theoretically meaningful relationships requires that certain restrictive assumptions be made. One such assumption is that all political parties want to maximize their long-term influence over the decision-making process.[1] This is not to say that there are not other goals which political party leaders might prefer, but even if they prefer other goals, political party leaders act as if this is their preferred goal. There are several reasons for them to act thus. No political party can hope to accomplish its goals unless it has sufficient influence over the decision-making process to manipulate the outcome of conflictual issues, especially with respect to the identification of governmental priorities and the allocation of resources. No political party can hope to exert a continuous impact on the decision-making process if it expends all of its influence in the short-term pursuit of some objective. Consequently, the preservation of a political party's long-term ability to exert influence is a prerequisite for the continued pursuit of other goals. The maximization of its influence in the long run is instrumental in increasing the probability that its pursuits end successfully. Thus, this goal must be pursued if parties are to have any hope of fulfilling their other political objectives.[2] Before undertaking an examination of the relevant theoretical, empirical, and experimental research which has already been done, it is necessary to define some basic terms.

The most essential concept used in this study is the notion of a coalition, which I define as a group of individuals (or group of groups) who share at least one goal and who agree to pool at least some of their resources in pursuit of that shared goal.[3] If the members of a coalition pool a sufficient quantity of resources to insure the attainment of their shared objective, then they belong to a winning coalition. If they are unable to achieve their shared goal, then they belong to a losing coalition.[4] A losing coalition can exist even if there is no winner, and of course, a winning coalition can exist even if there is no loser. Both winners and losers must exist only when the shared goal involves the distribution of private goods.[5] If the shared

A theory of coalition behavior

goal only involves the provision of collective goods, then winners and losers need not both exist.[6]

The provision of collective goods comprises an important set of goals sought by political coalitions. It is not a concern of the theory presented here, however, except to the extent that private goods are distributed in such coalitions as side payments stemming from the pursuit of the shared objective.[7] The theory is concerned with coalition behavior in competitive situations where the existence of a winner necessitates the existence of a loser.

Conditions encouraging coalition formation

In competitive situations, such as political contests, groups vie for control of scarce resources. In all such situations there are rules which specify, at the absolute minimum, the conditions which a contestant must satisfy in order to control those resources.[8] No participant can win without satisfying the demands established by the rules. In parliamentary democracies, for example, the rules often stipulate that a group must control a majority of seats in parliament before it can form a government. Whatever the specific rule may be in a particular contest, the important point is that competitive systems always define winning in terms of control of some specified resource, such as a particular number of supporters, a particular set of supporters, a particular skill, and so on.

When a single actor in the political arena satisfies the conditions required of a winner, then it has no incentive to join a coalition. That is, when an actor's relevant resource pool, or size, is large enough to give it monopoly control over decision-making, I assume that it does not share that control with anyone else.[9] If no solitary group is large enough to satisfy the requirements for winning, then a coalition is likely to form. When a coalition satisfying the rules for winning forms, the members control the allocation of the scarce resources. When a group of political actors form a winning coalition, all political groups outside their coalition can be deprived of any influence over the allocation or utilization of the scarce resources. Consequently, political contestants are better off in a winning coalition, even though they are required to share control over the benefits they secure, than in a losing coalition in which they gain nothing and in which they may be deprived of valued resources. Of course, actors are assumed to be better off outside a coalition if their individual size is sufficient to render them in control of the resources they desire.

If the conditions in a political system require that a coalition form, then each participant in that system must consider its utility in not joining any coalition, or joining one coalition in preference to another. In order for coalition members to maximize the probability that their preferences will

A theory of coalition behavior

be accomplished, the political actors must determine what the optimal strategic choices are.

Each political participant must know the extent to which it is willing to sacrifice its ideological or programmatic objectives when it is part of a government in exchange for increased success in acquiring the resources that bring it closer to monopoly control over future governments. Conversely, each participant must know the extent to which it will sacrifice its future size for the gratification that follows from immediate fulfillment of a specific policy objective. Without this knowledge, political actors cannot estimate the costs involved in choosing among options. This information alone is not sufficient to select a course of action.

Political contestants must estimate the impact each of their options would have on the probability that their goals will be fulfilled. They must be able to estimate the advantages and the disadvantages of each of their coalition options, including the merits of not joining any coalition at all. These estimates must not be based solely on the degree to which potential allies' goals are the same as one's own. If this were done, other variables which are crucial in selecting coalition partners would be ignored. The political skill and resources of one's potential partners is, for instance, of paramount importance in choosing among alternatives. All other things being equal, the probability of succeeding is directly related to the skills which can be brought to bear in pursuing particular goals. If the most skillful actors have opposing preferences, however, then selecting skillful partners may prove a hindrance rather than an aid in fulfilling one's own goals. Conversely, incompetent partners cannot be of much use even if they are willing to commit themselves to one's own goals. In fact, if they are sufficiently incompetent, or if skillful partners are sufficiently antagonistic to one's own preferences, then it may be more reasonable to join no coalition than to join a coalition whose net costs are greater than the costs of losing alone. In fact, I assume that the worst any political actor can ever be expected to do is to suffer the losses it would experience if it were in a coalition by itself.[10]

Coalitions that combine sufficient skills and resources to win, with complete agreement on priorities and principles, are rare, if not completely nonexistent. Consequently, coalition theories focus on rational decision-making in the face of incompatibilities among the participants. The resolution of these incompatibilities must be confronted during three stages of coalition politics: the coalition formation stage; the maintenance stage; and the termination stage. Each stage requires an assessment of the strategies to be employed, the benefits that can be acquired, and the liabilities attached to coalitions.

The questions one is likely to investigate during these stages are related to the effects that particular actions have on the characteristics or attributes

A theory of coalition behavior

of coalitions. In studying coalition formation, for example, one is likely to inquire as to the size of a coalition, the differences in the resources of its members, the characteristics of the actors excluded from the coalition, and so on. Most of the coalition literature is concerned with coalitions as dependent variables, and especially in terms of coalition formation.[11]

When one studies coalitions as on-going entities during the coalition maintenance stage, coalitions are treated as independent variables. They, along with many other variables, help account for such things as changes in the relative size of political parties, and in assessing shifts in attitudes and perceptions among political parties.

Coalitions in the maintenance stage also serve as intervening variables. For example, one might investigate the impact a party's leaders' general outlook has on the party's prospects for future growth, given that the party belongs to a winning coalition. If it is a very competitive party and it is in a winning coalition, is it likely to increase its size more rapidly than a very cooperative party in the same coalition or than a very competitive party in a losing coalition?

When coalitions are viewed as independent or intervening variables, they become entities which can contribute to an explanation of a wide variety of political processes. This aspect of coalitions cannot be understood until we understand the conditions which prompt political parties and other participants in the political arena to join coalitions in the first place. As a result, it is necessary to examine the literature on coalition formation for any insights it may suggest about coalition maintenance.

The episodic condition

In broad terms, the behavior of decision-makers is constrained by the resources at their disposal, the goals they pursue, and the political environment in which they function. When decision-makers cannot achieve their goals without forming a coalition, they naturally attempt to identify and join the coalition that is best for them. Within this context, most theories of coalition formation focus on the identification of each actor's best coalition: that coalition which maximizes their share of the payoffs and thereby increases the probability of achieving their goals.[12]

Which particular coalition, or set of coalitions, can maximize an actor's payoffs depends upon the particular environmental constraints that exist in the system and the particular distribution of resources that exists among the actors. Variations in these two conditions provide the basis for different coalition formation theories. Some theories, for example, are concerned with coalition formation in political environments that approximate the competitiveness of a zero-sum game.[13] Others focus on whether the total payoff available to any winning coalition is equal to the total payoff available to any other winning coalition, or whether they vary as a function of which actors are excluded from the winning coalition.[14] Still others are concerned with the effects that ideological differences have on the preferences actors express for different coalition options.[15]

One set of assumptions found in virtually all theories of coalition formation is that members of winning coalitions cooperate with each other in pursuit of whatever payoffs can be won, and compete against the losers to prevent them from securing any benefits or from withholding any losses.[16] All political actors are assumed to compete for membership in their best winning coalition during the coalition formation stage, but during the coalition maintenance stage, the members of the winning coalition are assumed to cooperate with each other in pursuit of their shared objective.

A consequence of these shared assumptions is that coalitions are viewed as short-term agreements intended to facilitate the fulfillment of some limited objective. Of course, the members of a coalition have additional goals with which their coalition is not concerned, and which are frequently the source of serious incompatibilities among partners in a winning coalition and provide the basis for the instability manifested by most coalitions. The presence of incompatible goals threatens the existence of any coalition and in many cases, proves to be the undoing of winning coalitions, sometimes prompting their termination even before the shared goal is accomplished.[17] Since all political groups necessarily have at least some incompatibilities, it is necessary for coalition theorists to introduce assumptions which make winning coalitions a viable means of fulfilling shared goals.[18] This viability is established by assuming that coalition partners set aside, albeit temporarily, the quest for their unshared goals.

> 'The stability of a coalition requires *tacit neutrality* of the coalition on matters that go beyond the immediate prerogatives. This makes the pursuit of power itself, i.e., control over future decisions, an ideal basis for coalition formation since it is an instrument for the achievement of widely ranging and even incompatible goals. Two members may realize their mutual goal antagonisms but such decisions lie in the future and the present alliance may make both better able to achieve a wide range of goals not all of which will be incompatible.'[19]

Implicit in the assumption of tacit neutrality is the condition that the pursuit of the shared objectives cannot, in the long run, detract from any coalition member's pursuit of its other, unshared, objectives. That is, the coalition's effects are restricted to the short-term distribution of benefits to all the winners, usually at the expense of the losers. In subsequent discussions this condition is called the *episodic condition*.

A theory of coalition behavior

The episodic condition is useful conceptually because it provides a basis for coalition formation among groups with at least partially incompatible goals. Since the very existence of more than one political group implies the presence of some incompatible goals, it is imperative that each theory of coalition formation has a mechanism – such as the episodic condition – that provides a basis for coalition formation in the face of incompatibilities.[20] Unfortunately, the utility of the episodic condition is limited to political situations in which short-term victories cannot harm any winner's long-term prospects for success.[21] This means that the episodic condition can be satisfied only when the distribution of a winning coalition's benefits cannot alter the relative probabilities among coalition partners that their unshared goals will be accomplished. If the relative probabilities of future success were altered in a winning coalition, then the future prospects of some members of the winning coalition would be enhanced at the expense of their putative partners, at least with respect to their incompatible goals, and that would violate the episodic condition.

In order to avoid this, at least one of two constraints must be imposed on the distribution of payoffs in winning coalitions. Either the benefits derived from victory must be ephemeral and incapable of application to future political contests, or else the payoffs must be distributed among the winners in exact proportion to their relative contribution to the resource pool which makes their coalition a winning coalition.

The first constraint allows some winners to get a disproportionately large share of the coalition's benefits provided those benefits do not become an integral part of the resource base, or size, of those winners. If the coalition's benefits are capable of conversion into the currency of influence in the political system, then the episodic condition would not allow them to be distributed disproportionately. That is, disproportionalities in the relative importance that the coalition's benefits hold for different winners can have no cumulative impact on the relative amount of influence the actors have in subsequent coalition formation situations.

The second constraint prevents potential losers from using side payments to purchase the support of pivotal actors, and thereby convert their status from losing to winning. If side payments were permitted (and if the first constraint did not obtain), the pivotal actor might enjoy a disproportionately large benefit in the winning coalition. Thus, the pivotal actor's benefits would be derived from two sources. First, it would receive its expected share of the coalition's benefits. Second, it would receive some portion of any remaining benefits that would otherwise go to its partner. The pivotal actor receives this portion as a side payment, or as an inducement to accept membership in a coalition in which its fair share is less than its fair share in another coalition. The inducement is offered, of course, because its partner prefers little or no payoff in the winning coalition to the loss it would suffer if it were in a losing coalition (including a coalition by itself). The first source of benefits for the pivotal actor appears to be consistent with the episodic condition, but the second source means that the system's resources are redistributed so as to give the pivotal actor a disproportionately large advantage over its partner in future coalition formation situations.[22] This violates the episodic condition.

The undesirability of the second constraint stems from the observation that the elimination of side payments is tantamount to removing politics from politics. That is, in the absence of side payments, there is little need for bargaining among potential members of a winning coalition since none of the actors are expected to accept less than their fair share of a coalition's benefits. Instead, each actor computes its percentage contribution to the strength of each coalition, and then determines the amount that each potential winning coalition will win. Once these computations are made, each actor knows what its just payoff is in each winning coalition. Since it cannot use any inducements to persuade other actors to form its most preferred coalition, each actor must hope that enough other actors will share its preference for the particular winning combination it favors. If they do, then the particular coalition forms and the benefits are distributed in accordance with the parity norm. The parity norm, of course, dictates that each actor receives a percentage of the total payoff equal to its percentage contribution to the resource pool of the winning coalition.[23] It is the most frequently observed sociological definition of a fair share.

Under the burden of these two constraints, the episodic condition eliminates the possibility that coalition participants use their short-term victories as a springboard to future successes. Instead, it restricts the motives of coalition participants to short-term considerations, such as the fulfillment of their shared objectives. Within the confines of the episodic condition, especially as it relates to tacit neutrality, participants in coalitions can not pursue power or any other benefits that might increase their control over future decisions. If they did, then some members of a winning coalition might move closer to monopoly control over future decisions than their partners do. This would, of course, violate the restriction that no member of a winning coalition can improve its long-term prospects at the expense of any other member of the winning coalition. That power cannot be pursued under the limitations of the episodic condition is easily demonstrated.

If the benefits derived from a winning coalition are distributed so as to preserve the initial relative distribution of resources among the winners, then the largest member of the coalition must get the largest share of the benefits. Of course, the ratio of this actor's size to that of each of its partners remains constant when such a distribution rule is applied (in accordance with the second constraint discussed above), but its absolute

A theory of coalition behavior

size moves closer to the system's definition of the size required to win. In fact, if the largest actor in the winning coalition was sufficiently close to that threshold at the outset, its proportionate share of the coalition's benefits could prove enough to guarantee it future control over the decision-making process. Whether it achieves such control or not, the apparently equitable distribution of the coalition's benefits places it closer to monopoly control than it was before. This is true even though the ratio of its size to the size of each of its partners remains constant. Thus, the future prospects of the largest member of a winning coalition are improved more than the future prospects of any of its partners provided that the parity norm is applied. Consequently, if the benefits derived from membership in a winning coalition can be converted into an integral part of the resource-base of the winners, then even the parity norm cannot assure all the winners that their future prospects are not being harmed by their present coalition. That is, the episodic condition can be violated even when the parity norm is observed, provided the participants are permitted to pursue power or other benefits that can yield control over future decisions.

If the parity norm is relaxed, then the actor who is most successful at acquiring a disproportionately large share of the winning coalition's benefits must necessarily do so at the expense of one or more of its partners (provided the first constraint is not imposed). This follows from the fact that the distribution of the payoff pie must be like a zero-sum game. If one participant gets a disproportionately large slice of the benefits, then some other participant or participants must receive a disproportionately small slice. Of course, if the benefits include the reallocation of power, or some other resource that redistributes the relative ability of each actor to influence future decisions, then those getting a disproportionately large slice of the pie benefit at the expense of their allies, thereby violating the episodic condition.

So long as the benefits derived from a coalition can contribute to an actor's prospects of controlling future decisions, one can expect that the distribution of benefits will, as noted above, manifest the characteristics of a zero-sum game.[24] Zero-sum games are at least partially, if not wholly, competitive. The episodic condition ignores this source of competition within coalition politics. Instead, it assumes that in winning coalitions where power can be redistributed, actors elect to remain neutral with respect to their unshared goals, even though that neutrality dictates that the distribution of benefits will aid some participants at the expense of others. This means that the episodic condition requires some winners to accept an erosion of their long-term influence in the interest of fulfilling the shared objective around which the coalition was formed. This is equivalent to requiring some winners to suboptimize their long-term prospects for fulfilling all their goals in exchange for the short-term gratification of fulfilling a smaller set of goals. Such a condition cannot be accepted if the postulated goal of this study is to be taken seriously. It seems more reasonable to eliminate the episodic condition and its attendant assumption that coalition partners necessarily cooperate with each other, and replace it with a condition that recognizes the importance of intra-coalition competition. Later in this chapter just such a condition is presented and its implications for short-term-oriented and long-term-oriented behavior are discussed. At that time it will become apparent that this new condition – the *redistributive condition* – does not differ substantially from the episodic condition so long as the focus is on the formation of coalitions, but that it differs very substantially with respect to the expected course of behavior during the coalition maintenance and the termination stages. One such difference, of course, is that the redistributive condition permits competitive behavior among coalition partners during the maintenance stage, while the episodic condition does not. Another important difference which stems from the redistributive condition is its assumption that coalition politics is an iterative process in which each coalition follows from, and is somewhat affected by, prior coalitions. The episodic condition, of course, focuses on the imperatives of the moment and not on future iterations of coalition politics. Consequently, the episodic condition assumes that each coalition in a series of iterations is an independent episode, unaffected by prior behavior or prior outcomes.

In order to see the effects these different assumptions have on the construction of theories of coalition behavior, let us examine the most salient episodic literature. When that task is completed it will be possible to develop a theory of coalition behavior under the constraints of the redistributive condition.

The episodic coalition formation literature

The most frequently studied questions in the coalition literature are concerned with explaining how actors select their coalition partners. Some of these studies focus on the distribution of payoffs as the key element while others are more concerned with the effects of social interaction on the inclinations of potential coalition members. Although the boundaries between these approaches are fuzzy, they provide a useful conceptual tool in organizing the coalition literature. Let us begin, therefore, with the literature that focuses on the distribution of payoffs, and then turn to those studies that are primarily concerned with social interaction under the constraints of the episodic condition.

There are two prevalent theoretical frameworks that focus on the distribution of payoffs as the determinant of coalition formation behavior: the minimum resource approach and the pivotal power approach.

A theory of coalition behavior

Minimum resource theorists, such as Riker and Gamson, hypothesize that participants in coalition situations prefer to form coalitions that are just large enough to win and no larger. Although both Riker and Gamson reach this conclusion, they do so by concentrating on different assumptions.

Riker's theory assumes that decisions concerning coalition formation are made within a zero-sum environment. It will be recalled that the zero-sum assumption stipulates that the net value of the winners' payoffs and the losers' losses is zero. It follows from this that the maximum possible value of a winning coalition that includes all the actors is equal to the null set composed of all the excluded actors. This value is, of course, zero. Similarly, if a winning coalition forms that includes all actors in the system except for one, then the maximum possible payoff that can be secured by the winning coalition is equal to the value of the lone loser. It follows from this that the size of a winning coalition's benefits increases as the value of the losers increases. The closer a winning coalition comes to having the minimal value required to win in accordance with the system's rules, the greater the value of the resources held by the losers and, therefore, the greater the possible benefit to the winners. That is, minimal winning coalitions can win more benefits than any other type of coalition.

While the benefits won by a winning coalition are maximized when it is a minimal winning coalition, it does not necessarily follow that each member of that coalition does better than it would in any other possible winning combination. Since rational behavior in this case requires that the individual participants attempt to maximize their benefits, rather than the benefits secured by the coalition as a whole, it is necessary to show that this can be done most readily in a minimal winning coalition. Riker accomplishes this task by permitting the actors to bargain with each other over the distribution of the total payoff. That is, he permits the total payoff to vary from winning coalition to winning coalition, and allows the use of side payments to manipulate the coalition preferences of some actors.[25] As Riker has demonstrated in his development of the strategic principle, so long as side payments are permitted, all the members of a minimal winning coalition can be more satisfied in that alliance than in any other potential winning coalition. Thus, given a zero-sum situation in which side payments are permitted, the most likely outcome is the formation of a minimal winning coalition. Riker has termed this observation the size principle.[26]

Gamson's model of coalition formation also leads him to hypothesize that the smallest winning coalition is most likely to form. His derivation of this hypothesis follows from the assumption that all potential winning coalitions in a given situation can win the same payoffs, and from the sociological observation that the distribution of payoffs among the members of the winning coalition is prescribed by the parity norm.[27] It will be recalled that the parity norm stipulates that each actor receives a share of the payoff that is equal to its contribution to the total resource pool of the coalition. Since Gamson's system keeps the value of the total payoff constant across coalitions, it follows that each actor can maximize its payoff only by maximizing the share it contributes to the total resources of the winning coalition. Of course, each member's share of resources is maximized in minimal winning coalitions.[28] Thus, while Riker reached this conclusion by permitting the payoffs available to winning coalitions to vary and by allowing side payments, Gamson's model reaches essentially the same conclusion by keeping the available payoff constant and by using the parity norm as the decision-rule governing the distribution of payoffs.[29]

Both Riker and Gamson have introduced interesting modifications to their basic theories. Riker hypothesizes that when coalitions are formed under conditions of imperfect information, the most likely winning coalition is the one perceived by the actors to be the smallest possible winning coalition. The more imperfect the information available to the actors, the larger the size of the subjectively minimal winning coalition.

Gamson modified his theory to take into account the role played by ideology in coalition formation, and introduced the notion of nonutilitarian preferences.[30] This notion suggests that when actors can select partners from among equally valuable potential allies, they prefer those actors whose ideology is most similar to their own. The evidence gathered by Gamson and others, however, indicates that nonutilitarian (or ideological) preferences enter the decision-making process under very limited circumstances. Several studies indicate, for example, that actors prefer to form coalitions that involve the fewest bargaining steps (that is, coalitions with two members are preferred to coalitions with three members which are preferred to coalitions with n members), rather than coalitions that include participants with the greatest ideological similarity.[31]

As we have just seen, minimum resource theorists focus their attention on the effect that the initial distribution of power has on coalition formation. Pivotal power theorists, on the other hand, are concerned primarily with differences in the ability of individual actors to convert losing coalitions into winning coalitions.[32] Although these two approaches are closely related, there are circumstances under which they lead to different predictions concerning coalition formation.

Let us posit a system with three actors, named A, B, and C. The distribution of resources among these actors satisfies the following two conditions: $A>B>C$, $A<B+C$. If a majority of the system's resources are required to form a winning coalition, then $A \cup B$, $A \cup C$, and $B \cup C$ all satisfy the definition of a winning coalition. According to Riker's theory, $B \cup C$ generally is the most likely coalition. Gamson would always hypothesize that $B \cup C$ is the most likely coalition. This follows from each actor's desire to maximize its share of the payoff. The share of the payoff given to

A theory of coalition behavior

each member of a winning coalition is assumed to follow the parity norm. B's contribution to $B \cup C$ is a larger percentage of the total resources than B's contribution to $A \cup B$, and so B prefers $B \cup C$. C's size is a larger percentage of the total in $B \cup C$ than it is in $A \cup C$, and so C prefers $B \cup C$. Since no one prefers a coalition with A, it follows that $B \cup C$ forms and that A is the loser.

Given the same distribution of resources, pivotal power theorists hypothesize that each of the three winning coalitions is equally likely to form. They contend that it is true that contestant A has more resources than B who, in turn, has more resources than C, but any combination of two actors is resourceful enough to form a winning coalition. That is, each actor is a potential member of two of the three possible winning coalitions. Consequently, each actor has an equal probability of entering a winning coalition. Thus, the inequality in the initial distribution of resources is not sufficiently large to give any one contestant an advantage or a disadvantage over any other.

Before turning to the research on coalition formation that focuses almost exclusively on social interaction, let us examine two models of coalition formation that combine aspects of the social interaction focus with aspects of the payoff maximization focus with particular attention to the models developed by Caplow[33] and Chertkoff.[34]

Caplow's theory, which is primarily concerned with coalition formation in a triad, is based on the following assumptions:

(a) actors prefer winning to losing,
(b) actors prefer to control winning coalitions rather than be controlled in them, but
(c) actors prefer to be controlled in a winning coalition rather than lose.

Caplow defines control in terms of the ordinal ranking of each actor's resources: more resourceful actors always control less resourceful actors. The notion of control in intra-coalition behavior is analogous to the notion of winning in coalition formation behavior. In a two-member winning coalition, the controlling actor is completely in control regardless of how close its partner is to it in resources. One might almost say that the controlling member of a coalition constitutes a winning coalition within the intra-coalition decision-making process.

In the situation with the three actors (A, B, and C) referred to above, Caplow hypothesizes that coalitions $A \cup C$ or $B \cup C$ are most likely to form. This follows from the assumptions mentioned earlier. C, as the smallest member of the system, recognizes that it cannot control either of its two potential coalition partners. Since C prefers winning to losing, it is reconciled to membership in any winning coalition it can enter. That is, C is

A theory of coalition behavior

indifferent between joining a coalition with *A* or joining a coalition with *B*. Like *C*, *A* has no preference between its options. If *A* joins a coalition with *B* or if *A* joins a coalition with *C*, the consequence is the same for *A*. Regardless of which winning coalition it enters, *A* will be the controlling member. *B*'s position is quite different from either *A*'s or *C*'s. If *B* joins a coalition with *A*, *B* will satisfy its preference for winning rather than losing, but it will not satisfy its preference for control. If *B* joins with *C*, it will satisfy its preference for winning and its preference for control. Since *B*, like *A* and *C*, is engaged in an episodic coalition situation in which it gets one and only one opportunity to select a preferred coalition partner, *B* naturally suggests forming a coalition with *C*.

In the hypothetical situation that was just described, there is some chance that *A* will offer *B* a coalition and there is some chance that *A* will offer *C* a coalition. There is also some chance that *C* will either suggest a coalition with *A* or with *B*. For *B*, however, there is no chance that it will suggest joining a coalition with *A*. Consequently, coalition $A \cup C$ can form (provided that *A* and *C* reciprocate each other's choices), and coalition $B \cup C$ can form (provided that *B* and *C* reciprocate each other's choices). There is no chance of $A \cup B$ forming since *B* would not reciprocate *A*'s bid. If *A* were unaware of *B*'s preference for controlling, then it is also possible that no coalition will form. This would happen if in a single episode *C* were to suggest a coalition with *A*, while *A* asked *B* to join a coalition with it, and *B* requested a coalition with *C*. Although this might occur under the constraints of a single, episodic coalition formation situation, it is demonstrated shortly that the probability that no coalition forms decreases rapidly if the coalition situation is iterative.

Caplow's model is unable to specify the relative frequency with which $A \cup C$ and $B \cup C$ are expected to form. Chertkoff has refined Caplow's basic model to add this information. Chertkoff suggests that the probability of *A* and *C* reciprocating each other's preference for one another is equal to one-half the probability that *B* and *C* reciprocate each other's preferences. It will be recalled that in any discrete episodic coalition formation situation, *A* and *C* are indifferent with respect to their winning coalition options.[35] Since losing is never preferred, one can expect all three actors to make a coalition bid in every episode. Thus, *A*'s probability of bidding *B* equals its probability of bidding *C*, which equals 0.5. *C*'s probability of bidding *A*, by the same reasoning, equals *C*'s probability of bidding *B*, which equals 0.5. Since *B* always prefers a coalition with *C* to a coalition with *A* in any discrete coalition formation episode, the probability that *B* suggests a coalition with *A* is zero, and the probability that *B* suggests a coalition with *C* is 1.0. Solving for the joint probabilities that any two actors reciprocate each other's bids, we find the following:

Let $p_Y(X)$ be the probability that some actor *Y* offers to join a coalition with

15

A theory of coalition behavior

actor X. Let $p(X \cup Y)$ be the probability that coalition $X \cup Y$ is formed. Let (No Coalition) indicate that no coalition is formed. Then,

$$
\begin{aligned}
p(A \cup B) &= p_A(B)p_B(A) &&= (0.5)(0) = 0 \\
p(A \cup C) &= p_A(C)p_C(A) &&= (0.5)(0.5) = 0.25 \\
p(B \cup C) &= p_B(C)p_C(B) &&= (1.0)(0.5) = 0.50 \\
p(\text{No Coalition}) &= p_A(B)p_B(C)p_C(A) &&= (0.5)(1.0)(0.5) = 0.25.
\end{aligned}
$$

If the actors are permitted to enter a new episodic coalition formation situation each time no coalition forms in a prior episode, then over several iterations of the independent coalition formation situations, the probability of remaining without a winning coalition must approach zero. That is, the probability that no coalition forms in any of a series of n independent coalition formation situations is equal to p (No Coalition)^n.[36]

Chertkoff's revision of Caplow's model fits the empirical coalition data concerned with triads better than any of the models discussed thus far. In addition, its focus on probability distributions and its recognition that no coalition may form in a given episode, facilitates the generalization of coalition formation theory to iterative coalition formation situations, provided each episode in a series of iterations is viewed as an independent event. While Chertkoff's approach does not allow resources to be redistributed as a consequence of any coalition formation experience, and it does not permit preferences to be altered as a consequence of prior experiences, his revision of Caplow's model at least allows variance in the probability distribution for each possible outcome as a consequence of the number of iterations that have occurred.

Other studies that do permit participants to consider prior experiences in making decisions in the present iteration have found similar results to those suggested by Chertkoff.[37] Although those studies do not assume complete independence between iterations, neither do they permit the benefits derived from membership in a winning coalition to increase the total resource pool actors bring to bear in future coalition formation situations. Instead, they keep constant the resources held by each participant, while permitting payoffs to accumulate in a currency separate from the resource pool. Under these circumstances one might expect that contestants act to maximize their share of the available payoffs. One might also expect them to focus their coalition bids on the individual actor who has been most likely to reciprocate their choices in the past. One might, therefore, expect A to learn never to suggest a coalition with B. In addition, whichever coalition was formed in the first episode – $B \cup C$ or $A \cup C$ – should be expected to occur in all future iterations. This latter expectation arises from the assumption that each actor learns to respond favorably to its successful prior actions. That these results do not actually occur is accounted for by introducing the notion that each participant attributes some utility to the loss of boredom that accompanies choice variability, or by suggesting that each actor's sense of justice leads it to give the earlier loser a chance to win some benefits. In an experimental study reported by Lieberman, for example, a triad was established in which two participants had 'a clear incentive to unite forces to the detriment of the third. In a majority of choices (70 per cent) the two did just that. However, in a sizable minority of choices (30 per cent) this prescribed behavior did not occur ... Some subjects felt it was not fair to do this.'[38] Thus, even when feedback is permitted, but benefits are not redistributive, the relative frequency with which various winning coalitions form approximate the predictions made by Chertkoff.

All the approaches to coalition formation that have been discussed thus far are concerned with identifying the mechanisms used by actors to assess the relative value of different coalitions. Until now, that value has been defined in terms of the distribution of the specific payoff which motivated the formation of the winning coalition. Another approach – the anti-competitive approach – focuses on benefits which appear to be external to the primary concern of the coalition as motivating factors in coalition formation.[39] The anti-competitive approach is most clearly visible in certain experimental games in which the players are asked to play the game repeatedly. Although the experimenter intends each play of the game to be an independent episode, the players act as if the entire experimental session, rather than the individual episodes, is the game. Because the players convert the episodic game into an iterative game, they become increasingly concerned about their social acceptability in subsequent rounds of play. In order to increase their acceptability, they bargain as little as possible, preferring to appear amicable and preferring to make coalition formation with them an inexpensive experience for their potential partners. Under these conditions, the players convert what was intended to be a constant-sum game into a variable-sum situation. Once this happens, decision-making models intended for use in constant-sum situations are no longer able to account for the behavior of the participants. In fact, the impetus for the development of the anti-competitive approach stems from the frequency with which outcomes unpredicted by the models discussed thus far occur when the same players are asked to play the same game with the same participants over a fairly long period of time. The principal pattern of behavior that emerges from anti-competitive studies is that players prefer to join coalitions with actors whose size is most like their own.[40] Perhaps this preference reflects the fact that 'lumpiness', or imperfect divisibility of payoffs, generally results in coalition benefits being divided in such a way that the smaller members of a winning coalition receive a disproportionately large share of the benefits more often than the larger members.[41] In

A theory of coalition behavior

a coalition of equals, of course, there would be no systematic difference in the expected distribution of benefits.

In summary, the episodic literature based on the minimum resource or the pivotal power approaches is concerned primarily with the maximization of payoffs; Caplow's and Chertkoff's concern with control focuses on the marginal utility of reciprocated choices; and anti-competitive studies concentrate on the marginal utility of positive social interaction in coalition formation situations.

Strategic behavior in the iterative literature

Most studies of coalition formation behavior, as I have already noted, assume that behavior in any one episode is unaffected by behavior in earlier episodes. Brief mention has been made of a few studies that introduce feedback into their investigation of iterative coalition formation situations. These studies permit actors to learn from their prior experiences, and to base their future actions on past outcomes. They do not allow the benefits secured in one coalition to become an integral part of the resource base that an actor can bring to bear in future coalition formation situations. That is, they relax the episodic condition's assumption of complete independence of episodes, but they do not accept the redistributive condition's assumption that benefits can be converted into the currency that defines size in a political system. Before turning to an exploration of the redistributive condition, more attention should be given to the empirical observations that result from learning processes in iterative coalition formation studies.

Earlier in this chapter it was suggested that rational participants in redistributive coalition situations have incentives to compete with their alliance partners. In selecting from potential allies, therefore, they should not assume that all other contestants intend to cooperate with them. Instead, rational actors in redistributive coalitions should identify the contestants who are most likely to be cooperative partners, and then should exploit those cooperative partners to the fullest possible extent. This is one of the most important inferences that follows from the elimination of the episodic condition. It is a somewhat different inference from those drawn by the non-redistributive, but feedback-oriented studies of iterative coalition behavior.

Anti-competitive studies have a particularly interesting implication for iterative coalition situations with feedback concerning prior behavior. They suggest that the rational actor is one who attempts to maximize his gains in the long run, rather than during each episode.[42] Many of the non-anti-competitive models lead to a similar implication for iterative games with feedback. Caplow, for example, distinguishes between the desire to maxi-

A theory of coalition behavior

mize one's advantage each time a payoff is distributed in episodic situations and the desire to maximize control over the entire length of a continuous coalition formation situation.[43] Gamson has made a similar argument in support of a relatively cooperative strategy in iterative coalition formation situations with feedback. He explains that:

'the benefits of competitive restraint are particularly apparent in experiments in which subjects take part in a prolonged sequence of plays of a coalition game. Under such circumstances... the entire experimental session rather than the individual play of the game is frequently the focus of the subject's coalition strategy. With such a focus the most selfish and exploitative player might well find that his best, long-run strategy involves deliberate restraint in seeking immediate advantage.'[44]

There is a fair amount of evidence to support Gamson's contention that cooperative actors are more likely to succeed in such coalition situations than are competitive actors. Hoffman, for instance, found that players who quickly forge a lead over others in an iterative game find themselves unable to locate coalition partners as the game progresses.[45] Others have duplicated this finding.[46]

To recapitulate, many researchers have drawn the inference that competitive behavior is most appropriate in episodic coalition formation situations without feedback, while cooperative behavior is most appropriate in iterative, feedback coalition formation situations. All of these studies, of course, assume that cooperative behavior can be expected after the coalition is formed, but before it achieves its specified goal. I have suggested, on the other hand, that somewhat competitive behavior can be expected during the coalition formation and the coalition maintenance stages of redistributive coalition situations. The source of this difference of opinion is that other studies of iterative coalition behavior assume that each actor's capabilities are unaffected by the distribution of payoffs within a winning coalition. I assume that the payoffs lead to a redistribution of capabilities and thereby alter the size of each actor in future coalition formation situations. Since this is so fundamental a distinction for this study, it seems appropriate to examine the implication of the redistributive condition in greater depth.

The redistributive condition

The purpose of the redistributive condition is to provide a basis for coalition formation among political groups, such as political parties or interest groups, that have at least partially incompatible goals. The condition

A theory of coalition behavior

stipulates that it is possible to convert the benefits derived from membership in a winning coalition into an integral part of a member's resource base. It does not require that a coalition's benefits are identical to the relevant resources of the particular political system in question, but rather that the benefits at least must be convertible into those resources. That is, the benefits must be convertible into the currency of political influence in much the same way that money is convertible into goods or services in the marketplace. Thus, money is not a good that one ordinarily wishes to purchase, although it is instrumental in purchasing desired goods. In the same way, the benefits derived from a coalition need not be the resources one wishes to control, but they must be instrumental in acquiring those resources.

The redistributive condition does not require that all benefits derived from membership in a winning coalition are convertible into part of an actor's resource base. This is particularly important because it means that maximizing one's share of the total payoff pie available in a winning coalition does not necessarily mean that one is maximizing control over future decisions. Thus, the astute politician may accede to the competitive demand of a naive politician for control over a large quantity of short-run benefits in exchange for control of a disproportionately large share of the long-term, redistributive benefits.

Finally, the redistributive condition does not require that all coalition benefits have comparable effects on all coalition members. A benefit which is of long-term value to one actor may be only of short-term value to another, and may be of no value to still another. For example, a political party might attempt to convince its coalition partners to pursue a particular policy with which it is closely identified. Such a party might believe that the successful implementation of that policy would enhance its prospects in subsequent elections. Another party might agree to pursue that policy because it felt the policy was desirable, even though the implementation of the particular policy would have no significance to its constituents. Such a party would derive a short-term policy benefit from the implementation of the particular program in question. It might not experience any long-term political benefits from its support for the policy. Another member of the same coalition might agree to pursue the specific policy in question simply because it perceived no cost that might be incurred by supporting it.

The first party in this example is able to convert the benefit it derives from the coalition's pursuit of its policy objective into increased political influence after a subsequent election. The second party is not able to convert the benefit derived from the implementation of the program into a politically significant payoff. The third party derives no benefit and suffers no loss, provided it need not compete against the first party in any future decision-making situation. If it must compete with that party in the future, then it has been naive in believing that it incurred no cost by acquiescing to the first party's policy goal. Any increase in a coalition partner's size necessarily means a decline in the relative position of the partner who remained constant. The important point to bear in mind, therefore, is that the effects of any given benefit need not be identical for each participant in a winning coalition.

The redistributive condition improves upon the episodic condition in at least three ways. Because the redistributive condition recognizes that pay-offs can alter each actor's future chances of fulfilling the goals it seeks that are not shared by some of its partners, this condition introduces the possibility that actors are motivated to join coalitions by their desire to compete with their putative partners. That is, the redistributive condition allows the coalition maintenance stage to serve as an arena for strategic maneuvering within the political system. Under these conditions, the stability of a coalition becomes a tool used by coalition partners not only to achieve the shared objective of the alliance, but also to improve their position at the expense of the actors in the losing coalitions and at the expense of their own partners in the winning coalition. Thus, the coalition maintenance stage can be used to sabotage a partner's efforts to enhance its future bargaining position, or to lower the costs of acquiring information about the decision-making process, the resources, and the intentions of one's 'allies'. The redistributive condition provides a basis for enhancing one's own position or undermining another actor's position without having to resort to the most costly forms of competition between declared foes. The assumptions of the episodic condition constrain actors to benefit themselves or undermine others during the coalition formation stage. The redistributive condition permits such behavior during the formation and maintenance stages of coalition situations. At the same time, the redistributive condition does not exclude the possibility that coalition partners might cooperate with each other during the maintenance stage; it just does not *require* such behavior.

The redistributive condition provides for the termination of a coalition before its ostensible goal is fulfilled. It does so by suggesting that the ostensible, shared goal of the coalition members disguises their actual intentions. Thus, while partnership in a coalition may imply that the agreed-upon goal is the basis for the coalition, the desire for redistributive benefits may be the actual incentive for continued membership, at least for some partners. If they find a better opportunity to secure such benefits in an alternative coalition, they may quit the first alliance even if such action jeopardizes the attainment of the shared goal to which they subscribed. Members of a winning coalition might also decide to terminate their alliance before the shared objective is fulfilled if they are convinced that the continued pursuit of the shared objective will disproportionately provide re-

A theory of coalition behavior

distributive benefits for some of their partners at their expense. Under the episodic condition, on the other hand, coalitions are terminated only when the shared objective is fulfilled, or when external constraints make its fulfillment too costly to warrant a continued effort. It cannot be otherwise because the episodic condition does not allow any incentive for joining a coalition other than the shared objective.

The redistributive condition improves on the episodic condition in a third way. As I have already hinted, the redistributive condition does not exclude the behavioral patterns permitted by the episodic condition, but it does permit additional forms of behavior under specific circumstances. Consequently, the redistributive condition can be applied to a larger set of political coalitions than can the episodic condition. In addition to being applicable to more coalitions, the redistributive condition allows a more detailed description of rational behavior than does the episodic condition. It allows us to speak about the strategies geared toward short-term maximization of benefits and the strategies geared toward long-term maximization of benefits. The redistributive condition makes it possible to explain behavior in the coalition maintenance and the termination stages, as well as during the formation stage.

The redistributive condition and coalition formation

As already noted, theories of coalition formation in non-redistributive, episodic situations generally hypothesize that the largest winning coalition is least likely to occur, that the smallest winning coalition is most likely to occur, and that intermediate sized coalitions have a probability of occurring which is intermediate. Although there are a great many ways to formulate the arguments for these hypotheses, they all agree that the process of selecting among potential partners is characterized by a significant degree of competitiveness (i.e. maximization of individual benefits). These observations are supported by the experimental and the empirical literature. The iterative coalition formation literature that assumes feedback effects, on the other hand, suggests that coalition formation is characterized by a high degree of restraint. In fact, the iterative coalition formation literature has observed that coalitions including the largest actor become very rare after a few iterations, even if the size of the coalition that includes such an actor is intermediate or small. Thus, in terms of the hypothetical triad discussed earlier, $A \cup C$ coalitions diminish in frequency over time, with $B \cup C$ coalitions becoming increasingly, though not exclusively, prevalent. The literature concludes that cooperativeness is more likely to lead to rewards in the long run than is competitiveness.

An unfortunate aspect of the feedback studies is their inability to dis-

A theory of coalition behavior

tinguish between the effects of an actor's size and the effects of an actor's strategy on its admissibility in winning coalitions. In particular, that literature cannot distinguish between players in coalition games who forge an early lead in the acquisition of non-redistributive payoffs because of their competitiveness and those who forge an early lead because of their largeness. An understanding of the source of this confusion is essential if one is to understand the coalition formation process in redistributive situations.

In the absence of redistributive effects, the most likely decision-rule governing the distribution of payoffs is the parity norm. A very large number of experimental studies reveal that this is the sociologically preferred decision-rule by most participants in coalition games.[47] Under the constraints of the parity norm, the largest constituent in a coalition would always receive the largest payoff. As a result of the large payoff it received, the largest constituent would forge an early lead in the acquisition of payoffs. This early lead does not stem directly from the competitiveness of the largest constituent in the winning coalition. Instead, the lead follows from the application of the parity norm. Of course, the largest actor, like all other actors in a winning coalition, selects the particular coalition it joins because that coalition gives it a larger share of the total payoff than does any other available option. Its search for the coalition in which its benefits are maximized is no more competitive than the comparable search conducted by all other rational actors. But even if it is suggested that the largest actor was more competitive than the others and should have sought an alternative coalition in which its benefits were suboptimized, the confusion would not be eliminated. Thus, the largest constituent might have followed one of three available options. It could have sought membership in (*a*) the coalition that maximized its share of the payoff relative to the other members and satisfied its expectation regarding the absolute payoff it would receive; (*b*) a coalition that maximized its share of the payoff relative to the other members, but did not satisfy its expectation with respect to the absolute payoff it would receive; or (*c*) a coalition that neither maximized its share of the payoff relative to the other members, nor satisfied its expectation regarding its absolute benefit.

The first coalition is, of course, the smallest winning coalition that includes the actor in question as a member. This is the coalition in which the largest constituent's size is most readily confused with its competitiveness. In this coalition, the largest constituent receives the largest absolute payoff it could expect from any coalition. As a result of the large payoff it receives, the largest constituent forges an early lead. Its absolute payoff stems from the application of the party norm, however, and not from differences in the competitiveness of the actors.

In the second coalition, the largest constituent has agreed to join a winning coalition in which the difference between its size and the sum of the

A theory of coalition behavior

sizes of the remaining constituents is not as great as it would be in the first coalition. In this coalition, the largest constituent's payoff is somewhat smaller than in the first coalition (provided that the total available payoff is constant across winning coalitions), but it is still larger than any other actor's payoff. Even though some restraint has been shown in choosing this coalition, the largest constituent still forges a lead over all the other actors in terms of the acquisition of payoffs. Consequently, membership in this type of coalition should also lead to the exclusion of the largest constituent in subsequent coalition formation situations.

In the third type of coalition the only significant change is the identity of the largest constituent. That is, the actor that has been referred to as the largest constituent in the two earlier coalitions simply is smaller than some other actor in this third type of alliance. This follows from the fact that its share of the total payoff is smaller than some other actor's share. Given the sociological preference for the parity norm, this is likely to occur only if another actor contributes a larger percentage of the total resource pool of the coalition. Thus, although the actor we were discussing does not forge an early lead, another actor does. That other actor is expected to be excluded from future winning coalitions. Of course, if the largest constituent in a winning coalition also is the largest actor in the entire system, then it does not have the option of joining a coalition of this type. Consequently, the absolutely largest actor in the system is restricted to the first two options, both of which are supposed to lead to its exclusion from subsequent winning coalitions.

As long as the parity norm is followed, the exclusion of the largest actor in the system from subsequent winning coalitions cannot be attributed to its competitiveness in the coalition formation stage. Regardless of which winning coalition it joins, the largest actor is required to accept the largest payoff if the parity norm operates. The payoff received by this actor is a consequence of its size and of the particular decision-rule that is most commonly applied to iterative, feedback coalition situations. The payoff is not a function of the strategic behavior of the actors. Since it is not, it makes sense for every actor, including the largest actor, to behave competitively during the coalition formation stage. By doing so, each actor focuses its attention on the set of coalitions in which its relative share of the payoff is maximized and in which its expected payoff is satisfied. The largest actor might as well follow this course of behavior since it has little hope, in any event, of being an acceptable partner for very long. If it can expect to be excluded from future winning coalitions, then it has all the more incentive to maximize its benefits while it is still an acceptable coalition partner.

When the redistributive condition is applied, it is possible to distinguish between the effects of size and the effects of strategic choices on an actor's

A theory of coalition behavior

admissibility to future winning coalitions. This is true because the identity of the actor playing the role of the largest actor in the system, or the role of the largest constituent in a winning coalition, can change from iteration to iteration. While the largest actor at any time might be excluded from the next winning coalition, that actor would not necessarily be the largest actor two or three iterations later. The redistributive effects of the winning coalition's benefits might, in other words, alter the identity of the actor playing the role of the largest actor in the system. Under these circumstances, it is the strategic behavior of each actor during each iteration that determines the point at which any given actor is likely to surface as the single largest actor in the system.

Since each actor wants to redistribute the system's resources so as to improve its own bargaining position in the future, no actor has any incentive to permit another actor to acquire monopoly control over future decisions. The largest actor at any one point is closer to monopoly control over future decisions than any other actor and is, therefore, the one most likely to be excluded from the next winning coalition. Because of this, rational actors seeking long-term maximization of their influence prefer to avoid becoming the largest actor in the system until the iteration in which they feel they can optimize their prospects for achieving their many unshared goals. They prefer to be large enough to have a substantial amount of influence in any winning coalition, but not so large that they lose their influence in future winning coalitions through the process of exclusion. Thus, while actors in redistributive coalition formation situations may behave competitively in their efforts to get into a winning coalition, they cannot afford to behave so competitively that their successes lead to their exclusion from future winning coalitions.

Since political actors have the option of competing with each other during the coalition maintenance stage, members of redistributive winning coalitions can manipulate the decision-rule governing the allocation of payoffs so that the extremely restrictive parity norm is not applied. That is, as the number of actors attempting to maximize their long-term influence increases, the utility of the parity norm decreases. As the utility of the parity norm decreases (because it forces more and more ambitious actors into a situation in which their payoff maximization occurs before the iteration in which they want their total payoffs to be maximized), actors have increasing incentives to avoid maximizing their total payoffs until some nth iteration. By eliminating the parity norm, the actors can manipulate their positions so that the most effective strategist would (a) be almost, but not quite, the largest actor in the system until some nth iteration; (b) be in a winning coalition across more iterations than any other actor; (c) make incremental gains in its share of the total pool of resources in the system; and (d) increase its total political influence by the nth iteration more than

A theory of coalition behavior

any other actor in the system. Thus, size is revealed as the most crucial element governing an actor's admissibility to a winning coalition during the coalition formation stage, while strategy during the coalition maintenance stage is most important in manipulating the resources each actor brings to future coalition formation situations. The first hypothesis of the theory follows from this discussion:

H1: Coalition formation behavior in redistributive situations is the same as coalition formation behavior in episodic situations. That is, minimal coalitions are most likely to form, with intermediate-sized coalitions being next most likely, and with very large winning coalitions being least likely to form.

The redistributive condition and coalition maintenance

The discussion of coalition formation suggests that the parity norm is an unlikely decision-rule in redistributive coalitions. This is especially true during the tenure of a coalition when the constituents have an opportunity to compete for those resources that can be converted into future political influence. The elimination of the parity norm is, in fact, a necessary condition for the success of those actors most interested in altering the status quo and in maximizing their political influence at some nth point in time. As I have already noted, the parity norm, or any other size-oriented formula for distributing a winning coalition's benefits, cannot benefit every member of the coalition in the long run. The largest actor is threatened with the probability that it will be excluded from future winning coalitions if it secures too large a share of the benefits before some nth iteration. The smallest members of a winning coalition find themselves slowed down in their efforts to attain a particular degree of influence by the nth iteration. The parity norm restricts their share of the benefits too severely, making it difficult for their growth in influence to progress at the rate they might desire. Since such a decision-rule is not clearly in the interest of any particular role player in a winning coalition, at least during the maintenance stage, there is little reason to believe that the parity norm is subscribed to when benefits are redistributive. This leads to the second hypothesis of the theory:

H2: There is no association between the distribution of redistributive payoffs in a winning coalition and the sizes of the actors in the winning coalition.

A corollary of this hypothesis and the earlier discussion of naive actors is that the distribution of all benefits – redistributive and short-term – may comply with the parity norm, even though the redistributive portion of those benefits do not.

If size is not the key variable influencing the distribution of redistributive benefits, what is? In order to answer this question it is necessary to focus on the strategic options available to political actors during the coalition maintenance stage.

During the earlier discussions of the redistributive condition, I emphasized that coalition participants who want to increase their long-term influence have little incentive to sacrifice potential political gains in the interest of the short-term policy gains that might be associated with the achievement of the coalition's shared objectives. Consequently, the shared objectives which allegedly provide the basis for the formation of the coalition are little more than a means to gain access to political benefits. Under these circumstances, the objectives that are clearly shared by political actors are the desire to maximize their long-term influence and the desire to minimize the long-term influence of all other actors. Of course, if these goals are held by more than one member of a coalition, then serious incompatibilities must exist within the coalition. Obviously, it is impossible for two actors to maximize their influence while minimizing the influence of all other actors. Thus, successful maximization of influence implies securing monopoly control over the decision-making process (that is, securing enough resources to form a winning coalition on one's own), and eliminating the need for coalitions with other actors. Since only one actor can secure monopoly control at some nth iteration, the postulated goal of this study is completely satisfied only if all actors save one have been eliminated from the decision-making process.

If the postulated goal is held by more than one member of a winning coalition, then the cooperativeness manifested among partners is little more than a façade for their competitive intents. When those competitive intents involve the redistribution of influence, grave risks are taken by each competitor. One such risk which has already been pointed out is that a competitor's share of the redistributive benefits may rise too quickly. If the redistributive benefits rise so quickly that the actor is excluded from future winning coalitions, it may find itself considerably weakened by the nth iteration. Even those benefits that it secured during its limited period of success may prove useless in future decision-making situations. Thus, if its rise is so swift that it is excluded from membership in future winning coalitions before it is able to convert its redistributive benefits into political influence, then those benefits have no positive impact on its future prospects. Quite the contrary, they have been the competitive actor's undoing. That is, the actor seeking to maximize its influence must be careful not to attain its maximum acquisition of benefits until it is able to convert those benefits into political influence. Consequently, the point at which an actor

A theory of coalition behavior

should attempt to maximize its size is at the end of a series of iterations, not at the beginning of such a series. If the series ends because of new elections, then the actor must have converted its redistributive benefits into electoral appeal. If the series ends with a redrawing of the system's rules, then the actor must have converted its redistributive benefits into legislative influence. Before the series ends, each actor continues to be somewhat dependent on its former partners, and on the internal workings of the political environment. Its former partners, of course, are not likely to be inclined to sacrifice their future bargaining position to satisfy their competitive partner. And the constraints imposed by the internal workings of the particular political environment can only be circumvented or escaped by defining a new political environment. It is exactly the function of elections, constitutional conventions and the like to redefine political environments. It is in that sense that such events mark the last in a series of iterations.

There are at least two means by which political actors may maximize their long-term gains while minimizing challenges to their influence either from within their coalitions or from outside them. As already noted, political actors may sap the resources of those who have been excluded from their winning coalition. But, they must also prevent their partners from doing the same. This may be accomplished by pursuing a strategy that involves terminating coalitions whenever it becomes apparent that the actor no longer can increase its resource base adequately from within the coalition,[48] it can increase its influence more effectively by joining a new coalition, or it can prevent others from increasing their influence relative to its influence by terminating the coalition. This suggests that a participant in a coalition can maximize its long-term influence by remaining in any given coalition just long enough to acquire an optimal quantity of redistributive benefits. Once those benefits are secured – and converted into political influence – it should attempt to terminate the coalition. By terminating the coalition, the actor deprives all the other members of the coalition from any additional opportunity to use the alliance to increase their influence.

Even if an actor can continue to increase its own resource base by remaining in a coalition, it might be wise to terminate the alliance, provided the actor is certain of membership in a new coalition that excludes at least some members of its earlier winning coalition. By joining a new coalition that does not include some of its former partners, the actor assures itself of access to redistributive benefits at the expense of all the members of losing coalitions. Of course, some of its former partners are included among the losers. Consequently, the actor is able to secure some benefits at their expense, thereby diminishing their influence. Under these circumstances, a hypothetical actor would first increase its influence at the expense of

A theory of coalition behavior

those outside the first winning coalition (that is, its partners in a new winning coalition), and then would increase its influence at the expense of those outside the new winning coalition (that is, its old coalition partners). The actor would not have to demand a disproportionately large share of the redistributive benefits in any one winning coalition to maximize its influence in the long run. On the contrary, it would be better off permitting those it hopes to exclude from subsequent winning coalitions to secure a disproportionately large share of the redistributive benefits. If they appear to increase in size too rapidly, they can easily be excluded in the future. By asking for no more than its fair share, an actor can grow slowly enough so that others may not perceive its rise until the nth iteration, by which time it may be too late for them to alter the effects of their earlier actions.

Such a strategy, of course, is filled with danger. The clearest source of risk in such an undertaking is that other actors will perceive the long-term consequences of the strategy before it can be successfully implemented. If this were to happen, then the actor pursuing this competitive, coalition-switching strategy would presumably be excluded from subsequent winning coalitions. Coalition participants can lack tolerance for this type of exploitative behavior just as they can lack tolerance for very large actors. The consequence is the same if one is excluded from access to winning coalitions because of one's size or because of one's competitiveness.

It follows from this discussion that actors seeking to maximize their influence in the long run must be careful not to maximize it at every iteration in the decision-making process. To do so is to maximize the probability that they will surpass the tolerance limits of their partners and find themselves excluded from access to future benefits. On the other hand, they cannot ignore the opportunity that redistributive payoffs afford them. They cannot simply accept a cooperative strategy that avoids any exploitative or manipulative behavior on their part. Such a strategy would only benefit the largest actors. It is they who must be most cautious about approaching monopoly control too quickly or too soon. Cooperative behavior cannot benefit ambitious, smaller contestants since it requires that they not attempt to alter the status quo. Therefore, ambitious actors must moderate their competitive acts so that the amount by which their influence increases in any single iteration either is imperceptible to their partners, or else is considered inconsequential by their partners. Such moderation involves combining cooperative actions with competitive actions. The exact mixture of the two depends upon the particular tolerance limits of the partners in question. Whatever those limits are, it seems that political contestants would do well to identify them and to operate as close to, but below them, as possible.

A theory of coalition behavior

The suggestion that a mixed strategy, incorporating cooperative and competitive actions, is a better long-term strategy than either a purely cooperative or a purely competitive strategy is central to the theory developed here. The implications of this strategy are explored in much greater depth and with considerably more precision in the pages that follow.

Strategic behavior in coalitions

A member of a coalition is cooperative if it demands no more than its fair share of the coalition's benefits, and it is predisposed to accept less than its fair share of the redistributive benefits in order to facilitate the achievement of the coalition's shared objectives. Cooperative actors prefer to focus the attention and resources of the coalition's constituents on the collective goal that all agreed to pursue. They prefer to satisfy their immediate policy goals and their long-term political goals. If this joint outcome cannot be satisfied, then they prefer to fulfill their immediate policy goals rather than gamble on the fulfillment of their political goals. Because of their preference for immediate policy gratification, cooperative actors prefer to apply the parity norm rather than face a costly bargaining process to determine how the coalition's benefits should be distributed. They will, however, sacrifice the parity norm – and accept less than their fair share of the politically useful redistributive benefits – if they believe such action will facilitate the achievement of their policy goals.

When cooperative actors are confronted with a partner who demands more than its fair share of the payoff (as defined by the parity norm), the cooperators meet that demand if it is not great enough, or frequent enough to push them beyond their tolerance limits. Cooperative actors are, by definition, better able to tolerate competitive demands for redistributive payoffs than are more competitive actors.

The cooperative strategy is oriented toward maximizing an actor's longevity in a winning coalition. If the strategy is successful, then the cooperator would maximize its long-term political influence by prolonging its membership in winning coalitions and by prolonging the accompanying access to some share of the redistributive benefits. This strategy is predicated on the notion that getting a very small reward for a very long time is more likely to result in long-term maximization than getting a larger share for a shorter time.

A member of a coalition is competitive if it always demands more than its fair share of the coalition's redistributive benefits, and it is predisposed to sacrifice the collective goals of the coalition in the interest of its own pursuit of redistributive benefits. Competitive actors prefer to allocate

A theory of coalition behavior

the redistributive benefits of coalitions without the restrictions imposed by the parity norm. Through their competitive demands, such actors attempt to convince their more cooperative partners that they are willing to disrupt the coalition's quest for the fulfillment of its collective goals unless they receive a disproportionately large share of the redistributive benefits.

Competitive actors, like cooperative actors, prefer to maximize the joint outcome of prolonging their membership in a winning coalition, and maximizing their share of politically useful benefits. Unlike cooperators, however, they prefer to maximize their acquisition of politically useful benefits to satisfying their policy goals. Because of their desire for political gratification, rather than policy gratification, they are unlikely to tolerate any competitive demands for political gratification on the part of their coalition partners. Consequently, their tolerance limits are easily surpassed, making coalitions involving only competitive actors extremely unstable.

The competitive strategy is very risky because competitors demand costly sacrifices on the part of their allies. Therefore, competitors who always pursue their private advantage at the expense of their partners can acquire a disproportionately large share of a coalition's redistributive benefits for a limited time only. Once they demand too large a share, or demand a disproportionately large share one time too many, they force their partners' tolerance limits to be surpassed. When this happens, the risk that the partners no longer have any incentive to remain in the coalition becomes extremely high. If the incentive to remain coalesced is low enough, the coalition will be terminated. When this happens, the competitor loses access to the coalition benefits they value. If this point is reached quickly enough, enough time may not have elapsed for the competitive actor to convert its disproportionately large share of the benefits into an integral part of its resource base: even the competitive actor might not enjoy more than a short-term political advantage from its strategy.

If a political actor pursues a mixed strategy – sometimes facilitating the attainment of the shared policy goals and sometimes demanding extra benefits in exchange for its support of those goals – it should be able to use the coalition to increase its resource base for a substantial period of time. In fact, by taking a more moderate stand and, thereby, reducing the probability that it surpasses the tolerance limits of its cooperative partners, the mixed strategist actually should acquire and convert more redistributive benefits in the long run than a completely competitive actor.[49]

The mixed strategist depends on two factors to insure its long-run success in coalitions. It depends on its ability to convince at least some of its partners that the infrequent extra payoffs it demands benefit their interests as well as its own. In particular, it must convince some of its cooperative partners that their opportunity to enjoy continued access to all the coalition's benefits – both the short-term policy-oriented type and the

A theory of coalition behavior

long-term redistributive type – depend on their satisfying the occasional extra demands of the mixed strategist. In addition, it relies on the high level of tolerance of at least some of its partners to facilitate the repetition of competitive demands. This is important because, unlike the completely competitive actor, the mixed strategist is attentive to the location of the tolerance limits of its partners. It behaves as competitively as it can without surpassing those limits. The competitive actor hammers away at its partners by making continuous demands without regard for the limits imposed by the rate at which its partners lose tolerance. Consequently, the mixed strategy actor is less likely to be cut off from future benefits as a consequence of its actions during a series of iterations than is the competitive actor and is more likely to survive as a coalition partner long enough to convert its redistributive payoffs into future political influence.

The argument just presented can be used to construct a calculus of expected payoffs, given different strategic orientations. The set of parameters that influence the expected payoffs also reveal the best strategy for any given combination of actors and the best combination of actors for any given preference for payoffs. The parameters include the lost tolerance for competitive demands and the length of time over which prior behavior is remembered or is considered relevant.

The probability that some actor i will receive a disproportionately large share of the redistributive benefits from some other actor j is described by the following *redistributive equation*:

$$p_i(Y)_n = (p(D_i)_n) \frac{X_j - \sum_{t=n-x}^{n-1} [(K_j)(f_i(D)_t)]}{X_j}$$

with the maximum $\sum_{t=n-x}^{n-1} [(K_j)(f_i(D)_t)] = X_j$

The probability (p) that actor i receives a disproportionately large share of the redistributive benefits (Y) at time n is indicated by $p_i(Y)_n$; $f_i(D)_t$ is the frequency (f) with which actor i demands (D) an extra share of Y benefits at time t. The range of t is from some immediately prior time period to some time $n-x$; $p(D_i)$ is the probability that a given demand D has come from i, and not from some other actor k, or l, or m. $p(D_i)$ is defined as

$$f_i(D)/\sum_{i=1}^{m} f_i(D).$$

Here X is the number of iterations over which actor j remembers or cares about earlier demands made by i; K_j is the proportion of j's tolerance for competitive demands that has been lost as a consequence of prior demands from i during each iteration that occurred during the previous x iterations; K_j can vary between 0 and 1.0. During the initial episode of a coalition situation involving j and i as partners, K_j is assumed to be 0 for all actors. This follows from the fact that there were no prior demands in the coalition that could have taxed any actor's tolerance. K_j is assumed to increase during the X relevant periods of behavior. K_j can be less than or equal to 1.0 after X iterations, although the relevance criterion requires that K_j cannot attain the value 1.0 until X periods have passed. Thus, as t approaches $n-1$, K approaches 1.0.

The redistributive equation simply states that actor i's probability of receiving a disproportionately large share of the redistributive benefits at the expense of j is equal to the probability that the specific demand under consideration at time n comes from actor i, discounted by the loss of tolerance on j's part caused by past demands made by i. It indicates that an actor's chances of success depend on how many other actors make competitive demands when i does. The more competitive demands being made at any point, the lower the probability that i's demand will receive a favorable response during that point in time. Consequently, i is better off in a coalition with actors disinclined to make competitive demands.

The closer i comes to its partner's tolerance limit, the more risk that is involved in making an additional demand for extra benefits. Consequently, i must determine the optimal level of competitiveness in terms of the frequency and sequence with which it can make competitive demands without experiencing serious problems with the discount term in the equation.

The equation recognizes the probability that actors do not have perfect memories, or that they are willing to ignore 'ancient' history. That is, the parameter X specifies the limits beyond which actors are no longer punished for their prior behavior. By selecting partners with short memories (that is, low X parameter values), and with tolerance limits that are lost slowly, one can maximize the number of competitive demands that can be executed successfully.

The ideal long-term strategy for any actor depends on its partners' X and K values, as well as on the propensity of its allies to demand extra benefits for themselves. The longer it takes a partner to lose tolerance, the more benefits that can be derived at that partner's expense by using a competitive strategy. On the other hand, no matter how quickly a partner's tolerance is exhausted, a cooperative strategy can never lead to the extra benefits that contribute to an actor's relative growth in influence. Without demanding extra benefits, there is no reason for an actor to expect to receive extra benefits.

Of course, participants in politics are neither perfectly tolerant, nor are they perfectly intolerant. When memories and tolerance are imperfect the mixed strategy is the best choice for contestants seeking to maximize their

A theory of coalition behavior

long-term control over the decision-making process. The degree of mix is governed by the exact magnitude of the parameters just discussed.

The redistributive equation provides a means by which we can calculate the probability that a given actor, under given circumstances, will receive a disproportionately large share of the redistributive benefits secured by its coalition. The equation does not tell us what circumstances actually arise, and therefore does not tell us what the most appropriate strategy is under those circumstances. This is an advantage in that it does not limit the applicability of the equation to a very restricted set of circumstances. It is also a disadvantage in that we want to generate probability estimates that can be applied to specific circumstances. The actual parameter values that arise are, of course, an empirical question. Therefore, reference to the empirical research in this area may prove helpful. Studies of iterative games – particularly prisoners' dilemma games – have been concerned with the length of time it takes a player to respond to a shift in an opponent's strategic choices. In an excellent review of the iterative prisoner's dilemma literature, Melvin Guyer notes that players tend to respond to each other in terms of the strategic response they received from their opponent in the immediately preceding iteration. They were less concerned with iterations more remotely situated in the past.[50] Actors receiving competitive demands from players who had been cooperative before tended to respond cooperatively to those demands. Actors receiving competitive demands from players whose immediately prior behavior was competitive, tended to respond competitively. That is, two competitive demands in a row were sufficient to exhaust the tolerance limits of the players over the span of iterations that they considered relevant.[51] In terms of the redistributive equation, this means the X parameter only spanned across one earlier iteration, and the tolerance limit of each player was exhausted by one earlier competitive demand during X. Using these empirically suggested parameter values, table 2.1 indicates the probability that a cooperative, a competitive, and a mixed strategy actor has of receiving a disproportionately large share of a coalition's redistributive benefits.

The computations assume the parameter values suggested above and that the three actors, but no others, were in the coalition together. The coalition lasts for six iterations, during which the competitor makes a demand at each opportunity, the cooperator never makes a demand, and the mixed strategist alternates between making demands and not making demands.

As can be seen from table 2.1, the cooperator never asks for and never receives more than its fair share of the payoff. Insofar as someone else does ask for and does get extra benefits, the cooperator is the one most likely to provide the resources for such side payments. There is a probability of 0.5 that the competitor will succeed in securing extra benefits during the first

A theory of coalition behavior

iteration, but this probability is reduced to zero for all subsequent iterations. The mixed strategist, on the other hand, alternates between a probability of 0.5 and a probability of zero from iteration to iteration. If it were to distribute its three competitive and three cooperative acts in any other sequence, its probability of success would be reduced, given the parameter values I have posited. For example, if it competed twice in a row, then cooperated twice in a row, then competed once and cooperated once, the mixed strategist probabilities would be 0.5, 0, 0, 0, 0.5, 0 for the six iterations. That is, its mean probability would be reduced from 0.25 to 0.167.

TABLE 2.1 *The probability of receiving extra benefits*

Iteration	Cooperator		Competitor		Mixed strategist	
	$f(D)$	$p(Y)$	$f(D)$	$p(Y)$	$f(D)$	$p(Y)$
$t1$	0	0	1	0.5	1	0.5
$t2$	0	0	1	0	0	0
$t3$	0	0	1	0	1	0.5
$t4$	0	0	1	0	0	0
$t5$	0	0	1	0	1	0.5
$t6$	0	0	1	0	0	0

Consistent with the results reported in the episodic literature these results suggest that in the first episode of an iterative situation, the competitive strategy is the best approach in bargaining for coalition payoffs.[52] The computations I have just reported, however, indicate that the competitive strategy is a poor strategy in subsequent iterations. Only the mixed strategy affords any chance at future extra benefits, given the parameter values used in table 2.1.

In the preceding discussion, it was assumed that all demands for extra payoffs were identical. This is, of course, a simplification of the variety of demands and payoffs that actually occur in coalitions. The equation for computing the probability that an actor's demands are satisfied can be generalized to introduce variance into the magnitude of the demands, as well as their frequency. This is done by redefining the discount term to reflect the magnitude of demands, and then counting the magnitude of each demand times its frequency. Thus, the greater the magnitude of a demand, the higher the probability that it will be rejected (that is, the greater $1 - p_i(Y)_n$). If competitors are inclined to demand larger benefits than mixed strategists, and are inclined to demand those benefits more frequently, then the relative advantage of the mixed strategy over the competitive strategy is even more distinct.

From this discussion the third hypothesis of this study follows:

A theory of coalition behavior

H3: An actor's share of a coalition's redistributive benefits decreases as the actor moves toward a purely cooperative or a purely competitive strategy. An actor's share of a coalition's redistributive benefits is positively associated with the degree to which the actor pursues a mixed strategy.

Risk-taking and strategic preferences

There are several inadequacies with the redistributive equation. Most serious of these is its failure to indicate the conditions under which an actor might rationally deviate from the mixed strategy. Rather than assume that deviations from this strategy indicate irrational choices, I prefer to explore the conditions which might lead to alternative strategic preferences. To do this, it is necessary to examine the three strategies with respect to the risk an actor takes that it will be ousted from a winning coalition, that it will not receive a disproportionately large share of the redistributive benefits, and that it will not be able to maximize the joint occurrence of remaining in a winning coalition and securing a disproportionately large share of redistributive benefits. In addition, it is necessary to examine the effect that risk-taking predispositions have in altering strategic preferences.

The first task is to understand the elements which enter the decision-making process when an actor is confronted with alternative strategies as a means to achieve the same end. In particular, it is important to understand the actor's assessment of the probability that a given outcome will occur if he selects one strategy as opposed to another, and to know how much value the actor attaches to the outcome. Finally, we must know the intrinsic value the actor associates with each of his strategic options. These elements may be combined in a single rational-choice *preference equation*. Solving such an equation permits us to evaluate the preferred strategy for any actor, given any set of goals. Riker and Ordeshook suggest the following equation for this purpose:

$$\sum_{a=1}^{r} [p_q(O_a) - p_s(O_a)]U(O_a) + (U_q - U_s) \text{ for } s \neq q$$

where q and s are alternative strategies, p_s and p_q are the probabilities that strategies s and q will result in the successful accomplishment of outcome a (hereafter O_a). U refers to the utility of an action or event. $U(O_a)$ is the value an actor attaches to outcome a, while U_q and U_s are the values an actor attaches to each of the contending strategies.

If the equation sums to a value greater than zero, given the pairwise comparison of the same two strategies across a set of desired outcomes, then strategy q is preferred to strategy s. If it sums to less than zero, then strategy s is preferred. Finally, if the equation sums to zero, the actor is indifferent between the strategies. Of course, this equation can be used to compare any set of strategies across any set of outcomes.[53] The utility of each outcome reflects the preference ordering the actor has with respect to the alternative outcomes before it, just as the utility of the strategies specifies the actor's strategic preference ordering.

One might conclude from the redistributive equation that all rational actors prefer the mixed strategy if their most preferred outcome is the joint maximization of their longevity in a winning coalition and their acquisition of extra redistributive benefits in that coalition. One might similarly infer that the cooperative strategy is preferred by actors who value most highly their continued membership in a winning coalition, while those who value the short-term acquisition of redistributive benefits might prefer the competitive strategy. As should be clear from the preference equation, such conclusions would be premature since a final assessment of an actor's preferred strategy cannot be made until more is known about the utility of each strategy, as well as its probability of yielding the desired outcome.[54]

Estimating the probability of achieving a desired outcome, given a particular strategy, is easier than determining the utility that a strategy has for different individuals. In the case of the three goals mentioned above, the redistributive equation is easily applied to determine the likelihood of remaining in the winning coalition, gaining a disproportionately large share of the coalition's benefits, or doing both. A glance at the discount term indicates the rate at which an actor approaches being ousted from the coalition, or being cut off from its benefits, as a consequence of the lost tolerance of its allies.[55] Clearly, the discount term for demands approaches zero most rapidly for competitive actors, followed by the mixed strategists. It barely deviates from 1.0 for cooperative actors. In terms of preserving one's membership in a winning coalition, the cooperative strategy is best and the competitive strategy is worst.

Acquiring an optimal level of extra redistributive benefits, and converting them into future influence, is most likely if one follows the mixed strategy. The probability of getting such extra benefits approaches zero if one is cooperative. The highly competitive strategy results in an initially high probability of gaining disproportionately, but this probability tapers off toward zero over several iterations. The number of iterations that must pass before it reaches zero depends upon the tolerance limits of its partners. With intolerant partners, the probability goes to zero quickly, while with tolerant partners, the probability of success goes to zero slowly. However, in the very long run, competitiveness is more likely to lead to a loss of access to those extra benefits than is a mixed strategy. Thus, in the very long run, at least, imperfect tolerance on the part of one's partners means that the mixed strategist has a higher probability of getting a dispropor-

A theory of coalition behavior

tionately large share of a coalition's redistributive benefits than does the competitive actor.

The probability of optimizing both one's longevity in a winning coalition and one's access to its redistributive benefits is determined by multiplying the individual probabilities associated with the components of this joint outcome. As should be evident from the above discussion, the fact that the cooperative strategy yields a probability of receiving extra benefits that approaches zero indicates that the joint probability for the cooperative strategy approaches zero. Similarly, the fact that the competitive strategy results in a probability of remaining in the winning coalition that approaches zero means that the joint probability for the competitive strategy approaches zero. Finally, the mixed strategy yields a joint probability whose magnitude is greater than zero. The exact value of this probability, of course, depends on the specific parameters in the system and so can range anywhere from a very low to a very high value. In relative terms, however, it is likely to be of moderate magnitude. This follows from the observation that the mixed strategist's probability of remaining in the winning coalition was moderate and that same actor's probability of securing extra benefits was moderate to large. A summary of these probabilities is found in table 2.2.

TABLE 2.2 *Strategic preferences and desired outcomes*

Strategy	Outcomes		
	Longevity	Benefits	Joint
Cooperate	$p \to 1$	$p \to 0$	$p \to 0$
Complete	$p \to 0$	$0 < p < 1$	$p \to 0$
Mixed	$0 < p < 1$	$0 < p < 1$	$0 < p < 1$

If it is assumed that an actor values each strategy equally, then the redistributive equation determines the strategy chosen by each actor, given its particular outcome preference ordering. An actor preferring to maximize its longevity as a member of a winning coalition would, for example, prefer the cooperative strategy to the mixed strategy and the mixed strategy to the competitive strategy. Since these preferences are transitive, it would also prefer the cooperative strategy to the competitive strategy. Those preferring to maximize their share of the redistributive benefits during any single iteration would prefer either the mixed strategy or the competitive strategy (depending upon the specific tolerance parameters in their decision-making system) as their first choice. The cooperative strategy would be their least preferred option. Finally, an actor that prefers to maximize the probability of achieving both outcomes (though not necessarily maximizing each outcome), prefers the mixed strategy to either the cooperative or the competitive strategy. Since the joint outcome is the postulated goal for this study, it is assumed that overall the mixed strategy is the most preferred option for an actor, provided the utility it attributes to each strategy is equal. But, it is very unlikely that each strategy is of equal value to an actor. In fact, a substantial body of research concerned with risk-taking motivations indicates that there are systematic differences in risk-taking preferences among individuals.

If attention is focused on the predisposition decision-makers have to take risks, several interesting observations may be made. One observation of particular interest here is that decisions involving a high subjective probability of failure and decisions involving a high subjective probability of success are more like each other than they are like decisions that involve a moderate subjective probability of success or failure. When the probability of failure or success is believed to be high, the decision-maker can be fairly confident about the outcome. Uncertainty occurs, on the other hand, when a moderately risky decision is made.

A few simple examples should help clarify these forms of certainty and uncertainty. An individual with money to invest may choose to place his money in an insured bank account, in mutual funds, or in an Irish Sweepstakes ticket. Money in the bank is almost certain to grow, although it will not necessarily keep up with inflation. There is virtually no risk that the money will be completely lost. The investor is, therefore, reasonably certain of enjoying a small increase in wealth as a consequence of his investment. Purchasing a ticket in the Irish Sweepstakes is almost certain to lead to a complete loss of the investment. On the other hand, should the ticket prove a winner, the financial gains can be substantial. Of course, if one were to calculate the investment needed to satisfy the random probability of winning, one would discover that in the long run, lotteries yield greater profits for those who run the lottery than for those who purchase tickets in it. Finally, placing one's money in mutual funds does not guarantee some increase in wealth, nor does it assure the loss of the investment. If one is skillful at selecting a mutual fund, substantial benefits can be enjoyed in the long run. In general, however, money invested in mutual funds grows faster than bank accounts, but less quickly than if one is successful in the Irish Sweepstakes. Thus, the probability of success is high and the value of the payoff, given success, is generally low when one undertakes behavior that is not risky. The probability of success is low, but the value of success is high when one undertakes behavior that is extremely risky. The probability of success, and the value of the benefits given success, are moderate when one undertakes behavior that is moderately risky.

Individuals motivated to take moderate risks, with the attendant un-

A theory of coalition behavior

certainty, would be somewhat predisposed to follow the mixed strategy. Individuals predisposed to maximize the certainty of an outcome would prefer either the cooperative or the competitive strategy, depending upon which particular outcome they were most inclined to pursue. Thus, those preferring to maximize their longevity as a member of a winning coalition should prefer the cooperative strategy, while those preferring to maximize their short-term share of a coalition's benefits should prefer the competitive strategy. If the joint outcome is preferred to either of these goals, and if a decision-maker prefers to maximize certainty, then the cooperative strategy and the competitive strategy may be preferred to the mixed strategy. This produces a situation in which the preferred strategy is more likely to lead to failure than the alternative strategy.

As noted earlier, the joint outcome is a restatement of the postulated goal on which this study is focused. The likelihood that the joint outcome is accomplished depends on the individual decision-maker's skill at manipulating the order in which he behaves cooperatively and competitively. The ratio of competitive to cooperative acts alone does not determine the probability that the mixed strategy will result in success. Thus, one can behave competitively half the time and behave cooperatively the other half the time and, given the parameter values from table 2.1, experience a range in the probability of overall success from

$$1/\{[\sum_{i=1}^{m} f_i(D)_{t_1}](n)\} \quad \text{to} \quad \{\sum_{t=1}^{m}[f_i(D)_t / \sum_{i=1}^{m} f_i(D)_t]\}/n$$

Given the specific values and actors in the coalitions represented in table 2.1, for example, a mixed strategy that alternates between cooperative and competitive acts results in a mean probability of success in any iteration equal to 0.25. A mixed strategy in which all competitive acts occur in sequence followed by all the cooperative acts, on the other hand, results in a mean probability of success equal to 0.083. In general, the mixed strategy yields the optimal possible level of benefits when one alternates the series of competitive and cooperative acts in exactly the proportion suggested by the rate at which the tolerance parameter increases. It is the skill involved in discerning one's partner's tolerance parameter that affects one's ability to maximize success in the long run. The competitive strategy, by way of contrast, allows no flexibility in the organization of responses. It is inattentive to the location of the tolerance parameters of all the members of a winning coalition. Consequently, the competitive strategy can succeed in the long run only if the competitor is lucky enough to stumble on the appropriate behavior for its partners. If it does succeed (and it will be recalled that the probability that it will achieve the joint outcome approaches zero), this does not indicate any skill on the part of the competitor; just luck. Similarly, if the cooperator succeeds in its pursuit of the joint out-

A theory of coalition behavior

come this is not a consequence of any particular skill or effort on its part. It is just a consequence of luck. This is true since no actor would have any clear incentive to reward the cooperator beyond its demands. Those demands are, by definition, minimal. Only the mixed strategy allows the actor consciously to manipulate the outcome by manipulating the sequencing of its competitive and cooperative actions. One might stumble on the mixed strategy by chance, and thereby succeed through luck, but this is probably less likely than one's following this strategy by design. While I prove this shortly, for the moment let me simply repeat that the other strategies, in their pure form, only allow one type of behavior – either competitive or cooperative – and so deny the actor any significant manipulative opportunities.

Need for achievement and risk-taking

What factors influence an individual's predisposition to value uncertainty or certainty? How do these factors influence the decision to pursue one strategy or another? One possible determinant of risk-taking preferences is a decision-maker's need for achievement. The way need for achievement, as a motivational pre-disposition, influences strategic choices is embodied in its definition: the desire to compete against a standard of excellence.[56]

Of course, it is difficult to measure one's performance against a standard of excellence when the decision-maker has little or no control over the outcome that results from his strategic choices. Cooperative choices and competitive choices do not give the decision-maker much control over outcomes. As is clear from table 2.2, the cooperative strategy results in near certainty that one remains in a winning coalition, that one gains extra benefits, or that one does both. Similarly, the competitive strategy results in fairly certain outcomes of at least remaining in a winning coalition or achieving the joint outcome. The mixed strategy results in uncertainty with respect to all three goals discussed in table 2.2. That is, it is difficult to assess one's success at competing against a standard of excellence when the inflexible cooperative or competitive strategies are followed. This is true because anyone choosing these strategies would be equally likely to experience the exact same outcome. It is not difficult to assess one's success at competing against a standard of excellence, however, when the mixed strategy is chosen. In that case, different individuals will experience different degrees of success, depending on their astuteness in organizing their competitive and cooperative acts. Consequently, decision-makers with high need for achievement (that is, a substantial need to compete against a standard of excellence) are more inclined to pursue the moderate risk, mixed strategy than are individuals with low need for achievement. This suggests the following hypothesis:

A theory of coalition behavior

H4: The higher an actor's need for achievement, the greater the tendency for the actor to prefer the mixed strategy.[57]

Hypothesis 4 suggests that actors with high need for achievement are expected to attribute a greater value to the mixed strategy than to the cooperative strategy or the competitive strategy. Actors with low need for achievement are expected to attribute a greater utility to the cooperative or the competitive strategy than they are to the mixed strategy. That is, they are expected to prefer risk-taking behavior that involves a high degree of certainty.[58] With this information it is possible to return to the preference equation and estimate the likelihood that an individual will pursue any one of these strategies given the value of the outcome being pursued, the value of the strategy being pursued, and the probability of fulfilling the outcome given one or another strategy. Table 2.3 suggests the expected preferences based on the following assumptions and conditions:

(a) For individuals with high need for achievement $U_{mx} > U_{co} = U_{cp}$, with mx = mixed strategy, co = cooperative strategy, cp = competitive strategy. U refers to utility.
(b) For individuals with low need for achievement, $U_{co} = U_{cp} > U_{mx}$.
(c) $U_j = 1$; $0 < U_l \leqslant 1$; $0 < U_b \leqslant 1$. j = joint outcome, l = longevity, b = benefits
(d) $p_{co}(O_l) > p_{mx}(O_l) > p_{cp}(O_l)$
(e) $p_{mx}(O_b) \geqslant p_{cp}(O_b) > p_{co}(O_b)$
(f) $p_{mx}(O_j) > p_{co}(O_j) \approx p_{cp}(O_j)$.[59]

Table 2.3 reveals several interesting results. Most important is that the mixed strategy is the most preferred strategy for decision-makers with high need for achievement in five of the six pairwise comparisons of strategies that include the mixed strategy. In the sixth case the preference ordering depends upon the exact magnitude of each value rather than just the ordinal ranking of the values. Even in this one case, the mixed strategy cannot be the least preferred strategy for achieving the specific goal (that is, maximizing longevity). Thus, decision-makers with high need for achievement prefer the mixed strategy to all other strategies when they pursue the short-term maximization of benefits and when they pursue the long-term maximization of benefits embodied in the joint outcome. They prefer the mixed strategy and the cooperative strategy to the competitive strategy when the goal being pursued is the longevity outcome.

Decision-makers with low need for achievement are confronted with considerable ambiguity in their efforts to select a strategic option. Only with respect to the longevity outcome do they have a clear first choice – to cooperate. In the case of the maximization of short-term benefits they are undecided between the competitive strategy and the mixed strategy. With respect to the joint outcome, the decision-makers with low need for achieve-

A theory of coalition behavior

TABLE 2.3 *Need for achievement and strategic preferences*

Probabilities	Low n-ach utilities	Strategic preference	High n-ach utilities	Strategic preference
$[p_{co}(O_l) - p_{cp}(O_l)]U_l > 0 + (U_{co} - U_{cp} = 0)$	= Cooperate	$(U_{co} - U_{cp} = 0)$	= Cooperate
$[p_{co}(O_l) - p_{mx}(O_l)]U_l > 0 + (U_{co} - U_{mx} > 0)$	= Cooperate	$(U_{co} - U_{mx} < 0)$	= ?[a]
$[p_{mx}(O_l) - p_{cp}(O_l)]U_l > 0 + (U_{mx} - U_{cp} < 0)$	= ?	$(U_{mx} - U_{cp} > 0)$	= Mixed
$[p_{co}(O_b) - p_{cp}(O_b)]U_b < 0 + (U_{co} - U_{cp} = 0)$	= Compete	$(U_{co} - U_{cp} = 0)$	= Compete
$[p_{co}(O_b) - p_{mx}(O_b)]U_b < 0 + (U_{co} - U_{mx} > 0)$	= ?	$(U_{co} - U_{mx} < 0)$	= Mixed
$[p_{mx}(O_b) - p_{cp}(O_b)]U_b \geqslant 0 + (U_{mx} - U_{cp} < 0)$	= ?	$(U_{mx} - U_{cp} > 0)$	= Mixed
$[p_{co}(O_j) - p_{cp}(O_j)]U_j \to 0 + (U_{co} - U_{cp} = 0)$	= Indifference	$(U_{co} - U_{cp} = 0)$	= Indifference
$[p_{co}(O_j) - p_{mx}(O_j)]U_j < 0 + (U_{co} - U_{mx} > 0)$	= ?	$(U_{co} - U_{mx} < 0)$	= Mixed
$[p_{mx}(O_j) - p_{cp}(O_j)]U_j > 0 + (U_{mx} - U_{cp} < 0)$	= ?	$(U_{mx} - U_{cp} > 0)$	= Mixed

[a] ? indicates that the preference is unknown: in these cases the preference depends on the exact value of the probabilities and the utilities, rather than on their ordinal ranking. Strategic preferences in these cases are unlikely to reflect a systematic pattern among individuals, at least so far as the variables specified here are concerned. These cases differ somewhat from those situations where the decision-makers are reported to be indifferent between choices. In the indifferent cases, it is also unlikely that there are systematic differences related to the variables I have specified (assuming that the underlying assumptions are correct), but this uncertainty on our part would not be altered by knowing the exact values of the entries in the preference equations. If the assumption of equal utilities for the competitive and co-operative strategies were relaxed and replaced with the assumption that they are almost equal, the cases that indicate indifference would become ?.

A theory of coalition behavior

ment are hopelessly deadlocked. Almost any idiosyncratic external input might be sufficient to sway some low need for achievers toward the competitive, some toward the cooperative, and still others toward the mixed strategy. Thus, while any individual in this group may manage to select an option, the group as a whole is not expected to manifest any particular strategic preference when it comes to the joint outcome.

Over time, individuals within the low need for achievement group are expected to alter their strategic preferences in response to small changes in idiosyncratic, exogenous factors. Consequently, many decision-makers with low need for achievement may appear to follow the mixed strategy in that a random distribution of strategic acts manifests some of the characteristics of that strategy. The important difference is, of course, that the mixed strategy involves the proper manipulation of actions to operate within one's partner's tolerance limits; it does not simply involve long sequences of one and then the other pure type of behavior, nor does it involve haphazard decisions to cooperate or compete. Consequently, low need for achievement decision-makers are likely to suboptimize their long-term gains by not using the various strategies in a systematic, goal-attaining way. Decision-makers with high need for achievement, on the other hand, systematically prefer the strategy that results in the long-term maximization of political influence. This suggests the fifth hypothesis for this study.

H5: Political actors with high need for achievement are more likely than political actors with low need for achievement to succeed in maximizing their long-term influence over the decision-making process.

Organization and success

The presence of a predisposition to take moderate risks, such as exists in individuals with high need for achievement, does not guarantee success in acquiring the benefits afforded by the joint outcome of preserving one's membership in a winning coalition and continuing to receive a disproportionately large share of the coalition's redistributive benefits. It does guarantee success, at least if this theory is correct, when an actor's estimation of the probability of success associated with each strategy is accurate. If an actor incorrectly perceives the riskiness of the competitive strategy, for example, it might erroneously select that strategy thinking that competitive behavior involves only a moderate risk of failure. For the assessment of riskiness to be accurate, the estimating actor must be in a position (*a*) to gauge the tolerance limits of its allies; (*b*) to evaluate the credibility of any threats it might issue; and (*c*) to assess the amount of time it needs to convert any benefits it acquires into an integral part of its resource base. That is, an actor must have the organizational wherewithal to make

A theory of coalition behavior

reasonable estimates of its capabilities and of the likely responses by its partners. Thus, high need for achievement and implementation of a mixed strategy are particularly likely to result in the long-term maximization of a political actor's influence provided the actor is in a position to use the mixed strategy meaningfully. Idle threats can only hasten the actor's passing of its partners' tolerance limits without prompting any concessions from them. Threats that are taken seriously, on the other hand, can result in handsome rewards in the long run. This can be restated in the form of a hypothesis:

H6: Political actors predisposed to pursue the mixed strategy, with the organizational capabilities necessary to identify the optimal application of that strategy, and with the motivational predisposition to take the risks involved in the optimal application of that strategy are most likely to acquire a disproportionately large share of the redistributive benefits in their coalitions. Consequently, they are most likely to increase their political influence in the long run.

Coalition termination

The coalition termination stage has been alluded to frequently in the discussions of coalition formation and coalition maintenance. It is appropriate now to examine this stage more extensively.

When an actor cannot increase its capabilities relative to its partners, and when some of its partners can still increase their capabilities in the coalition, then the actor cannot improve its position, and might lose part of its excess benefits by remaining in the coalition. If it is an essential member of the alliance then it can terminate the coalition by withdrawing its support, cutting its partners off from access to the extra benefits which it can no longer acquire, and depriving the coalition of the margin required to win.

Such an approach to coalition is, of course, filled with uncertainty. So long as the actor remains in the coalition, it has access to at least some benefits, even if not a disproportionately large share of them. In addition, so long as an actor is in the winning coalition it is likely to benefit, or at least not lose, relative to those actors outside the winning coalition. On the other hand, by withdrawing an actor increases its ability to manipulate the precoalition formation situation to gain access to a coalition that excludes some of its former partners. If it can enter such a coalition, then its long-term prospects are improved even if it manages to get its fair share of the payoff and no more. This follows from the observation that an actor that always gets a fair share of the redistributive benefits can gain continuously, while an actor that wins sometimes and loses sometimes may

A theory of coalition behavior

find that its losses offset its gains in the long run. Of course, if an actor can gain access to a maximum number of winning coalitions and gain a disproportionately large share of the redistributive benefits in most, if not all, such coalitions then it should do best of all. It would do worst by being systematically excluded from all winning coalitions (as might happen to an overly competitive actor), or by systematically accepting less than a fair share of a coalition's benefits in exchange for continued membership (as might happen to a cooperative actor). In any event, if an actor terminates one coalition and then joins another that excludes some of its former partners, it puts itself in a position to diminish the influence of some of its former allies. It does so by extracting, as the cost of losing, some of the redistributive benefits they secured in earlier coalitions.

The most significant danger involved in pursuing a coalition termination strategy such as I have just described is that one could easily surpass the tolerance limits of all other actors in the system. This would occur if one were overly competitive and manipulative in one's coalition dealings or if one enjoyed too rapid a rate of growth in one's resource base (provided that one's size were not so great that one becomes essential to any winning coalition). A skillful actor might avoid these pitfalls, at least until some nth iteration during which it achieves monopoly control over the decision-making process, or becomes an essential member of future winning coalitions, or at least becomes as influential as it can. The risks involved, and the skills required to regulate the costs and benefits of such a strategy are, of course, conditions that are attractive to decision-makers with high need for achievement. On the other hand, actors motivated by a desire for social acceptance, such as some cooperative actors, are considerably less inclined to follow this strategy.[60] This suggests that the risk-taking propensities associated with high need for achievement are likely to predispose an actor to the potentially optimizing strategy for coalition termination, as well as the optimal strategy for manipulating payoffs within coalitions. These same actors are also most likely to compete at the optimal level during the coalition formation stage since they are most inclined to value the manipulations, trades, and compromises that characterize successful bargaining for membership in a winning coalition.

Actors who rigidly hold to their initial demands, or who are unwilling to compromise their goals, are unlikely to find partners who are sufficiently compatible with them so that they can gain access to winning coalitions. Thus, political actors with low need for achievement are most likely to secure membership in winning coalitions when their partners pretend to share similar goals to theirs. Assuming that political ideology is unassociated with need for achievement, this means that coalitions are likely to include decision-makers with low need for achievement as a resource to be exploited by high need for achievement partners. Of course, if the

A theory of coalition behavior

decision-makers with low need for achievement recognize this intention they will balk at the opportunity to join such 'partnerships', unless they value the potential policy payoffs sufficiently to sacrifice consciously their share of the redistributive payoffs.

Summary

I have suggested a theory of behavior in coalitions that is based on the notion that some benefits derived from coalitions become an integral part of the resources that actors bring to bear in future decision-making situations. Given this redistributive condition, and assuming that actors want to maximize their long-term influence over the decision-making process, the hypotheses are: (*a*) The largest actor in a political system at any point in time is the least likely actor to gain membership in a winning coalition. Intermediate-sized actors have an intermediate probability of belonging to a winning coalition whereas small actors have the highest probability of being members of winning coalitions. (*b*) The redistributive benefits of winning coalitions are not distributed in accordance with any size-related formula such as the parity norm, but in response to the demands of the individual constituents of the winning coalition. Those demands vary from extremely competitive demands for continuous enjoyment of extra redistributive benefits to extremely cooperative behavior, characterized by demands for the fulfillment of the collective policy goals of the coalition rather than the private political goals of the constituents. (*c*) Actors following a mixed strategy, sometimes demanding the pursuit of the coalition's collective policy goals and sometimes demanding the satisfaction of the actors' private political goals, gain a disproportionately large share of their coalitions' redistributive benefits. These benefits are, through the careful manipulation of the mixed strategy, converted into increases in the actors' long-term influence. Thus, actors following the mixed strategy do better in coalitions, and in subsequent political contests and decision-making situations, than do more cooperative or more competitive actors. This is especially true if the actor has the organizational capacity to implement the mixed strategy effectively. The effectiveness of the implementation of this strategy involves the appropriate timing of competitive and cooperative acts, as well as the accurate assessment of the tolerance limits of one's partners and the credibility of one's demands. (*d*) The motivational predisposition of an actor to take moderate or extreme risks has a substantial impact on its inclination to implement the mixed strategy in the most effective way. More specifically, the higher the need for achievement of the actor, the greater the inclination to undertake strategic maneuvers that require skill rather than luck on the part of the actor. In addition, the higher the need for achievement of the actor, the greater the inclination

A theory of coalition behavior

to undertake actions that require using its organizational capacity to identify and operate as close to the tolerance frontiers of its partners as is possible. Finally, (*e*) the inclination of an actor to pursue the appropriate strategy during the coalition formation stage, the maintenance stage, and the termination stage are all related to the risk-taking propensities of the actor. Those actors predisposed to take moderate risks are most likely to pursue an optimizing strategy during each stage of coalition politics.

3. The Indian context: 1967-1971

Why India?

India, perhaps more than any other political entity, embodies a wealth of diverse coalition settings and experiences. Indeed, it is a microcosm of the conditions prevalent in a variety of political systems dependent on coalition politics for the performance of the functions of government. For these reasons, India is a most appropriate place in which to test a theory of coalition behavior. Probably there is no other political system with as great a potential for developing diverse forms of government as India.[1] Certainly, it can be said that no other nation has experienced the diversity of governments that India has since 1967.

The widely differing coalition experiences that the Indian states have undergone provide an abundant opportunity for the examination of a broad spectrum of generalizations. Since 1967 there have been more than twenty different coalition governments in the Indian states. In West Bengal, and to a lesser extent in Kerala, these governments have been based on common programs agreed to by primarily leftist political parties. In Orissa, on the other hand, there has been a coalition between ideologically like-minded parties of the right. In Uttar Pradesh, Bihar, Madhya Pradesh, Haryana, and the Punjab the coalitions have consisted of parties with disparate ideologies.

The Indian experience encompasses a very diverse set of coalition governments in terms of the number of political parties involved in the various state alliances. In Orissa, for example, there was a two-party government, while in West Bengal, a coalition of no less than fourteen parties was formed. The sizes of the other coalition governments have fallen at various intervals between these two extremes.

The Indian experience is representative of the scope of coalitions in other ways as well. For instance, one of the aspects of coalition politics that has attracted considerable attention is the tendency for parties to aggregate themselves either into grand coalitions or into minimal winning coalitions.[2] Both types of alliances occurred in India between 1967 and 1971.

There are other compelling reasons for considering India a suitable arena for the study of coalition behavior. The Indian experience provides examples of national political parties vying for increased national status, and regional political parties competing for increased attention to their more limited goals. This facilitates an examination of the relationship between developments at the state level and changes at the center. It also enhances the investigation of the relationship between environmental constraints and the growth and development of political parties.

The Indian context: 1967–1971

The actors

Between 1952 and 1967 the Congress Party's support gradually withered; with the exception of 1957, the party continuously lost seats and votes to the opposition. Yet, until 1967 the Congress proved remarkably able to maintain control both at the center and in the provinces. This was true even though the party rarely polled a majority of votes in either the state assembly (Vidhan Sabha) or national parliamentary (Lok Sabha) elections. A breakdown of the Congress vote by election, assembly, and state is given in appendix I.

In 1967 the election results took on a radically new complexion. Not only did the Congress continue to lose votes, it also lost its majority of seats in eight states. Within a few months of the elections, defections from the Congress ranks deprived the party of its majority in another two states. Once the Congress monopoly of power was broken, state after state began a search for a viable alternative government. Only in Madras did an alternative present itself in the form of a single-party government. In one province – Rajasthan – no government was formed and so President's Rule was implemented.[3] Eight other states decided to experiment with coalition governments. It is the governments in these eight states that are the focus of this study.

As the Congress Party declined over the years, many All-India parties hoped to form their own governments in the provinces. Others did not consider this feasible and so declared their desire to develop alliances with other parties. It was their hope that through the mechanism of coalitions they would be able to replace the Congress Party as the ruling force in the states, and, eventually in Delhi. The various parties began to formulate a variety of election strategies, each geared toward the removal of the Congress Party from power. An examination of the pre-election orientation toward coalitions of each of the All-India parties will help clarify some of their later actions.

The Bharatiya Jana Sangh. Among those parties opposed to pre-election alliances is the nationalist, traditionalist, militantly pro-Hindi/Hindu Bharatiya Jana Sangh. The Jana Sangh has long taken the position that cooperation with other parties is possible after elections, but that the election period is an opportunity for the party to gain popularity, educate the masses to its ideology, and expand its organization by contesting seats on its own platform, unencumbered by election alliances. This was the case in 1967 when Deendayal Upadhyaya, the late General Secretary of the party, explained that in the Jana Sangh's view 'alliances and adjustments may serve a temporary tactical purpose, but cannot provide the ideological inspiration to inculcate a spirit of service, sacrifice and sustained effort.' He

The Indian context: 1967-1971

went on to explain that the Jana Sangh 'has looked upon elections not merely as an opportunity to capture power by democratic means, but also as an opportunity to educate the people. We [sic] have been trying to achieve the first objective without sacrificing the second.'[4]

While most other parties were attempting to forge pre-election alliances to defeat the Congress, the Jana Sangh felt it was more important to present its own program and so remained aloof from most such arrangements. Its attitude toward pre-election fronts, however, should not be construed as implying a distaste for post-election alliances. Quite the contrary, the events proved that the Jana Sangh was eager to participate in such alliances.

At the close of the fourth general election in India (1967) it became apparent that the Jana Sangh would have to cooperate in coalition governments, even with their arch enemy – the Communist Party of India (CPI) – if they wanted to prevent the Congress from ruling. The opportunity to control some of the machinery of government was welcomed by the party, even if it meant cooperating with allegedly anti-nationalist forces (such as the CPI, and the allegedly separatist Akali Dal in the Punjab). Whereas in April of 1967 the Jana Sangh was still declaring its unabashed opposition to electoral alliances and adjustments, by December of that year the party claimed that:

'from the very beginning the Jana Sangh kept the doors open and declared its willingness to arrive at adjustments with other parties. At the same time a proviso was added to the effect that there would be no adjustment with the Communists, Muslim League, and other antinational parties. But this stipulation was thoughtfully kept apart from the ideological position.'[5]

Keeping it apart from the 'ideological position' meant that the party was able to justify its participation in coalition governments with the very parties it had earlier branded as being anti-national or communal. The coalitions were justified and legitimized to the Jana Sangh's supporters by claiming that the party joined because that was the only way to maximize their potential for emerging as a viable one-party alternative to the Congress by the next general election. Thus, the party's leaders declared that they must possess the 'self-confidence which permits a growing party to play the game of politics, and on the basis of which it can use every agreement and adjustment to gain increased strength and prestige and overtake other parties'.[6]

The Jana Sangh formula for success was to join coalitions, but only with the intention of using the coalitions to strengthen its own hand at the expense of its alliance partners. The Jana Sangh's leadership argued that their political enemies could be more readily undermined from within the government than from outside the government.[7] In short, the Jana Sangh

The Indian context: 1967–1971

claimed that its strategy would enhance the achievement of the party's program in the long run, even if it appeared to undermine the party's customary position in the short run.

The Jana Sangh's attitude toward coalition governments is consistent with its position toward pre-election alliances. Because it openly admits that the party intends to use coalitions for its own advancement, Jana Sangh partners should not be surprised by its unwillingness to formally align with them during the elections. As the 1969 midterm polls drew near, the Jana Sangh once again expressed its customary opposition to interparty cooperation. It maintained that:

> 'in a parliamentary democracy, coalitions can be accepted only as a matter of political compulsion. Every political party naturally aspires to gain strength enough to rule by itself. . . . So, in the U.P. poll, the Jana Sangh has decided to strive for an absolute majority and thus be able to shape the destinies of this largest state in the country in accordance with its own plan and programme.'[8]

Naturally, when it failed to achieve a majority, the party once again eagerly sought membership in ruling coalitions.

The Jana Sangh, being a pragmatic political party, does not adhere rigidly to its policy against election alliances. When it believes that such an alliance will further the party's efforts to overtake other parties, then the Jana Sangh does join pre-election alliances. For example, the Jana Sangh participated in a pre-election alliance with the Akali Dal in the Punjab during the 1969 midterm poll. In that case, the Jana Sangh was clearly the weaker party and stood to gain much more than it could possibly lose. As the party explained, in another context, 'It is often the major partners who have to sacrifice the most, both in terms of ideology as well as of political interests'.[9]

After the split in the Congress Party in late 1969, and particularly during the period immediately before the 1971 general election, the Jana Sangh made several attempts to forge an alliance with the Congress (O) and with the Swatantra Party. This is in keeping with the party's desire to promote the polarization of political forces in India. The Jana Sangh, with its tight-knit and competent organization, would very likely stand to gain from such a polarization of forces.[10] It might very well emerge as the leading voice of the right in Indian politics.

The general attitude of the Jana Sangh toward coalition politics, at least as it has been expressed in party publications, is one of cautious tolerance. The party is cooperative when that appears to be the best strategy for its own ends, and it is competitive when competitiveness seems to benefit it the most.[11] In later chapters the extent to which the party's leaders and actions

The Indian context: 1967–1971

support a mixed competitive–cooperative mode of behavior is examined and an attempt is made to determine if this strategy has been effective in maximizing the gains of the Jana Sangh.

The Swatantra Party. The Jana Sangh attitude toward coalition politics is neither typical of the position of most parties, nor even of the political party closest to it in ideology. The Swatantra Party is a laissez faire, nineteenth-century liberal party, with a strong admixture of Indian aristocrats and other traditionally oriented leaders.[12] It is a newer party than the Jana Sangh, with an older leadership.[13]

The Swatantra Party is much less willing to compete on its own in electoral politics than is the Jana Sangh. Thus, while the Jana Sangh was focusing its attention on how it could come to power, Swatantra was formulating a strategy to remove Congress from the seats of government. The difference in these two positions is quite important. The Jana Sangh perceived the fourth general election primarily as an opportunity for it to grow. Swatantra responded to the election in negative terms. It was not so much concerned with its own growth as with preventing the further growth of the Congress Party.

Early in its existence, Swatantra recognized that no one party was likely to provide a viable alternative to the Congress in the short run. Swatantra, therefore, accepted the principle of pre-election alliances well before the fourth general election. In 1964, the party declared that 'if the Congress Government in New Delhi has to be displaced in 1967, considerable progress will have to be made between now and then in the direction of increased and closer cooperation between democratic opposition parties'.[14] The party was not, however, surrendering its own aspirations for power to the common cause against the Congress. In the same breath, Swatantra also maintained that 'there is no reason why, as is sometimes feared, the Party's initiative in this direction should be a reason for any slackening in our organizational efforts, which should enjoy the highest priority among our tasks'.[15] Whether this was an accurate assessment remains to be seen. At this point it must suffice to point out that 56 per cent of Swatantra Party elites, when asked if they felt that pre-election alliances were harmful to the successful development of the party's organizational wing, responded yes ($N=9$).[16] In any event, Swatantra's affinity for pre-election alliances is in keeping with its desire to pursue a short-term goal – the ouster of the Congress Party from power.

In keeping with its declaration of 1964, and with the spirit of its election manifesto in 1967, Swatantra attempted to forge pre-election alliances with other rightist parties, such as the Jana Sangh, the Jan Congress (in Orissa), and others. In Orissa their efforts proved so successful that the Swatantra Party emerged as the major party in the state's coalition government.

The Indian context: 1967–1971

Following this success, and despite the failure of its policy in other states, Swatantra continued to support the notion of program-oriented pre-election alliances as the only legitimate basis for the formation of coalition governments. In an article in *Swarajya*, an official publication of the Swatantra Party, Francis Meckery wrote: 'Any coalition without a minimum programme on which the parties are committed to the extent of compromising their other necessarily diverse and even mutually opposing objectives, is without a *raison d'être* for its existence.'[17]

Swatantra, like the Jana Sangh, is opposed to communism. C. Rajagopalachari, the elder statesman and founder of the party, often branded both of India's major communist parties as 'public enemy number one'. Despite this opposition, Swatantra has also found it necessary to join coalition governments that included the CPI, but, unlike the Jana Sangh, Swatantra quickly found itself unable to continue to participate in those governments and so withdrew. Whether the withdrawals were the result of a reawakening of its ideological purity, or whether they resulted from the recognition that the Party was being outmaneuvered by its partners remains to be seen.

Following the split in the Congress Party, Swatantra, like the Jana Sangh, made efforts to foster closer ties with the Congress (O). Since the split, and particularly as the fifth general election approached, Swatantra considered that wing of the old Congress Party to be a natural ally, and a potential coalition partner.

In later chapters we will examine the extent to which Swatantra's short-term strategy has succeeded in accomplishing two of the party's goals: (a) the ouster of the Congress from the seats of government; and (b) the development and expansion of the Swatantra Party's base of support.

The Praja Socialist Party. The Praja Socialists (PSP), like Swatantra, seemed to consider the first task of the fourth general election to be the ouster of the Congress Party. To this end, the PSP encouraged alliances between progressive, national, secular parties. Like the two parties already discussed, the PSP was not eager to cooperate with the communists. In West Bengal, in 1967, fourteen socialist and Marxist political parties organized into two united fronts that contested the elections against the Congress Party. The PSP decided not to join either front because they were both led by communists.

Following the elections, the PSP joined coalition governments in West Bengal, Bihar, and Uttar Pradesh, in pursuit of its policy to oust Congress governments. In all three of these states the communists were partners in the alliance. In other words, the PSP, like the Jana Sangh and Swatantra, agreed to participate in governments with the communists, even though they refused to cooperate with the communists before the elections. On the

The Indian context: 1967–1971

other hand, the Praja Socialist Party refused to join the Orissa coalition because it was composed exclusively of rightist parties.[18]

With the passage of time, the PSP became more and more disillusioned with the functioning of non-Congress coalition governments. It recognized from the start that it could not participate in an administration led by rightists. After only a brief period of time, the party's experiences in the West Bengal ministry convinced it that the PSP could not work with leftists, such as the Communist Party of India (Marxist) (hereafter, CPI(M)) either. Thus, by June of 1968, Sunil Das, one of the leaders of the West Bengal branch of the PSP, wrote that it had become

> 'evident after some time that the dominant partner in the united front, the Marxist Communists, sought to channelise the forces unleashed after the disappearance of Congress monopoly [sic] of power with the objectives of subversion of the democratic process, undermining people's faith in the parliamentary methods, weakening the administrative fabric in the border states and liquidating other political parties and their mass organisations, particularly the trade unions'.[19]

Obviously, the PSP was no longer able to turn either to the right or to the left in its quest for alliance partners.

By 1970 the party had all but given up on the usefulness of pre-election alliances and coalition politics. A resolution of the party's annual conference in 1970 declared that 'the country has entered what may be described as the dangerous decade – a period of ever changing loyalty, unstable alliances and counter-alliances, united fronts and coalitions in which the participants freely conspired against one another'.[20] Under these extremely competitive circumstances, the PSP preferred to remain aloof from simple anti-Congress coalitions. Instead, the PSP moved to the position that only rigidly ideological alliances and fronts are capable of replacing the Congress Party as a viable form of government so long as no single party emerges as an alternative. Prem Bhasin, the PSP's General Secretary, summed up the position of the party by saying that 'make-shift arrangements like alliances and fronts with groups and parties with basically different outlook and objectives would not serve the purpose and temporary success would be followed by a long period of bitterness and frustration'.[21] This was the conclusion of a party that experienced that bitterness and frustration.

In later chapters we will see to what extent the PSP responded to its coalition experiences in an acquiescent, cooperative way, and to what extent it responded competitively.

The Samyukta Socialist Party. For most parties, alliances and coalitions are mechanisms through which they may implement, at least partially, their

The Indian context: 1967–1971

ideology and goals. For the Samyukta Socialist Party (SSP), anti-Congress alliances have been a part of their ideology, an end as well as a means.

Dr Rammanohar Lohia, the late leader of the SSP, was probably the first prominent politician in India to call for the formation of non-Congress alliances composed of all opposition parties. Lohia argued that regardless of the ideological differences between the opposition parties, they all shared at least one common goal – the removal of Congress from power. He felt that all other differences should be set aside in pursuit of that common goal.

The call for non-Congressism became the hallmark of the SSP during the 1967 elections. From 1965 through 1967, the party developed a formula by which disparate parties would be able to work together to form non-Congress governments. The SSP suggested that the opposition parties join together in pre-election alliances, and agree to distribute legislative constituencies in accordance with the past performance of the various allied parties.[22] The pre-election alliances were, according to the party's 1967 election manifesto, to be based on time-bound, minimum programs.[23] The minimum program was intended to establish the basic areas of agreement within which the non-Congress coalition governments might be able to function.

The SSP attempted to legitimize the notion of all-inclusive non-Congress coalitions by arguing that the left–right distinctions commonly drawn in politics are meaningless. They argued that aspects of the 'rightist' Jana Sangh program, such as the language policy, are more radical than aspects of the 'leftist' communist programs and, of course, vice versa. The alliances were further justified to the SSP's supporters by maintaining that through such alliances each of the non-socialist parties would be educated to the errors of its ways. This education, in turn, would lead to a gradual movement of the rank and file away from those parties and in the direction of the SSP and other socialist parties.[24]

The results of the 1967 elections encouraged the SSP to believe that it was following the proper path. Om Prakash Deepak and Roma Mitra, two leading figures in the SSP, evaluated the results of the non-Congressism strategy in 1967 and wrote that:

'in all the states where the Congress got between 35 and 40 per cent of the votes, and the major opposition parties had an electoral understanding, the Congress was reduced to an insignificant minority (Kerala and Madras). It was defeated in those states where the opposition had even a partial understanding (Bengal and Rajasthan), but won where the opposition had no understanding, as in Madhya Pradesh and Haryana.'[25]

The SSP, like the other opposition parties, had to decide after the general election whether or not to continue to pursue the strategy of non-Congressism. Unlike the other parties, it was not a question of whether the SSP had

The Indian context: 1967–1971

succeeded in gaining power that would determine their decision. Rather, it was a question of whether the Congress had been permanently removed from the government. The SSP leadership was divided on this question, and so it is difficult to determine to what extent the party continued to be committed to anti-Congressism. During the 1969 midterm polls the SSP did continue to pursue the Lohia strategy, but after the split in the Congress Party, the SSP leadership became severely divided. In some states, such at Uttar Pradesh, the leadership decided that the Indira Gandhi-led wing of the Congress was to be opposed in accordance with the Lohia strategy, while in other places, such as Bihar, the party leaders refused to participate in an alliance with the Jana Sangh, Swatantra, and Congress (O) against Indira Gandhi.

The SSP leadership gave emphasis to non-Congressism both as a strategy for winning support specifically for the SSP, as well as a strategy for taking power away from the Congress. In later chapters the extent to which the SSP succeeded in increasing its power through the use of coalition politics is examined.

The Communist Party of India. In many ways, the CPI attitude toward coalition politics has been similar to that of the Jana Sangh. Although the communists have long supported united fronts of 'left and democratic' parties, they were adamantly opposed to cooperation with the rightist parties. Yet, like the Jana Sangh, the CPI reinterpreted its position after the 1967 elections so as to legitimize its participation in coalition governments with the Swatantra Party and the Jana Sangh. Thus, in reviewing the results of the fourth general election, the party leaders declared:

> 'We were right in rejecting any united front including the Jana Sangh or Swatantra Party or both. But our attitude towards adjustments was a bit too rigid and inflexible. We thought that such adjustments would lower our prestige in the eyes of the masses. No left party seems to have suffered in these elections on account of such adjustments. Some have definitely gained. We should have taken a flexible line and tried for adjustments at least on "no-contest-and-no-support" basis in a number of places.'[26]

The CPI position is similar to that of the Jana Sangh in that they both hoped to gain the same thing, in the same way, from the coalition experience. The CPI perceived the coalitions as an opportunity to expand their mass organizations and their mass influence. And they were quite pleased, at least immediately after the election, with their position and their opportunity to carry this goal to fruition. The party concluded that in the fourth general election:

> 'The prestige of the left and democratic parties has enormously gone

The Indian context: 1967–1971

up... This enables the left and democratic parties to influence the future course of the development more than any other anti-congress force.'[27]

With the passage of time, the CPI became much less willing to cooperate with the rightist parties. Their return to a more rigid position has become most apparent since the splitting of the Congress Party. Whether this is a result of the leadership's belief that the CPI can gain more for itself by cooperating with the Indira Congress, or a genuine feeling of distaste for the rightists remains to be seen.[28] Later on, the CPI's mixed competitive–cooperative strategy is examined in an effort to determine how successful the CPI has been in increasing its influence through coalition governments.

The Communist Party of India (Marxist). The CPI(M), which is largely composed of dissidents from the CPI, was formed in the wake of the Sino-Indian War of 1962. It attracted many of the younger, more militant, and more Maoist-oriented of the members of the CPI. The CPI(M) was more 'revolutionary' than the CPI, especially in terms of its attitude toward cooperation with other parties.

The CPI(M), like the CPI, supported the formation of left and democratic pre-election united fronts. The party believed that through electoral alliances it would be possible to defeat the Congress, and most efficiently utilize its own resources to maximize its own gains. The CPI(M), more than any other party, was sensitive to the effects of electoral politics on the expansion of the party organization. Perhaps because the CPI(M) is less committed than the other parties to promoting change exclusively through elections and other constitutional means, the party's leaders examine almost all actions in terms of the effect they have on the party's mass base. Thus, in the CPI(M)'s review of the 1967 election, it maintains that election fronts are important because without them:

'we will be dispersing our resources and thus will not be in a position to win seats to the extent possible and hence we will not be in a position to utilize the parliamentary forum effectively. Further, by too much extending our contests, apart from the difficulty of winning these seats, even the difficulties of maintaining and consolidating the contacts which we will be forging during the election campaign itself, has to be taken into consideration.'[29]

Following the election, the CPI(M) continued to pursue the policy of united fronts among leftist parties. It also continued to be adamantly opposed to cooperation with the rightists. While many of the other leftist and rightist parties were reassessing each other in the light of the compulsions of the political situation, the CPI(M) continued to declare that 'unless these parties are totally excluded from the anti-Congress democratic fronts, and the people are rescued from their pernicious political influence, the danger of disruption of the democratic upsurge, and distortion and diversion of the economic political crisis for reactionary ends cannot be averted'.[30] Party actions, as well as rhetoric, underscore its determined opposition to the rightist parties. The CPI(M) did not, for instance, participate in any coalition cabinets in which the Jana Sangh or Swatantra Party were represented, although it did give legislative support to alliances including these parties.

The CPI(M) did, however, participate in the Kerala coalition where the Muslim League was a constituent. That party certainly is not a 'progressive' political force in India from the point of view of the CPI(M). Then why did the Marxists agree to share cabinet responsibilities with them? The decision was not altogether inconsistent with the CPI(M)'s principles, although it might appear to have been. In Kerala, the CPI(M) was the major constituent of the coalition. As such, and because of its great emphasis on organizational work, the party was able to utilize its leadership position to expand its mass base. It was able to take advantage of labor–management grievances and peasant–landlord conflicts, often at the expense of the trade unions and peasant organizations headed by its coalition partners. Consequently, it sacrificed very little in admitting the Muslim League into the coalition, while benefiting from the added strength and stability which the League was able to bring to the alliance.

Following the 1969 midterm polls and the subsequent split in the Congress Party, the CPI(M) – unlike most of the other major opposition parties – did not seriously alter its electoral strategy or its coalition strategy. The party did not give its support to either faction of the Congress. In fact, it labeled parties, such as the CPI, as revisionists for aiding the Indira Gandhi wing of the Congress.

As with the other parties, the extent to which the CPI(M)'s strategy has yielded gains for the party is examined when the analysis of the strategies pursued in the coalition governments is reported.

Summary. In examining the basic attitudes of six All-India parties toward coalition politics, four distinct coalition preferences have been found. The Jana Sangh and Swatantra Party both prefer a right of center alliance, including each other, the Congress (O), possibly the Bharatiya Kranti Dal (BKD), and some small local parties such as the Jan Congress (in Orissa) or the Janata Party (in Bihar).

The CPI and CPI(M) prefer a leftist coalition including the SSP, PSP and several smaller parties, such as the Republican Party of India; the Revolutionary Socialist Party of India; the Forward Bloc, and others. The CPI also considers the Indira Ghandi-led Congress (R) as an appropriate partner, while the CPI (M) does not.

The Indian context: 1967–1971

The Praja Socialist strategy called for a centrist, socialist alliance including the SSP and appropriate members of either Congress. The SSP, on the other hand, supported the continuation of Dr Lohia's anti-Congressism strategy.[31] It reconciled anti-Congressism with the split in the Congress by generally opposing whichever Congress was in power. This means that it usually supported the 'less socialist' Congress (O). Leaders such as Raj Narain explained this support by maintaining that Dr Lohia's strategy will not have succeeded until the Congress monopoly of power has been broken at the center.

The six parties which have been discussed also differ in terms of the degree to which they are willing to cooperate with each other. Of course, for the SSP this was not really a problem. They were willing to cooperate with any party that would accept a time-bound minimum program.

The Jana Sangh and the CPI have been the most willing of the five remaining parties to set ideological differences aside, if only temporarily, in the interest of forming non-Congress coalition governments. They have generally done so in the belief that being in the government would promote their own advancement. Since the split in Congress, however, both parties have become much less willing to cooperate with each other and other 'unlikeminded' parties.

The Praja Socialists were initially willing to experiment with non-Congressism and cooperate with all opposition political forces. They learned very quickly, however, that this required too many fundamental compromises on their part and so gave up that strategy. Since then, they preferred to remain outside of administrative coalitions which included the CPI(M) or the rightist parties, although they were willing to lend legislative support to such alliances.

Finally, both the Swatantra Party and the CPI(M) have seldom diverged from their ideological paths to join coalition governments with parties of markedly different political persuasions from their own.

The coalition environment

It may now be helpful to examine the circumstances under which the coalition governments came into existence; especially the environmental factors which distinguished those states with coalitions from the rest of the country.

The most obvious distinguishing characteristic between the states that had coalitions and those that did not is that people in the states with alliances gave greater support to the opposition parties. It will be helpful to identify some of the characteristics of the people who gave their support to the opposition parties.

The four leftist All-India parties appealed primarily to lower middle and

The Indian context: 1967–1971

lower class voters. The communists concentrated their efforts on the laboring classes and, more recently, on the small or unpropertied peasant farmers. The SSP, and to a lesser extent the PSP, concentrated their efforts on the downtrodden sectors of Indian society: the lower castes, the unpropertied, the women and youths.[32]

Swatantra derived its support from medium and large landowners. A post-election study found that 54.9 per cent of those who voted for Swatantra legislative assembly candidates in 1967 owned five or more acres of land. Only 29.7 per cent of Congress supporters possessed holdings that large.[33] In general, Swatantra derives much of its support through the use of many local notables – aristocrats, zamindars, and other traditional patrons.[34] The Swatantra electorate is relatively uneducated,[35] rural, and often propertied. The Jana Sangh, in contrast, draws much of its support from urban areas, and from educated voters.[36]

Income. Since most of the support for the leftists comes from the poorer sectors of society, and since the Swatantra notables are probably able to mobilize many of their poorer 'clients', it is likely that the opposition parties win more votes than the Congress in the poorer states.

It seems reasonable to postulate that the opposition does particularly well in the poorer states because of strong feelings of disaffection for the Congress among the voters in those areas. This factor was probably especially important in the poorer states in 1967 because there was widespread famine in India at that time. The voters in these states were most dependent on the wealthier provinces for food and other essentials. Therefore, they were keenly sensitive to the inequitable distribution of resources in India under the stewardship of the Congress Party. In any event, this was a large part of the explanation for opposition votes offered by the Indian political elites interviewed in connection with this study.

In table 3.1, the states are dichotomized on the basis of whether they fall above or below the mean for per capita income. They have also been dichotomized on the basis of whether they fall above or below the mean in the percentage of valid votes cast for Congress candidates for legislative assembly seats.[37] Yule's Q, a measure of one-way association, is used to determine the extent to which a large Congress vote is associated with a high per capita income in India. As was suggested, there is a very strong tendency for the poorer states to vote for the opposition. Q is 0.89 ($N=15$).

As the election results reveal, Congress often fails to win a plurality of votes while still securing a majority of seats. Therefore, it still must be ascertained if those states where the opposition parties were able to convert their large percentage of votes into a majority of seats were the poorer states.

The Indian context: 1967–1971

TABLE 3.1 *Association of per capita income by state with the size of the Congress vote*

Income	Congress vote	
	High	Low
High	7	1
Low	2	5

In eight provinces, Congress won a majority of the seats in the legislative assemblies in 1967. In another eight, the opposition gained control of a majority of seats. Table 3.2 examines the relationship between income and the percentage of seats won in fifteen of the states. Haryana has been excluded from the analysis because per capita income data were not available. Once again the evidence indicates that the opposition parties do better in the poorer states, though not as dramatically as it did above. Yule's Q for table 3.2 is 0.38.

TABLE 3.2 *Association of per capita income by state with the distribution of assembly seats*

Income	Majority for Congress	Majority for opposition
High	5	3
Low	3	4

Following the elections, Congress was able to form governments in nine states – Andhra Pradesh, Mysore, Assam, Jammu and Kashmir, Haryana, Maharashtra, Madhya Pradesh, Gujarat, and Uttar Pradesh. In Rajasthan, where the opposition won a majority of seats, President's Rule was instituted after the governor ruled that no group was able to form a government. In Tamilnadu, the DMK was able to form a government on its own. In the remaining states – the Punjab, Bihar, West Bengal, Kerala, and Orissa – opposition parties joined together to form coalition governments. These states were soon joined by Uttar Pradesh, Madhya Pradesh, and Haryana, where defections caused the fall of the Congress administrations. What characteristics did these eight states with coalition governments share that help account for the emergence of non-Congress governments? It should follow from tables 3.1 and 3.2 that coalition governments are more likely to occur in states below the mean on per capita income in India.

Table 3.3 presents the relationship between per capita income and whether a state had any coalition governments. These were not all states in

The Indian context: 1967–1971

which the Congress had done particularly badly during the elections, though for many of them that was the case. They are all states in which there was discontent with the Congress administration. In the case of five of them, the discontent was manifested by the defeat of the Congress during the elections. In the other three that discontent was manifested in the form of defections from the Congress ranks. Once again there is substantial support for the contention that the poor feel the greatest dissatisfaction with the Congress Party. Yule's Q is 0.76, indicating that a below average income is associated with the advent of coalition governments.

TABLE 3.3 *Association of per capita income with the emergence of coalition governments*

Income	Coalition	
	No	Yes
High	6	2
Low	2	5

Number of candidates. India is often described as a single-party-dominant political system.[38] This label stems from the observation that the Congress Party controlled the central government and almost every state government in India up to the 1967 elections, even though the Congress rarely won a majority of votes. The Congress Party's success at securing large numbers of seats is generally attributed to the division of the opposition vote among a large number of candidates in most constituencies. It is suggested, therefore, that the percentage of votes won by the Congress Party is inversely related to the number of candidates contesting an election in any particular state, while the number of seats won by the Congress Party is directly related to the number of candidates contesting against them.

Both statements are supported by the evidence. Where more candidates contested, Congress won a smaller percentage of the vote, but a larger percentage of seats. The product–moment correlation between the percentage of votes received by the Congress and the number of candidates per constituency is -0.46 ($N=16$). The correlation between the number of candidates and the percentage of seats won by the Congress is 0.41 ($N=16$). That is, as the number of candidates in a constituency decreases, the probability that the Congress will be defeated increases. Furthermore, there is a modest association between having an above average number of candidates in a state and having a Congress-led government ($Q=0.33$).

The most effective way to keep the number of candidates per constituency small is for political parties to form pre-election alliances. In the

The Indian context: 1967–1971

four states where the opposition parties made extensive use of pre-election alliances – including West Bengal, Orissa, Kerala, and Madras – the Congress was defeated at the polls, and fairly stable governments were formed. In the five other states where non-Congress governments were formed – including Uttar Pradesh, Haryana, Madhya Pradesh, the Punjab, and Bihar – the absence of pre-election alliances resulted in an above average number of candidates per constituency. In fact, the Congress actually formed the government immediately after the election in three of these states.[39] In all five of these states, the opposition parties were forced to pay a high price in order to form, or maintain, their governments. Thus, with the exception of the Punjab, the governments of these states were, from the very start, dependent on the support of defectors from the Congress Party for their survival. The support of these defectors was purchased by giving them important cabinet positions. In fact, in four of these states even the chief ministership was turned over to politicians who defected from the Congress Party after the election. These costs were not experienced in the states that made use of pre-election alliances.

It seems reasonable to conclude that the relative unity of the opposition parties was an important factor in the emergence of non-Congress governments. In the states where pre-election alliances helped limit divisions in the opposition vote, the Congress was handily defeated.[40] In every state where the Congress Party won a majority of seats the opposition parties had failed to form pre-election alliances.

Other factors. Given what is known about the supporters for the opposition parties, it is expected that the states with large minority or downtrodden populations gave greater support to the opposition parties.[41] In fact, this expectation is supported by the evidence. The percentage of religious minorities living in a state is substantially correlated with the percentage of seats won by the opposition parties ($r=0.57$). But does this relationship stand when the states are dichotomized on the basis of whether they did or did not have coalition governments?

As table 3.4 shows, there is a strong association between the percentage of religious minorities and the formation of coalitions. Yule's Q for the relationship is 0.72.

To complete the examination of the relationship between the advent of coalition governments and the presence of significant cleavages in the states, the proposition that there is a positive association between the percentage of scheduled castes/tribes living in a state and the formation of non-Congress coalition governments is investigated. This association is even stronger than is the association between religious minorities and coalition governments. Q is 0.89 for the relationship presented in table 3.5.

These two findings are important because they indicate the areas of

TABLE 3.4 *Association between the distribution of religious minorities by state and the presence of coalition governments*

	Coalition	
Percentage of religious minorities	Yes	No
High	5	2
Low	2	5

TABLE 3.5 *Association between the distribution of scheduled castes and scheduled tribes by state and the presence of coalition governments*

	Coalition	
Percentage of scheduled castes/tribes	Yes	No
High	6	2
Low	1	6

greatest potential defeat for the Congress. Where the religious minorities are small, and therefore not very visible, social cleavages and conflicts do not appear to be very severe. On the other hand, when a large percentage of a state's population is from minority groups, then the opposition parties, with their special appeal to distinct religious, caste, or social groups, are likely to be quite successful.[42] The same holds true whether the cleavage is based on religious, caste, or tribal lines.

Other variables generally considered as indicators of development – such as literacy, urbanization, and number of radio receivers per thousand population – support the contention that coalitions were more likely to occur in the less developed, more disaffected states. These variables, however, do not seem to be as closely associated with the victory of non-Congress forces as the attributes discussed above. The literacy rate in the states, for instance, is only moderately associated with the formation of coalition governments ($Q=0.43$). It is completely unassociated with the performance of the Congress in the elections. A large percentage of urban dwellers is weakly associated with Congress success in the elections ($Q=0.23$). Finally, as the number of people per radio receiver in a state increased, the probability that the Congress would be defeated in that state in 1967 also increased ($Q=0.30$). These three indicators – literacy, urbanization, and radio receivers – suggest that the less access the population has to mass media, and other non-personal sources of political information, the more likely they are to support the opposition parties.

The Indian context: 1967–1971

Summary. In this section a series of propositions linking the relative deprivation and disaffection of the people in the Indian states to the likelihood that they would defeat the Congress Party at the polls or afterward were tested. The evidence indicates that the disaffection of the people in the poorest states, combined with the strategy of pre-election alliances of many opposition parties, were important environmental factors which created the impetus for non-Congress coalition governments after the 1967 election.

The states

In the first two sections of this chapter the attitudes of six All-India parties toward interparty cooperation, and the environmental factors which eventually compelled those parties to confront the difficulties of working with one another, were examined. In this section, a brief review of the important characteristics and events of the coalition governments in India between March 1967 and late 1970 is undertaken.

Although eight states, including the Punjab, Haryana, Madhya Pradesh, Bihar, West Bengal, Orissa, and Kerala, had non-Congress coalition governments, only seven are examined. Haryana is excluded from the analysis because no All-India party participated as a member of its coalition cabinets. In Appendix II, where this project's research design is elaborated, a further explanation is offered for the elimination of Haryana from the study.[43]

The Punjab. Following the 1967 general election, the Punjab Vidhan Sabha (legislative assembly) was extremely divided. Although the Congress emerged as the single largest party, with forty-eight of the 104 seats in the assembly, their strength was not adequate to form the government. The opposition parties were in a position to displace the Congress if they could arrive at a mutually satisfactory program. Seven parties and six independents succeeded in coming together and drafting an eleven-point minimum program on which to base their government. The seven parties were the Akali Dal (Sant), with a strength of 24; the Akali Dal (Master), with 2 seats; Jana Sangh with 9; CPI with 5; CPI(M) with 3; the Republican Party of India (RPI) with 3; the SSP with 1; and 6 independents, for a total strength of 53 legislators.

Not all of these parties received representation in the cabinet. The initial composition of the cabinet included one independent (who was a military hero of the 1965 war with Pakistan), one member of the RPI, one Jana Sanghi and two representatives, including the chief minister, from the Akali Dal (Sant). After a rather short time the cabinet was expanded to include Satya Pal Dang, a leading member of the CPI. Several independents and a Congress defector were also given positions in the administration, but below the cabinet rank.

The Indian context: 1967–1971

Within one month after the election, the Punjab had a coalition government including both the Jana Sangh and the CPI. Despite the ideological diversity of the government, and despite crisis after crisis, it remained in power until late November 1967. As the relations between the organized parties in the alliance worsened the government became increasingly dependent on Congress defectors for its survival. The chief minister found it necessary to offer cabinet posts and other lures to attract members away from the Congress and to the coalition. The *Times of India* reported on June 29, 1967 that the leaders of the united front felt that since the Congress was trying to bring down their government, they had to seek additional support by making attractive offers to legislators who were willing to defect from the Congress in favor of the coalition. This was exactly what was done.

In the struggle to preserve his government, Gurnam Singh, the chief minister, continually expanded the ministry. In May of 1967, for example, he reshuffled and expanded his ministry, bringing in one Congress defector as a cabinet minister, two Congress defectors as ministers of state, and three defectors as deputy ministers. Following this reorganization, the coalition ministry consisted of seventeen members, six of whom had defected from the Congress Party.

The defections continued and reached a new height on November 22, 1967 when seventeen members of the coalition withdrew their support and formed the United Punjab Janta Party (UPJP). Among those joining the UPJP, and thereby depriving the coalition of its majority, were seven members of the Akali Dal (Sant), three members of the RPI, one from the Master Akali Dal, two former Congress defectors, and four independents. Sri Lachman Singh Gill, the leader of the new group, secured support from the Congress, thus enabling him to form a new government.

The Gill ministry, like the united front before it, was to be plagued by the problems of defector politics. Initially the new government stated firmly that defectors would not be brought into the ministry (which was particularly bold since all of the members of the UPJP were defectors). As time passed they wavered on this point. This wavering brought on a new crisis. The government's Congress supporters exerted a great deal of pressure on the Gill ministry, hoping to discourage the chief minister from using ministerial posts as a means of attracting defectors. Of course, the Congress' reason for taking that position was, at least partially, its fear of further defections from its own ranks.[44] Finally, amid differences between the constituents on what the government's relationship to the Congress Party should be, and who should be in the ministry, Congress withdrew its support and the government fell.

In August of 1968 President's Rule was instituted in the Punjab. A few months later midterm elections were held and once again the Congress

The Indian context: 1967–1971

failed to secure a majority of seats in the legislative assembly. Table 3.6 shows the distribution of seats by party in 1967; at the time President's Rule was instituted; and after the 1969 midterm poll.[45]

TABLE 3.6 *Representation in the Legislative Assembly of the Punjab*

Party	Strength in 1967	Strength during President's Rule	Strength in 1969
Congress	48	43	38
AD (Sant)	24	20	43
Jana Sangh	9	9	8
CPI	5	5	4
CPI(M)	3	3	2
RPI	3	0	0
AD (Master)	2	1	0
SSP	1	1	2
PSP	0	1	1
Swatantra	0	0	1
Janata	0	20	1
Independents	9	1	4
Total	104	104	104

Following the election, the Akali Dal (Sant) and the Jana Sangh formed a coalition ministry supported by the CPI, CPI(M), SSP, Swatantra, and one independent. Having learned from his past experience, chief minister Gurnam Singh did not bring defectors into the new cabinet. In fact, most cabinet expansions were primarily used to bring additional Akali Dal (Sant) members into the ministry, thereby strengthening the hand of the chief minister. This government was more stable than the previous coalition.

Uttar Pradesh. As in the Punjab, the 1967 election left politics in Uttar Pradesh in a state of flux. Neither the Congress, nor the Samyukta Vidhayak Dal (SVD or united front) of opposition parties were able to claim majority support in the legislature. The balance of power in the 425 member state legislative assembly lay with a few uncommitted independents. After much negotiating, and some coercion, the Congress Party under the leadership of C. B. Gupta succeeded in wooing sufficient support to form the government.

Just a few weeks after the formation of the ministry, Charan Singh (who was a very prominent Congressman), and seventeen of his supporters, crossed the floor, announced the formation of the Jana Congress, and brought down the C. B. Gupta government. It would be unfair to suggest that Charan Singh's aisle crossing was prompted solely by opportunism, though the value of being in a pivotal position was not lost on him.[46] As early as March 7, a week before the formation of the Congress government, Chaudhuri Charan Singh announced his candidacy for the leadership of the Congress Party. He had decided to challenge C. B. Gupta because he felt that:

> 'In its long strides and, over a considerable time now, the State has lacked a person at its helm who could discipline the vast bureaucracy on its pay-rolls. Administration of law and order, particularly in the rural areas, is far from satisfactory. . . Far worse than this record of failure and incompetence is the fact that people have lost faith in the sincerity of our professions, with the result that the atmosphere of Uttar Pradesh today is full of portents. A storm may break over our heads any day. I offer myself as a candidate because I believe I can meet this challenge successfully.'[47]

It is fitting that Charan Singh became the vehicle by which the Congress government was toppled. With the fall of the Congress ministry, the governor of the state called upon the SVD – composed of the Jana Singh, Swatantra, PSP, SSP, CPI, RPI, and the newly formed Jana Congress – to form the government. Although the Jana Sangh, as the largest constituent in the SVD, normally would have designated the chief minister from their ranks, it was decided that Charan Singh of the Jana Congress should become chief minister. As a result of this decision, Charan Singh not only caused the fall of the C. B. Gupta ministry; he also was given the opportunity to demonstrate his ability to meet the challenges of running the government.

The cabinet was composed of representatives from all points on the political spectrum. Jana Sangh, Swatantra, and to a lesser extent Jana Congress, represented the right, while the PSP, SSP, and CPI represented the left. With an alliance of such disparate interests, internal bickering was bound to occur. In fact, the history of the coalition was one of threats and counter-threats to resign among the ideologically disparate parties.

The SSP was dissatisfied with the pace at which the government was implementing important programs. On June 26, 1967 it gave the government an ultimatum: either the government would exempt uneconomic holdings (i.e. landholdings of 6.25 acres or less) from land revenue, or the party's forty-four member contingent would withdraw its support. After long debates back and forth, the SSP resigned in late November of that year. On the same day, the CPI minister and deputy minister both resigned from the cabinet in support of the SSP position, but assured the government of their party's continued support. The SSP gave no such assurance.

The Indian context: 1967–1971

Without the support of the SSP, Charan Singh's coalition government would have lost its majority in the legislative assembly. Recognizing the necessity of SSP support, the Jana Sangh and the Swatantra Party – the two parties at greatest odds with the SSP on the question of land revenue – agreed to compromise their positions on the land revenue issue. While they both favored the abolition of land revenue on large holdings as well as small, they agreed to accept the SSP proposal as a first step toward their broader goal. By October, the chief minister had also agreed to implement a modified version of the SSP land revenue program. He agreed to reduce the charge by 50 per cent on holdings of less than 6.25 acres.

In the meantime the SSP and the CPI ministers, satisfied with the compromise, withdrew their resignations. The communists, however, resigned again in November of 1967, this time over the government's use of the Preventive Detention Act (PDA) against trade unions. In what must be considered an unusual meeting of the minds, the Jana Sangh national executive commitee supported the CPI's complaint against the use of the Preventive Detention Act. They went so far as to ask Charan Singh to release those held under the PDA so that the CPI might rejoin the cabinet. When the government failed to respond appropriately, the Jana Sangh leadership threatened to withdraw its support from the coalition ministry. The united front, of course, could not afford to lose the support of its largest constituent, and so an amicable solution was found for the use of the Preventive Detention Act.

At an earlier stage in the tenure of the coalition, a rift arose between the government and the Swatantra Party. The Swatantra leadership was disturbed because Charan Singh retained Akhtar Ali Khan in the cabinet after his resignation from the Swatantra Party. Eventually Charan Singh yielded to the Swatantra leadership on this point, and Akhtar Ali resigned from the cabinet. Despite his resignation, the Swatantra Party withdrew from the coalition. Their withdrawal resulted both from their dissatisfaction with Charan Singh's handling of the Akhtar Ali case, and their general displeasure with the communists in the SVD. It is interesting to note that Charan Singh did not make a significant effort to regain the support of the Swatantra Party, though he did respond rather quickly to demands from more important constituents in the coalition, such as the SSP and the Jana Sangh. Swatantra was a very minor member of the alliance and could not seriously threaten the stability of the SVD even by resigning. The SSP and the Jana Sangh, on the other hand, were essential to the survival of the alliance since without their support the SVD would have lost its majority. Thus, Charan Singh was willing to lose the support of members of the coalition so long as they could not threaten his government's security.[48]

Some time after the withdrawal of the Swatantra Party, the CPI resigned from the coalition. After their resignation there was speculation that Swatantra might rejoin the SVD. They did not and this caused severe problems for the party. Swatantra's failure to re-enter the government, coupled with other differences that had arisen among the party's leadership, led to the defection of several key members to Charan Singh's party – newly named the Bharatiya Kranti Dal (BKD) – thereby solidifying the undoing of the Swatantra Party in Uttar Pradesh.

By early 1968, the differences between the SVD constituents reached crisis proportions. Charan Singh declared that his party was not committed to the nineteen-point minimum program which formed the basis of the coalition. He contended that the minimum program was drawn up by the other members of the united front prior to his defection from the Congress Party. Since he was not consulted at that time, he did not feel obligated to implement those parts of the program which he either did not support or did not consider practical.

As if matters were not bad enough, Charan Singh also announced a reshuffling of his cabinet in which the Jana Sangh lost three major portfolios; the PSP was angered by the appointment to a cabinet post of a former defector from the PSP, and several independents and even BKD members were angered because they were left out of the newly constituted cabinet. By this point, almost all hope of patching up the differences between the parties in the alliance had been lost. Charan Singh, who had been selected chief minister because of his reputation for fair play and integrity, was now being accused by the Jana Sangh of using dictatorial methods to get his way.

In the wake of similar accusations from the SSP and other parties, Charan Singh offered to resign for the third time during his tenure as chief minister. The members of the coalition, however, were unable to agree on an alternative leader. After more bickering, the chief minister submitted his resignation to the governor of the state, writing that:

> 'A coalition of so many disparate elements necessarily involves an adjustment with principles. But adjustment or compromise implies a limit also. In my case, this limit has been reached.'[49]

President's Rule was instituted and after no political group was able to demonstrate its command of a majority in the legislature, midterm polls were held. Charan Singh, and the BKD, emerged from the coalition relatively untarnished in the eyes of the public. The press and the electorate seem to have felt that it was the other parties, and not Charan Singh, that had compromised their principles in the coalition. The BKD was perceived as being composed of sincere politicians who risked their political security inside the Congress Party in order to pursue what they felt was right. In any event, most indications suggest that Charan Singh and

The Indian context: 1967–1971

his followers were given credit for the accomplishments of the popular SVD ministry, while the other constituents were blamed for the bickering which eventually led to its downfall. As table 3.7 demonstrates, the All-India parties suffered severe defeats in Uttar Pradesh in 1969, while the BKD scored a stunning victory.

TABLE 3.7 *Representation in the legislative assembly of Uttar Pradesh*

Party	Strength in 1967	Strength during President's Rule	Strength in 1969
Congress	199	192	211
Jana Sangh	98	93	49
SSP	44	44	33
CPI	13	13	4
Swatantra	12	8	5
RPI	10	6	2
PSP	11	11	2
CPI(M)	1	1	1
BKD	0	27	99
KMP	0	0	1
HMS	0	0	1
Independents	37	27	17
Total	425	422	425

After the elections, President's Rule was replaced with a Congress-led government. Once again C. B. Gupta assumed the position of chief minister. After a great deal of negotiating in which Charan Singh first appeared to support Gupta's Congress (O) and then appeared to support the Congress (R), C. B. Gupta resigned as chief minister in late 1970, turning the position over to Charan Singh. Charan Singh later resigned the chief ministership, although he remained in the coalition government.

Bihar. Probably no state has suffered from greater instability and unbridled opportunism than has Bihar. Between 1967 and 1970 the state had six governments, as well as President's Rule on two occasions. Although there were great ideological differences among the constituents of the coalitions in Bihar, these differences were no greater than they had been in Uttar Pradesh or in the Punjab, where governments were able to survive for a reasonable period of time. Bihar differed from these states in the number of regional parties involved in the government, and the opportunism and ambition of the late Raja of Ramgarh.

Following the 1967 election, a coalition of the SSP, PSP, CPI, Jana Sangh, Jana Kranti Dal (JKD) and independents formed the government.

The SSP was the largest constituent in the united front. Despite this, the chief ministership was given to Mahamaya Prasad Sinha, a leader of the Raja of Ramgarh's Jana Kranti Dal. The JKD was primarily composed of former Congressmen. In fact, the chief minister, like most other members of the JKD, was a defector from the Congress Party.

During the first few months that the SVD was in power it experienced several minor disputes. Yet it still succeeded in attracting defectors and in performing the functions of a government. The arrival of new defectors frequently prompted expansions of the ministry so as to provide a reward for those who crossed the aisle from the loyal opposition to the government. Among those given cabinet positions in exchange for their support were the Jharkhand Party, the Republican Party, and several Congress defectors. These cabinet expansions led to some disagreement between the chief minister and the Jana Sangh. Although the Jana Sangh favored a small ministry, and the chief minister favored a large ministry, the Jana Sangh did not press the point in the early days of the alliance and so a crisis was averted.

The first major test of the government's stability came in December of 1967 as a consequence of a strike of sugar workers at the Rohtos Industries factory in Dalmianagar. When the factory was shut down by the management, the PSP raised a cry of protest which eventually led to their resigning from the coalition. After the PSP escalated the issue to the point of crisis, the chief minister exerted his influence, and succeeded in having the factory reopened. The PSP, having had its demand satisfied, withdrew its resignations.

The resolution of the Rohtos Industries strike did not return the SVD to a state of calm. While the strike was going on, and even before, other forces were attempting to oust the coalition from power. The most notable effort to topple the government came from B. P. Mandal, who organized a new political group – the Shoshit Dal – and was busily luring supporters away from the SVD. Finally, in January of 1968 he succeeded in withering the SVD's fragile majority to the point where the government could no longer survive. With the support of the Congress Party, Mandal toppled the SVD and formed his own government. Within two months, however, he suffered from counter-defections and once again the SVD was called upon to form a ministry.

The new coalition government was headed by Bhola Paswan Shastri, a defector from the Congress who was affiliated with the Loktantrik Congress Dal (LCD). The LCD enjoyed the support of sixteen defectors in addition to the chief minister. Besides the LCD, the new government was supported by the SSP, PSP, BKD, Jana Sangh, CPI, CPI(M), Democratic Congress Party, the RPI, and a section of the Jharkhand Party (which had split into the Jharkhand and the Hul Jharkhand).

The Indian context: 1967–1971

The formation of the Paswan government reopened many of the rifts that had been developing between and within some of the constituent parties. As already noted, only part of the Jharkhand Party supported the new government. This represented an important split in that group. The BKD, which included many of the former members of the JKD, was divided on whether to support the ministry or not. The former chief minister, Mahamaya Prasad Sinha, was opposed, while the Raja of Ramgarh and his followers were in favor. As he had done so many times before in his political career, the Raja broke with his party – the BKD – and together with his followers joined the Paswan ministry.[50]

The PSP was also divided on whether to support the ministry or not. Baswan Singh and his supporters favored entering the ministry, while the party's state president, Suraj Narain Singh, and his supporters opposed entering the ministry. After consultations with Peter Alvares of the national executive committee, the PSP agreed to enter the government. H. V. Kamath, chairman of the PSP's central parliamentary board, explained that the party decided to join the ministry because three of its four preconditions had been met and because the PSP wanted 'to prevent the return of the Congress to power and to avert President's Rule'.[51]

At least temporarily after the resolution of internal party disputes, the ministry was constituted successfully. However, the Raja of Ramgarh, who had several law suits concerning his farming and mining interests pending against him, was quite discontent with the new coalition government. During the first SVD government's tenure he had been given control of the Public Works Department portfolio, which included the mines and metals departments. This put the Raja in a position to influence the progress of the law suits against him. In the second SVD he was not given charge of mines and metals. Thus, his position vis-à-vis the pending court cases was seriously threatened and naturally he was upset. On June 16, 1968 he resigned from the cabinet, ostensibly because of poor health. It was generally known, however, that he was very dissatisfied with the way portfolios had been allocated in the Paswan ministry.[52] On June 17, the *Times of India* reported that 'in Congress organization, it was rumored that the Raja had been offered Deputy Chief Ministership in an alternative Congress cabinet to be headed by the present opposition leader, Mr. Mahesh Prasad Sinha'. The Raja must have found this a very tempting offer. In any event, on January 26 Bhola Paswan Shastri resigned as chief minister, and demanded the dissolution of the state assembly, charging 'the Public Works Department Minister and leader of the Janata Party, the Raja of Ramgarh with "pressuring me directly and indirectly for acceptance of certain conditions, the acceptance of which will go against the interests of the State and its people' ".[53] In an editorial in the *Patriot*, the SVD experience was summed up in the following way:

The Indian context: 1967–1971

'Paswan is honest and courageous, but nobody in Bihar or outside was prepared to see the inclusion of the Raja and his brother in the Government as anything but opportunism. The Raja who had been able to get his terms from Mr. Mahamaya Prasad assumed that he could demand from Mr. Paswan a higher price. This amounted to Deputy Chief Ministership and the Mines portfolio for himself and withdrawal of the innumerable cases filed against him and members of his family by the Bihar government.'[54]

Following the resignation of the Paswan ministry, President's Rule went into effect, and midterm polls were held. After the election, Bihar again underwent a period of serious instability. In February of 1969, a Congress-led coalition, supported by Swatantra, the Janata Party, Jharkhand, and the Shoshit Dal, was sworn into office. The Congress, fearing pressure from other political parties, convinced the Raja of Ramgarh to stand aside in the Cabinet in favor of his less 'infamous' brother. This arrangement was acceptable to the Raja. While his brother became a cabinet minister, he continued to exert veto power over the actions of the coalition. As leader of the Janata Party, the Raja controlled enough seats in the legislative assembly so that he could topple the government at his pleasure. Thus, regardless of the nature of his official position in the coalition, the Raja of Ramgarh continued to be a major source of both power and of disagreement.

Many of the constituents of the new government were quite displeased with the coalition's relationship with the Raja. Swatantra's three-man delegation, for instance, threatened to withdraw its support if the government refused to discontinue its efforts to whitewash the corruption charges which were pending against the Raja. Other parties, including the Congress, raised complaints against the undue influence of the Raja. The situation degenerated considerably when it was learned that the Supreme Court had withdrawn the petition for receivership of the Raja's properties. Many of the constituents of the coalition were convinced that only the chief minister could have succeeded in convincing the Court to take such action.[55]

At the same time, the Congress was suffering from internal dissension. Harihar Singh, the chief minister, attempted to iron out the differences within the coalition by expanding his cabinet to include many of the dissident points of view. This strategy proved successful for a fair amount of time, but at the expense of the government's effectiveness. The *National Herald*, in an editorial on June 19, 1969, reported that the Bihar cabinet was so huge and unwieldy that the government ground to a standstill. As they put it, 'the instinct to survive has made the chief minister expand the ministry, and the same instincts may induce him to accommodate a few more disgruntled legislators in the ministry'. Despite the chief minister's instinct for survival, his government was defeated in the legislature on June 21 when several members of the Shoshit Dal and the Hul Jharkhand voted with the opposition.

After the fall of the Harihar Singh government, another SVD ministry led by Bhola Paswan Shastri was sworn in. Recognizing the dysfunctional effects of ever-growing ministries, the SVD agreed to limit the size of the cabinet to 11 per cent of the legislature. There was disagreement, however, on the exact purpose of limiting the size of the cabinet. Some, such as the chief minister, felt the action was intended only to restrict the ministry to a manageable size, thereby insuring the efficient functioning of the government. Others, such as the Jana Sangh, understood the size limit to be directly intended to prevent the accommodation of defectors in the ministry. They felt that in this way the government would be assured greater stability.

The differences in the interpretation of the 11 per cent ceiling on the ministry were of more than academic interest. Thus, on July 2, 1969, less than two weeks after the ministry was formed, the Jana Sangh contingent of thirty-four legislators withdrew its support from the SVD because two Congress defectors were given cabinet posts. With the withdrawal of the Jana Sangh, the Paswan ministry lost its majority and the government fell. President's Rule was once again imposed in Bihar and remained in effect until mid-1970 when a new coalition came to power.

Table 3.8 shows the distribution of seats in the state legislature after the 1967 election, in June of 1968, and again after the midterm poll.

West Bengal. The West Bengal coalition experience differs markedly from the three states discussed so far. First of all, the coalition was much less of an *ad hoc* response to the decline of the Congress Party. The fourth general election in West Bengal was contested by the Congress Party and by two well organized pre-election coalitions. Following the election, the two coalitions, one led by the CPI and the other by the CPI(M), agreed to merge and form a united front ministry. Unlike the other three states examined thus far, the West Bengal government was not headed by a politician who defected from the Congress after its electoral defeat. Although Ajoy Mukherjee, the chief minister, had left the Congress to found and become the leader of the Bangla Congress, he had done so prior to the election and so contested his legislative assembly seat on the Bangla Congress ticket. The West Bengal ministry also differed from the others in that there were far fewer ideological differences between its constituents than in the Punjab, Uttar Pradesh, or Bihar. No rightists participated in the two pre-election alliances, and no rightists were invited to join the ministry.

TABLE 3.8 *Representation in the legislative assembly of Bihar*

Party	Strength in 1967	Strength during President's Rule	Strength in 1969
Congress	128	105	118
SSP	68	56	52
Jana Sangh	26	24	34
CPI	24	24	25
JKD (BKD)	24	3	5
PSP	18	16	18
CPI (M)	4	4	3
Swatantra	3	0	3
RPI	1	1	2
LCD	0	23	9
SD	0	37	6
Janata	0	18	13
Hul Jharkhand	0	0	7
Jharkhand	9	0	6
FB	0	0	1
RSPI	1	1	0
Independents	12	6	16
Total	318	318	318

The relative unity and exultation which prevailed during the first few weeks of the coalition was not to last long. In the Naxalbari district of Bengal a crisis situation erupted in March of 1967. Jotedars in the area were allegedly being compelled to join the CPI(M) or to move out of the district. Simultaneously, many landless farm workers began seizing land with the support and encouragement of the CPI(M). As tensions mounted in the Naxalbari district, violence erupted and became widespread. With the situation continuing to deteriorate, the chief minister ordered police intervention in the area. He did so without consulting the other members of his ministry despite the stipulation in the coalition's minimum program that called for the withholding of police intervention in areas where there was a legitimate grievance between peasants and landlords.

Despite the presence of the police, the situation in the Naxalbari district continued to degenerate until the government was finally confronted with a full-scale revolt. The central government, aware of the lawlessness which prevailed in the Naxalbari district, and conscious of the strategic importance of the area, ordered the banning of all weapons in the region. Once again a decision aimed at terminating the struggle in the district was taken without consulting the members of the united front, though Ajoy Mukherjee, as chief minister, was consulted by the central government.

The Indian context: 1967–1971

The CPI(M) was infuriated at not being consulted. This was a quite natural reaction for several reasons. The CPI(M) had considerable political influence in the Naxalbari district. The leaders of the CPI(M) expected, therefore, that as a standard procedure the government would consult them before taking any action. In addition, the CPI(M) had insisted on including the clause in the minimum program that restricted the use of police power in cases considered to be legitimate class struggles. The applicability of this clause, as already noted, was not adequately discussed among the constituents of the coalition prior to the use of police pressure in the Naxalbari district. Finally, the CPI(M), aside from being a major power in the Naxalite area, was the single largest constituent in the united front. As such, they felt they should have been consulted before the government took any major action. Despite their open dissatisfaction with the behavior of the chief minister they decided to remain in the government while openly resisting certain of its policies both from within the cabinet and also through the use of hartals (i.e., general strikes) and other forms of public protest.

While the rift between the CPI(M) and the rest of the united front widened over the situation in Naxalbari, the cabinet was facing a crisis from the SSP quarter as well. The SSP, with the support of the Bangla Congress, CPI, PSP, Forward Bloc, and others, demanded the appointment of a scheduled caste member to the cabinet. Kashi Kanya Maitra, the SSP's only cabinet minister, threatened to resign if the demand was not met. Five parties in the front, including the CPI(M) and the RSP, were opposed to any expansion of the ministry, regardless of the merits of the case. This difference of opinion was resolved on June 10, while the Naxalbari Revolt was accelerating into crisis proportions, when the united front unanimously decided to expand the cabinet to accommodate a Harijan.

The first few months that the front was in power revealed the tenuous nature of the agreements among the constituents. The CPI(M) was particularly sensitive to the severity of the situation, especially as it related to the party's role in the Naxalbari Revolt. As a conciliatory gesture intended to legitimize their own position and to reduce tensions in the front, the CPI(M) expelled the Naxalites from the party. While this action did help reduce tensions, many of the constituents were extremely disillusioned with the coalition, and with the CPI(M) in particular. Ajoy Mukherjee was most dissatisfied of all. For several months after the Naxalites began their revolt, there was speculation that Ajoy Mukherjee would resign as chief minister. It was believed that he was negotiating with the Congress Party in the hope of forming a non-Communist coalition supported by them.[56]

The evidence indicates that the chief minister's negotiations progressed fairly rapidly and amicably. Most observers, including many of the leaders of the united front, were convinced that Ajoy Mukherjee intended to resign from the united front on October 2. An emergency session of the united front committee had been called for that day, and it was believed that the chief minister would use the opportunity to tender his resignation. However, when the designated day arrived, the emergency session was cancelled, and Sri Mukherjee did not resign.

On the fourth of October, the chief minister received assurances from the CPI(M) that they would extend their fullest cooperation in restoring agrarian and industrial peace to the state. In light of these assurances, and after consultation with the members of the front, the chief minister announced on October 5 that he would not resign. At the same time, he accused the CPI(M) of being responsible for the lawlessness in the state. They, in turn, accused him of having participated in a conspiracy with the central government to overthrow the popular united front government. According to the CPI(M), the conspiracy even included plans to use military force if it became necessary.

As can well be imagined, the relations between the constituents of the united front were extremely strained. On November 3, P. C. Ghosh, a cabinet minister and prominent figure in the government, resigned from the ministry. His departure from the coalition was followed by the resignation of seventeen members of the legislative assembly, thereby reducing the united front to a minority. On November 21, 1967, the governor dismissed the Ajoy Mukherjee government because the chief minister repeatedly failed to call an early meeting of the state assembly to test his claim that he still controlled a majority.

On the same day, P. C. Ghosh was sworn in as chief minister at the head of a Congress supported government. Apparently, the Congress had finally succeeded in replacing the united front with a non-Communist coalition government. However, the Ghosh government was soon racked by internal and external dissension; dissatisfaction within the coalition arose over the continued leadership of Atulya Ghosh in the Congress Party, and over the distribution of portfolios in the ministry. When negotiations failed to resolve the differences within the new government, Ashutosh Ghosh and eighteen members of the legislative assembly withdrew their support from the P. C. Ghosh ministry and announced the formation of the Indian National Democratic Front (INDC). The new front received support from the 132 members of the old united front; P. C. Ghosh had lost his majority. On February 15, 1968, the governor of West Bengal reported to the President of India that it was not possible for the state to be governed in accordance with the constitution, and so President's Rule was instituted.

President's Rule continued until midterm elections were held in which, as table 3.9 indicates, the Congress was soundly defeated. The united front,

The Indian context: 1967–1971

TABLE 3.9 *Representation in the legislative assembly of West Bengal*

Party	Strength in 1967	Strength during President's Rule	Strength in 1969
Congress	127	137	55
CPI(M)	43	43	80
BC	34	16	33
CPI	16	16	30
FB	13	13	21
SSP	7	7	9
PSP	7	4	5
Jana Sangh	1	0	0
Swatantra	1	0	0
RSP	6	6	12
LSS	5	5	4
INDF	0	10	1
SUC	0	0	7
Gorkha	0	0	4
RCPI	0	0	2
WP	0	0	2
FB (M)	0	0	1
PML	0	0	3
Independents	20	22	11
Total	280	279	280

and the CPI(M) in particular, scored an impressive victory in the election. Shortly thereafter, the front was again invited to form a government. The new government, led by Ajoy Mukherjee, soon fell upon difficult times. A rift quickly surfaced between the Bangla Congress and the CPI(M) over the powers of the chief minister, and the role of collective leadership in a coalition cabinet. Extremely hostile threats and accusations were made between Ajoy Mukherjee and the Home minister, Jyoti Basu of the CPI(M). The situation reached such proportions that the chief minister found it necessary to go on strike personally against his own government. The CPI(M) was once again accused of fostering lawlessness and of exploiting its position in the government for party ends. The CPI(M), on the other hand, accused the Bangla Congress and other members of the front of failing to implement many of the more progressive aspects of the common minimum program. The policy which was subject to the greatest amount of hostile exchanges was, once again, the issues of whether or not the government should withhold police intervention when peasants and landlords, or workers and employers were engaged in allegedly legitimate struggles.

The accusations and counter-accusations continued until early 1970

The Indian context: 1967–1971

when the government finally fell and President's Rule was imposed on West Bengal.

Orissa. Like the coalition in West Bengal, and also in Kerala, the Orissa government was based on a common minimum program and a pre-election alliance. Unlike those other two states, however, the Orissa front consisted of two rightist parties; the Swatantra Party and the Jan Congress.

The Orissa experience was markedly different from all of the other coalition ministries in India. Following the 1967 election, the two-party alliance enjoyed a fairly small, but stable majority (i.e. 75 out of 140 seats). With only a few minor exceptions, there were no important divisions within the coalition that could have threatened its continuation. Because of its size and harmony, the alliance permitted the parties to implement much of their agreed upon program.

Despite the secure majority which the alliance controlled, and despite the harmony among the constituents, the Swatantra Party made repeated efforts to gain the additional support of the PSP.[57] Apparently some of the leaders of the Orissa branch of the Swatantra Party were afraid that their partners, the Jan Congress, might abandon them and return to their former colleagues in the Congress Party.[58] While it is difficult to say if this fear was well-founded, subsequent events have at least demonstrated that the alliance between the two parties was fairly tenuous. Thus, though the government survived for the entire time period between the fourth and fifth general elections, the Swatantra Party and the Jan Congress were unable to coordinate their electoral campaigns in the 1971 election, and so both suffered a serious setback.

Madhya Pradesh. The Congress Party succeeded in securing a majority of seats in the Madhya Pradesh state assembly during the fourth general election. However, the chief minister, D. P. Mishra, who had been implicated in several cases involving corruption, was unable to maintain his majority for very long. G. N. Singh and thirty-four supporters defected from the Congress and lent their support to the newly formed SVD (Samyukt Vidhayak Dal – literally, united legislative party; SVD refers to the set of parties that agreed to participate in a legislative coalition). Without the support of those thirty-five MLAs (i.e. members of the state legislative assembly), the Congress no longer controlled a majority and so the government fell.

Once the Congress was out of power, the SVD was called upon to form a coalition government. The Rajmata of Gwalior, in her role as the leader of the SVD, designated G. N. Singh as the chief minister of the new government.

In addition to the defectors, the coalition was supported by the

The Indian context: 1967–1971

Rajmata's supporters in the KVD, the Jana Sangh, SSP and the BKD. As with so many of the other coalition governments, the Madhya Pradesh SVD enjoyed a fairly small majority. The chief minister recognized this fact and set out to strengthen his government. On August 2, just a few days after taking the oath of office, G. N. Singh reported that 'I will have a ministry as big as is needed to make it stable.'[59] That is, he intended to use ministerial appointments as a lure with which to attract new supporters, and insure the loyalty of old supporters of the SVD.

Following his own advice, the chief minister almost immediately began to expand the ministry. On August 4, a thirty-one man ministry was sworn in amid speculation that it would be expanded even further if (*a*) the SSP decided to participate in the ministry; (*b*) the PSP decided to participate in the ministry; or (*c*) more defectors were needed from the Congress.[60] It was on the issue of cabinet expansion that the government was to experience its first important rift. This very issue would continue to plague it throughout its tenure in office.

The Jana Sangh, being a rather large contingent in the SVD, wanted cabinet posts to be distributed in proportion to the strength of representation of the constituents in the coalition. (As table 3.10 indicates, this would have meant substantial representation for the Jana Sangh.) The chief

TABLE 3.10 *Representation in the legislative assembly of Madhya Pradesh*

Party	Strength in March 1967	Strength in March 1968
Congress	167	122
Jana Sangh	78	64
SSP	10	9
PSP	9	9
Swatantra	7	0
JC	2	0
CPI	1	1
LSD (Rajmata)	0	35
Congress defectors	0	52
Independents	22	3
Total	296	295

minister, on the other hand, was very sensitive to the demands of the defectors and so opposed any set formula for allocating ministerial positions. The Jana Sangh finally agreed to relax its demand for proportionality in return for the Home portfolio as well as other important positions. Although a prominent Congress defector in the cabinet threatened to resign if he were not given the Home portfolio, the chief minister succumbed to the Jana Sangh's pressure on this issue.

During the next several months, the ministry experienced only minor disagreements. It continued to expand its strength by attracting Congress defectors, and giving many of them cabinet posts. During this period of relative calm the defectors became the single largest contingent in the coalition. They organized themselves into the Lok Sevak Dal which was also joined by the Rajmata of Gwalior and her supporters.

As time passed, both the Jana Sangh and the SSP became dissatisfied with the size that the coalition had attained. Both parties offered to vacate ministerial seats in order to reduce the size of the government and insure its stability. It quickly became evident that the Jana Sangh was especially unhappy with the continued expansion of the cabinet. On April 25, 1968 seven Jana Sangh ministers resigned, ostensibly to participate in the Kutch Satyagraha.[61] However, initially only two ministers were expected to resign and so the act was interpreted as an indication of the Jana Sangh's dissatisfaction with the government. The *Hindustan Times* pointed out that 'the Jana Sangh would prefer mid-term polls to a further expansion of the Council of Ministers'.[62] Whether the Jana Sangh dissatisfaction resulted from its weakened position in the cabinet, or from a genuine concern for the inefficiencies produced by such a large ministry is hard to say, but it is clear that the party was very unhappy with developments in Madhya Pradesh.

That the Jana Sangh was displeased with the state of affairs was underscored by comments of Virenda Saklecha, the party's leader in Madhya Pradesh (as well as the deputy chief minister in the G. N. Singh cabinet). He reported that following the Kutch Satyagraha the Jana Sangh would rejoin the ministry only if it were agreed that (*a*) when the head of a department is to be appointed, the appropriate cabinet minister would be consulted; and (*b*) all of the constituent units of the SVD had to be consulted on all major policy decisions. Apparently, the party was disgruntled by the undue influence being given to the defectors in the Lok Sevak Dal at the expense of the other important constituents, not least of which was the Jana Sangh.

In July the Jana Sangh rejoined the ministry, but this did not end the government's problems. At almost exactly the same time, the SSP resigned because of the government's failure to implement an ordinance to abolish land revenue on uneconomic holdings. In the meantime other members of the SVD were dissatisfied because several members of the cabinet had threatened to defect back to the Congress. It was proposed that 'the ministry should be shed of such defectors as had favoured return to the Congress'.[63] Shedding them, however, would have upset the chief minister's balance of power, particularly since many of those ministers who were

The Indian context: 1967–1971

considering a return to the Congress were 'among the Ministers most loyal to the chief minister himself'.[64] In the wake of these accusations and threats G. N. Singh offered to resign on grounds of poor health. He was persuaded, however, to continue in office in order to prevent the return of the Congress to power.

Again in October of 1968 the chief minister talked of resigning, and sixteen ministers threatened to join him. He did not resign. Instead, he continued to expand his ministry, primarily by appointing his own supporters to cabinet posts. Once again a crisis erupted over cabinet expansions. The Jana Sangh, in the meantime, demanded control of the education portfolio, and that the size of the ministry be limited to thirty-six. The chief minister seemed willing to give the Jana Sangh the portfolio they wanted only if he could nominate the Jana Sanghi to whom it would go. The Jana Sangh, fearing defections in its own ranks, was not willing to accept such a compromise. The chief minister recognized the severity of the situation and in an attempt to improve his position reshuffled the ministry. It should be added that by this point the ministry was already very much biased in his favor. Of the thirty-six members, twenty-three were Congress defectors, seven were from the Jana Sangh and two represented the SSP.

The Jana Sangh, seeing its position weakening, and becoming increasingly discontent with the coalition, accused three members of the ministry of corruption. This made the crisis situation which prevailed all the more severe. Both the Jana Sangh and the Rajmata wanted at least six ministers, including those accused of corruption, dropped from the ministry. The chief minister, fearing the repercussions of such an action, preferred to simply redistribute the portfolios among the existing ministers. This, of course, was not an adequate solution as it neither cleared the accused ministers, nor satisfied the demands of the Jana Sangh and the Rajmata of Gwalior. The coalition government had clearly reached the precipice. As the *Statesman* reported on October 31, 1968: 'By all counts, Mr. Singh is in a predicament. If he drops some of his colleagues the defectors may revolt. If he does not do so, it may mean the end of his ministry.'

A temporary solution to the dilemma was found when twenty ministers, including nineteen Congress defectors, resigned on November 2. Although this could have been a disaster, the chief minister succeeded in turning it to his advantage. Mr Singh redistributed the portfolios which had been held by the twenty resigning ministers among the three remaining ministers from his own party. The seven Jana Sanghis, two members of the SSP, and the three supporters of the Rajmata in the cabinet received no new portfolios.

After a great deal of delay, the cabinet was reconstituted in January of 1969, and the three ministers against whom the Jana Sangh had preferred charges were again in the government. The reconstitution of the ministry did little to ease the tensions between the chief minister and the Jana Sangh. It was felt by many, including some of the former Congress defectors, that the reconstituted cabinet went too far in centralizing all power in the hands of the chief minister and his most loyal supporters.[65] Finally, in March of 1969 the rift became too wide to be tolerated and G. N. Singh resigned his office. Raja Naresh Chandra Singh was designated as the new chief minister. He took office with even less support than had G. N. Singh. Thus, the new chief minister did not invite the SSP or the Jana Sangh to join the ministry because both of their national executive committees had decided to seek midterm polls in the state rather than support the SVD. This meant that the new government did not have the support of the two largest organized parties (other than the Congress) in the state.

Within the same month that the Raja became chief minister, his efforts at gaining the support of more defectors, and thereby insuring himself a majority failed and his government fell. On March 27, Shyama Charan Shukla of the Congress Party became chief minister after D. P. Mishra, the former chief minister who had been implicated in several corruption cases, was pressured into stepping down in his favor. G. N. Singh and his supporters promptly returned to the Congress fold after the collapse of the SVD.

Kerala. The Kerala coalition, like the West Bengal coalition, was based on a pre-election united front of leftist parties. As a result of the joint efforts of the members of the united front, the Congress was resoundingly defeated in 1967 and a coalition with a rather stable majority was formed. The new government was supported by the CPI(M), CPI, SSP, Muslim League, RSP, the Kerala Socialist Party (KSP), and the Karshaka Thozhilali Party (KTP). Besides a minimum program, the parties agreed to formulate a code of conduct and to constitute a co-ordinating committee to insure the smooth functioning of the government.

Despite the efforts of the constituents to minimize friction, a dispute emerged very shortly after the swearing in of the government. When the portfolios were distributed among the constituents, P. K. Kunju of the SSP was given the finance ministry. He was not, however, given control of the sales tax department which had traditionally been part of the finance minister's domain. Instead, the CPI(M)-led ministry assigned the department to Mrs Gouri Thomas, the CPI(M) revenue minister. The SSP became infuriated over this breach with custom, but agreed not to resign over the issue. Nevertheless, the incident left the SSP with a feeling of bitterness toward the CPI(M) party. Mr Kunju expressed that bitterness in September of 1967 when he said, 'Frankly speaking, I do not approve of

The Indian context: 1967–1971

anything that the present government does.'[66] Quite clearly, he and his party no longer felt themselves wholly committed to the united front. Yet, four days later he was reported as saying that no rift existed in the cabinet and that the government, under the leadership of E. M. S. Namboodiripad of the CPI(M), would continue to rule for a full five-year term.

Conditions in the coalition remained fairly stable until a division emerged in the SSP. The national executive committee of the party had ordered all of its cabinet ministers throughout India to resign from their posts and join in the Kutch Satyagraha. Both P. K. Kunju and P. R. Kurup, the two SSP ministers in Kerala, refused to resign. Kunju explained that the Kutch settlement was an international question and, therefore, it would be more appropriate for the SSP's members of parliament to resign first. The SSP leadership did not accept Kunju's argument. Since they felt that the two SSP ministers had breached party discipline, the SSP asked Sri Namboodiripad, the Kerala chief minister, to relieve both Kunju and Kurup of their ministerial responsibilities, claiming that they no longer represented the views of the SSP. Mr Namboodiripad refused to honor the request. He maintained that he welcomed all progressive support, regardless of its affiliation. In the face of this rebuke, the SSP was left with no choice but to withdraw its support from the ministry. Their withdrawal caused a major split in the SSP ranks, with about half of the SSP MLAs in Kerala leaving the party and joining the newly formed Indian Socialist Party (ISP).

At about the same time, in May of 1968, further trouble erupted in the ministry. T. V. Thomas, a minister from the CPI, was publicly dissatisfied with the CPI(M)'s lack of responsiveness to directives from the united front's coordinating committee. He maintained that the CPI(M) leadership was making too many unilateral decisions for the united front. Mr Thomas was, in return, accused of being a fifth columnist by the CPI(M). Despite their obvious differences, the constituents ignored the accusations to which they had been subjected, at least for the time being, and the government continued to function fairly well.

In late 1968, however, the differences between the constituents, especially the CPI and the CPI(M), became more serious. The chief minister accused T. V. Thomas of attempting to form an alternative government. This, and other events, led to continuous harassment between these two major constituents of the united front during the next several months.

On April 28, 1969, the CPI threatened to withdraw from the front because of the alleged interference by the CPI(M) in the functioning of the CPI ministries. This charge was reiterated by M. N. Govindan Nair, a CPI minister, on May 7. In the wake of these accusations, E. M. S. Namboodiripad accused several cabinet ministers of corruption. At the same time, other members of the front charged two of the chief minister's supporters

The Indian context: 1967–1971

with corruption. Before these accusations could tear the alliance asunder, a temporary calm set in while Mr Namboodiripad was out of the state receiving medical treatment for several months. Upon his return, the battle between the CPI and the CPI(M) was resumed with full gusto. On October 17 two CPI, one RSP, one ISP, and two Muslim League ministers resigned. The other ISP minister had stepped down earlier, pending the outcome of an investigation into corruption charges against him. Mr Wellington, a supporter of the CPI(M), also quit the cabinet after the chief minister, under pressure, ordered an inquiry into corruption charges against him. With the resignations of these ministers, the chief minister lost much of his support in the legislative assembly. Thus, after almost three years in office, E. M. S. Namboodiripad resigned as head of the government.

The Namboodiripad ministry was replaced with a minority government, supported by the CPI, Muslim League, ISP, RSP, and the Kerala Congress. This government quickly ran into difficulties over whether to readmit P. K. Kunju into the cabinet following the dismissal of corruption charges that had been brought against him. Ordinarily, the CPI-led ministry would not have hesitated to reinstate him, but the dismissal of the case against Kunju was based on a technicality. Because of the nature of the dismissal, there were many in the front who felt that Kunju's name had not really been cleared. Furthermore, the interim finance minister was well thought of by members of the ministry, and he was not inclined to resign. The result of this was a further split in the ISP, and severe friction in the minority government.

After several more months of struggling, the CPI-led Kerala mini-front finally fell in late 1970. Later the state was once again ruled by a CPI-led coalition government, this time with the Indira Gandhi branch of the Congress Party as one of the major constituents. At the time of this writing, that coalition is in its third year of stable government.

Summary. Our brief examination of the coalition experiences in seven states suggests the presence of several common problems. With the exception of Orissa, each coalition suffered more or less severely from defector politics. Even in Orissa, the coalition would not have been possible without the defection from the Congress Party of the members of the Jan Congress.

In four of the seven states the chief ministers had defected from the Congress Party. In three of those states, the chief ministers had defected after the outcome of the election was known. In two of the states, the opposition was deprived of a majority of the seats in the legislative assembly until the defections occurred.

Besides defector politics, many of the coalitions were plagued by the belief that stability would come from constantly expanding the ministry so as to accommodate new, and often very opportunistic, supporters. In Madhya Pradesh this tactic succeeded in keeping the government in power for quite a long time, but it prevented the ministry from doing very much for the people. In Bihar it lent neither stability nor dignity to the coalition governments. The belief that stability could be achieved by luring supporters with offers of cabinet positions was widespread, even though it is not at all supported by the events. In fact, the correlation between the number of governments a state had, and the average size of its ministries is 0.46, indicating that large ministries were accompanied by frequent turnovers in government. Small ministries, on the other hand, were accompanied by governmental stability.

Finally, with the exceptions of Kerala, West Bengal, and Orissa, the coalition governments were composed of very disparate political elements. Although they shared the common desire to oust the Congress Party from power, and although they were willing to forgo at least some of their major programs to do so, in the long run most of them found that they were unable to work together. Even where there was a great deal of ideological homogeneity, as in West Bengal and Kerala, parties often found their ambitions at conflict with one another. This may very well have been the most important factor contributing to the fall of the united front ministries in India.

In the final analysis, it seems to have been the case, almost everywhere and for almost everyone, that the quest for power, rather than the desire to implement programs, led both to the formation and the dissolution of the coalition ministries. Each coalition required the constituents to surrender their own dreams of power for collective rule. Very few of the parties were prepared to make such a commitment.

4. Size and coalition politics

In the second chapter it was postulated that political parties join coalitions to maximize the long-term increase in their political influence. I suggested that the attainment of this goal depends on behavior during three stages of coalition politics. During the coalition formation stage, each party's primary concern is to gain membership in a winning coalition. During the maintenance stage, parties are concerned with influencing the decision-rules used to distribute the coalition's benefits. When coalitions enter the termination stage, parties are again concerned with optimizing the point at which their benefits give them a disproportionately large advantage over their putative allies. Strategic behavior was thought to be the major factor influencing the allocation of redistributive benefits in the latter stages of coalition politics. In the coalition formation stage, on the other hand, the size of parties was thought to influence their access to membership in winning coalitions. Because none of the benefits available during the latter stages of a coalition can be secured by actors outside the coalition, the first empirical concern of this study must be to ascertain which political parties are most likely to become members of winning coalitions. Do those same considerations influence the allocation of redistributive benefits during the coalition maintenance stage? The particular considerations investigated in this chapter concern the relationship between the size of political parties and their success in entering winning coalitions and in securing redistributive benefits.

The meaning of size

Size is a complex concept. A party's size can be related to its electoral popularity, its legislative representation, or its participation in a ruling government, among other things. The resources required to be successful in each of these areas are somewhat different. A party's electoral popularity, measured as the percentage of votes that it wins, is an indicator of the party's influence among the mass electorate. Votes reflect some of the mass organizational capacity of a political party. This relationship is especially evident in India because of the important role played by vote banks in influencing electoral outcomes.[1] The proportion of votes that a party receives does not necessarily reflect differences in party influence in other sectors of the political system.

The number of legislative seats that a party wins is a good indicator of its influence in legislative politics, but not necessarily as good an indicator of a party's mass base of support. Thus, given a decision-rule that requires

Size and coalition politics

a plurality for a candidate to be elected to a legislature, two parties receiving identical shares of the vote across several constituencies cannot necessarily expect to receive equal shares of the legislative seats. Some parties are more successful at converting their votes to seats than are other parties. The Congress party, for instance, managed to convert every 1 per cent of the legislative assembly votes it received in 1952 into 1.6 per cent of the legislative seats. In 1957 and 1962 the ratio was 1.4 per cent of the seats to 1 per cent of the vote. In 1967, this conversion factor was 1.2:1. The average ability of all other parties to convert votes into seats during the same four general elections was 0.54:1, 0.64:1, 0.68:1 and 0.86:1. That is, while the Congress secured a disproportionately large percentage of seats relative to its share of the vote, the other parties, on average, secured a disproportionately small percentage of seats, relative to their share of the vote. Still, the two indicators are related to each other. Among fifty-nine of the political party units – including twenty-eight state branches of national parties and twenty-eight local or regional parties – in the seven states included in this study, 66 per cent of the variance in the share of seats won in 1967 is accounted for by the percentage of the vote that was won in that same year ($r=0.81$).[2]

The number of legislative seats that are won goes beyond the share of votes in indicating a political party's ability to convert its popularity into effective action. If a party's share is sufficiently large it may secure monopoly control over the decision-making process.[3] Thus, a party with a large number of supporters, but with little ability to use them effectively, is unlikely to exert substantial influence on the legislative process. A party with fewer voters, on the other hand, can exert considerable influence in the legislature provided it converts a disproportionately large share of its votes into seats.[4] Consequently, votes are not useful as an indicator of legislative influence, although the number of seats held by a party is a relevant indicator of its legislative strength and, to a lesser degree, of its mass popularity.

Political influence cannot be measured in terms of seats alone. Two parties holding equal numbers of seats may be very different from each other in terms of their ability to influence the government's priorities and its allocation of resources. A large party outside the government, for example, may have less political influence than a much smaller party in the government. Thus, membership in a ruling government assures a party of at least some influence over the determination of priorities and the allocation of resources. Representation in a ruling government is, therefore, an important indicator of the relative influence of parties, both in terms of legislative decision-making and in terms of the bureaucratic manipulation and implementation of those decisions.

It should be clear that the three indicators of size – votes, legislative seats, and degree of representation within a ruling government – cannot be used interchangeably: each measures a different aspect of a party's size and so each is reserved for questions dealing with the relevant aspect of size. Votes, and the ratio of votes converted to seats, will be reserved for discussions of a party's popularity and organizational capabilities, representation within a legislature is used as a measure of a party's size during the coalition formation stage; while a party's representation in the ruling government indicates its size during the coalition maintenance and coalition termination stages.

Temporal framework

Any study concerned with the investigation of change must identify a temporal framework within which change may occur. For the purposes of this investigation, the selection of time-periods is especially important. The prevalence of defections from one party to another in India makes it imperative that time-periods are selected which reflect more than minor perturbations in the legislative representation of the parties.[5]

Three time points are used as the temporal referents for the measurement of party size, and for the assessment of the redistributive benefits acquired by the parties.

Restricting the analysis to so few intervals sacrifices some detail and will inevitably lead to our overlooking many interesting events. These losses, while unfortunate, are more than outweighed by the benefits attached to such an approach. If more attention were paid to every fluctuation in the distribution of size-related resources, the analysis would be lost quickly in a morass of idiosyncratic, often unimportant, shifts and counter-shifts in party size. By identifying a small set of important intervals, it is possible to compare shifts in party size under fairly comparable circumstances, facilitating the generalizability of the results.

Between 1967 and early 1974 the number of legislative seats controlled by the Indian political parties fluctuated during four elections. These include (*a*) the fourth general election in India, held in 1967; (*b*) the midterm elections held in six of the seven states included in these analyses;[6] (*c*) the fifth general election, held in 1972, in which four of the seven states under investigation were required to participate; and (*d*) the midterm elections conducted in Uttar Pradesh and Orissa in 1974. The latest of these elections is so recent that only sketchy data are available.

There are important differences among the three remaining elections. Only in 1967 were all seven states under investigation required to participate in the elections. The 1967 election did not occur because of a governmental crisis, but simply because it was scheduled to take place by law. Unlike earlier general elections, however, the fourth general election

Size and coalition politics

created a major realignment of political influence in India. For the first time, well over half the population of India was ruled by parties other than the Indian National Congress. Indeed, the very notion of India as a single-party dominant political system was most forcefully challenged by the results of the election.[7]

The midterm polls were radically different from the 1967 election. The most important difference stems from the conditions which led to the calling of midterm polls. These elections were necessitated by the failure of the political parties to provide adequate governments in several states. Unlike the 1967 election, the midterm polls are not a normal part of the electoral schedule, and they would not have occurred had the coalition governments proved able to maintain their parliamentary majorities. The midterm polls differ from the general election in another important way. Midterm polls are called in response to the exigencies of the states. Thus, four states had midterm polls in 1969, one state had them in 1970, and two states had midterm polls in 1971 (including one state – West Bengal – which also had them in 1969). General elections, on the other hand, generally occur in all states at the same time.

The fifth general election, held in 1972, followed shortly after midterm polls to elect a new national parliament. Only four of the states with which we are concerned held legislative assembly contests during the fifth general election. They all held elections to the Lok Sabha in 1971, however. Because Lok Sabha elections are not an important concern of the size-related hypotheses, detailed analyses of this election are reserved for subsequent chapters.

The instability which prompted the midterm elections stemmed, in part, from the prevalence of defection politics in India after 1967. Although changes in legislative size due to defections reflects some change in a party's immediate influence, defectors do not generally develop any long-term loyalty to a party other than their original party. Consequently, defections generally are not important in terms of long-term changes in political influence. Nevertheless, occasional reference is made to their short-term impact.

The meaning of benefits

As was noted in the discussion of the episodic condition and the redistributive condition, coalitions offer their members two types of benefits, only one of which is convertible into subsequent political influence. In operational terms, the non-redistributive benefits are uncorrelated, or worse yet, negatively correlated, with a party's subsequent performance in elections and in coalitions. The redistributive benefits are positively associated with the subsequent performance of a party in elections and in future coalitions.

Size and coalition politics

The most obvious place to identify such benefits is within the coalition cabinets. The assignment of cabinet portfolios is one of the most important political decisions that coalitions make. Some portfolios are obscure, with little access to patronage, of little interest to most constituents, and with little appeal to the media. Other portfolios are so essential to the workings of government that their control places a political party in an excellent position to undermine the efforts of some of their partners and reward the efforts of others. The ministers of finance in the Indian states, for example, exert so much control over the expenditure of funds that they can regulate the success or failure of programs by releasing or withholding appropriations. The ministers of agriculture have such great influence over so vital a sector of every Indian state's economy that they too can manipulate the political prospects of many of their allies. A minister who advertises the good works that are done under his directorship is likely to gain support for his party. This is likely to have an important effect on the party's future growth, especially in constituencies where the party needs only a little more support to win. On the other hand, the ministry of tourism, controlling resources that are of no consequence to most constituents, is not likely to give a politician very many redistributive benefits.

The above discussion of cabinet portfolios suggests that some cabinet portfolios have a redistributive effect, and others do not. In evaluating the benefits a party derives from its membership in a coalition, therefore, I will examine its share of all portfolios, cabinet-level portfolios, redistributive portfolios, and its actual change in legislative representation from election to election.

Size and coalition formation

In chapter 2 we hypothesized that a party's admissibility as a member of a winning coalition in any single iteration depends upon its size. In particular, our expectation is that very large parties have the lowest probability of gaining admission, while intermediate-sized parties have an intermediate probability of gaining admission, and small parties have a high probability of gaining admission to winning coalitions. This hypothesis, and related propositions, may now be tested.

In the discussion which led to the development of the first hypothesis some attention was given to the role played by ideology in coalition formation. The empirical literature indicates that ideology plays a small role in coalition formation. In the case of India, a test that discriminates between size and ideology is somewhat difficult to construct. During the period studied here, several parties subscribed to a policy known as non-Congressism. The purpose of this policy was to deprive the Congress Party of monopoly control over the decision-making process in the states and,

Size and coalition politics

eventually, in the national parliament. As a consequence, the Congress was excluded from membership in pre-election alliances and in most post election coalitions. The Congress was, not coincidentally, the largest political party in most places where the non-Congressism strategy was applied. Therefore, one cannot conclude without additional information whether the Congress was systematically excluded from coalitions because of its size or because of an ideological bias against the Congress.

The additional information which is required involves the use of survey techniques to ascertain the motives which prompted the application of the non-Congress strategy. For this and other purposes, reliance is placed on interviews I conducted between September 1969 and June 1970. The subjects of the interviews were prominent members of All-India parties in those states where their parties had participated in coalition governments. Prominent members were defined as (*a*) the President, Vice President, or Secretary (or their equivalent) of a state branch, or the national branch, of the All-India parties discussed in chapter 3; (*b*) any person who represented an All-India party as a full cabinet minister in a coalition government (but not as a deputy minister or a state minister); or (*c*) any person who was named as a principal leader by a majority of the leaders satisfying the above two criteria. For details concerning the interview data, and other aspects of the research design, see appendix II.

Before undertaking a systematic analysis of the importance of size and the importance of ideology in influencing the coalition formation behavior of the Indian parties, let us examine the non-Congressism strategy more closely. The late Dr Lohia, of the Samyukta Socialist Party (SSP), is generally recognized as the founder of the non-Congressism strategy. His views on the purpose of the strategy are helpful in clarifying any confusion between non-Congressism as an ideological approach and as a size-oriented approach.

Lohia noted that 'It should be possible for every non-Congress party to combine. For to run a government we require not a like mind but a few common policies.' He went on to explain that:

> 'No sane person should want to associate just yet with a pack of people who have been wasters of national energy and resources. The Congress must go through a period of remorse and repentance. They must disgorge the wealth which they have accumulated although nothing can be done about the heaps of money that they have wasted.'[8]

The Lohia view of non-Congressism reflects the attitude that the Congress is an unacceptable coalition partner because of its size or wealth, not because of its ideology, and it would not be acceptable until its resource base was reduced through a process of disgorgement. The emphasis was completely on Congress's politically useful resources, not on a change in

Size and coalition politics

the Congress party's ideology. It is expected, therefore, that the emphasis on the non-Congress strategy should be greatest in those states where the Congress Party was strongest, and should be weakest in those states where the Congress was weakest. After examining the evidence for hypothesis 1, I will examine the relationship between attitudes toward non-Congressism and the size and ideological preferences of the coalesced parties.

Hypothesis 1 might be tested in several ways. One might treat each political party, or indeed each individual politician, as a separate actor and compute the random probability of such an actor entering a winning coalition. Alternatively, all the relevant parties could be reduced to a set of protocoalitions in the pre-coalition formation period.[9] The propensity of the protocoalitions to enter winning coalitions could then be related to their size.

The former approach has the advantage of requiring the least transformation of reality. On the other hand, it is threatened by the morass of idiosyncratic shifts in party size as defectors came and went, or as parties rose and fell. These frequent fluctuations make it difficult to ascertain the actual size of each party just prior to the formation of a winning coalition. In addition, this approach oversimplifies the relationships among parties. It assumes that each party's likelihood of entering a coalition is strictly a function of its individual size, rather than the size of the political group that is committed to it. Thus, focusing on individual parties ignores the very real groupings which were formed in the pre-election period. It would lead us, for example, to classify the Gorkha League and the Swatantra Party as in approximately the same size category in West Bengal in 1967. The Gorkha League elected two members to the state legislative assembly while the Swatantra Party elected one. The Gorkha League, however, was a member of a large pre-election united front. All the members of this front were committed to pursue a winning coalition as a united group; not as individual political actors. The Swatantra Party had no such alliance and, therefore, had no additional legislative 'clout' beyond its one legislator.

The protocoalition approach focuses attention on the political groupings that acted as a unit in pursuit of membership in a winning coalition. It identifies the size of coordinated groups of political actors, rather than the size of individuals. Consequently, the protocoalition approach is sensitive to the underlying coalitional significance of each party, rather than just their apparent influence. There are difficulties inherent in this approach as well, however. For one thing, it is often difficult to identify the members of a protocoalition. If all parties formed explicit pre-election alliances, which they do not, this difficulty would be somewhat resolved. Instead, parties join state-wide pre-election alliances with some parties; agree to electoral adjustments in a large number of constituencies with some

Size and coalition politics

parties; and agree to electoral adjustments in very few constituencies with still other parties. One solution to this difficulty is to define protocoalitions in terms of each party's preferences for other parties along a salient dimension. Although such simplifications are always risky, I attempt to organize the Indian parties along a right–left continuum. My concern is less with their exact spatial location, than with their position relative to the Congress Party. Thus, I assume that all parties left of the Congress are more like each other than they are like parties to the right of the Congress, and vice versa.

This assumption does less injustice to reality than one might expect. It will be recalled, for example, that the Praja Socialist Party was disgruntled with its coalition experiences with the extremely leftist CPI(M). Nevertheless, the leaders of the PSP repeatedly supported coalitions that included the CPI(M), and even more extremist parties. Yet, they refused to participate in the Orissa coalition with the rightist Swatantra Party. One might infer from this that the PSP – probably the most centrist of the left-of-Congress parties – perceived a greater affinity for the extreme leftists than it did for the rightists. Of course, this does not suggest that leftists and rightists found it impossible to cooperate with each other. As has already been noted, there were far more ideologically disparate coalitions than there were ideologically homogeneous coalitions. The assumption simply recognizes that 'likeminded' parties are more likely to coordinate their actions than are 'unlikeminded' parties.

There are almost no instances of rightist parties intentionally excluding other rightist parties from winning coalitions, while admitting leftists into the same alliances. Although this is somewhat more common among the leftist parties, especially since the Congress Party split into two factions in 1969, it is still unusual to find leftist parties excluding other leftist parties from their coalitions, while coalescing with rightists. One does find a few recent examples of a leftist party – the CPI – coalescing with the more leftist wing of the Congress – the Indira Gandhi-led Congress (R) – while excluding the CPI(M). There are instances of such behavior in West Bengal and in Kerala. But these few exceptions are far outweighed by the number of cases of cooperation among ideologically similar parties in the *preformation* period.

In order to test the various size-related formulations concerning coalition formation, I use this modified protocoalition concept to divide the Indian political parties into a triad. In order to do this, the following additional assumptions are made:

(*a*) The Indira Gandhi-led Congress Party is a single protocoalition.
(*b*) Political parties to the right of the Congress generally act as if they are a protocoalition.

Size and coalition politics

(c) Political parties to the left of the Congress generally act as if they are a protocoalition.
(d) Defectors from a winning coalition who succeed in terminating the winning coalition comprise a protocoalition.
(e) Those parties that remain in a terminated coalition after it has suffered defections comprise a protocoalition.

The first assumption recognizes the relatively independent course the Congress Party has followed in elections and in other precoalition situations. The Congress occasionally agrees to local electoral adjustments, but it does not subscribe to extensive pre-election alliances. Of course, with its enormous organization and resource pool it can afford to operate as a lone protocoalition.

The second and third assumptions have already been discussed. It should be noted that among the All-India parties, the Swatantra Party and the Jana Sangh qualify as rightists, while the Samyukta Socialist Party, the Praja Socialist Party, the CPI and the CPI(M) qualify as leftists. Although some might object, I consider most nonsecular parties – such as the Muslim League, the Hindu Maha Sabha, and the Akali Dal – to be rightist parties.

The fourth assumption refers to defectors only during the period in which they are defecting away from one coalition and toward another. The fifth assumption is true by definition.

In constructing the analyses, I modify these assumptions slightly in the case of West Bengal and Kerala, especially since the 1969 split in the Congress Party. Neither of these states have particularly viable rightist protocoalitions. Instead, they have CPI-led and CPI(M)-led protocoalitions. Because the rightists are too weak to form important protocoalitions, some rightist parties belong to a protocoalition led by a leftist party. The Muslim League in Kerala, for instance, belongs to a protocoalition led by the Communist Party of India. In these states, I assume that the two communist parties each lead their own protocoalition. The independence of these protocoalitions is highlighted by their behavior since 1969. In Kerala and in West Bengal the CPI-led protocoalition has coalesced with the Congress Party, and has excluded the CPI(M) and its followers from the winning coalitions.

The size of any one protocoalition is assumed to be equal to the sum of the legislative seats held by the political parties that comprise the protocoalition. It should be noted that only three of these protocoalitions can exist at one time. The Congress Party is a protocoalition whenever it is not part of a winning coalition. Similarly, the right and left protocoalitions exist whenever there is no winning coalition. Once a coalition is formed, it replaces the political groups that comprise it and becomes a single entity itself. Consequently, the right, left, or Congress are not protocoalitions

Size and coalition politics

when they are part of a winning coalition that is terminated as a consequence of defections. During such times, the remaining members of the formerly winning coalition are treated as a protocoalition. The defectors are treated as another protocoalition during the termination stage of coalition politics.

In order to establish the relationship between size and coalition formation it is necessary to examine situations in which large, intermediate, and small protocoalitions all had an opportunity to belong to a winning coalition. To satisfy this requirement, I focus on coalition situations in which any two of the three existing protocoalitions, which I call A, B, and C, could have formed a winning coalition. This condition is satisfied if the distribution of seats among the protocoalitions satisfies two conditions. These conditions are that $A>B>C$, $A<B+C$.

There have been approximately twenty coalitions in the seven states included in this study since the fourth general election. Of these, twelve meet the triadic capabilities assumptions required for my analysis of coalition formation. The others involved ideologically 'likeminded' parties that secured a majority of seats as a group through the careful use of pre-election alliances. In these cases, such as the Swatantra–Jan Congress alliance in Orissa in 1967 or the CPI–CPI(M) cooperation in Kerala in 1967, there were no rival protocoalitions large enough to form a winning coalition. Let us turn our attention, therefore, to the remaining twelve coalitions.

Eight of the twelve coalitions were of the $B \cup C$ type, three included an A and a C protocoalition, and only one was between protocoalition A and protocoalition B. In the first iteration all winning coalitions were between a B and a C protocoalition. That is, in Bihar, Madhya Pradesh, Uttar Pradesh, the Punjab, and West Bengal, a combination of any two protocoalitions would have been sufficient to form a winning coalition. In each of these cases, the A group – the Congress Party – was excluded from the initial winning coalition. After the initial set of coalition terminations, four states experienced a second wave of coalition formation situations that meet the assumptions of this inquiry. In Bihar a coalition formed between the Congress Party and a group of defectors. By the time this coalition formed, the Congress had been reduced to a B protocoalition, with the defectors comprising a C protocoalition. The parties that remained associated with the old winning coalition were an A protocoalition. In Uttar Pradesh, the Bharatiya Kranti Dal and the Congress (O) formed a coalition in which the Congress (R), as the A protocoalition, was excluded. In the Punjab a very short-lived legislative coalition between the Congress and defectors was formed. In this case, the Congress Party was the largest protocoalition, while the defectors were the smallest protocoalition. Finally, in West Bengal, a legislative coalition betwen the Congress and a

Size and coalition politics

set of defectors briefly formed and maintained a government. As in the Punjab, the Congress was an A protocoalition and the defectors were a C protocoalition.

By the time a third set of iterations were entered upon, all possible combinations emerged. In Kerala, the Congress Party and the CPI-led protocoalition formed an alliance, excluding the CPI(M) and its supporters. This was the only instance of an $A \cup B$ coalition. In the Punjab, the rightists and the leftists managed sufficient cooperation in the legislature to maintain a coalition government that excluded the Congress Party. Congress was the middle-sized protocoalition. In Bihar, the groups that made up the original winning coalition during the first iteration again came together in a $B \cup C$ alliance.

These results suggest several interesting conclusions. Foremost, of course, is that the distribution fits excellently with the expectations of hypothesis 1. The most prevalent winning coalitions were minimal winning coalitions including the smallest and intermediate protocoalitions. The least prevalent were those including the two largest protocoalitions. In fact, the actual distribution of memberships was four for the A group, nine for the B group, and eleven for the C group. Since in all twelve cases of coalition formation, $A>B>C$ and $A<B+C$, the random expectation for any one protocoalition is that it would enter eight winning coalitions. The actual distribution is substantially different from that. This indicates that the pivotal power argument is not supported by the evidence, while the minimum resource and control approaches are supported to some degree.

The distribution of coalitions during the initial iteration lends considerable support to the minimal winning hypothesis suggested by Riker and Gamson. The developments during subsequent iterations suggest support for Chertkoff's iterated extension of Caplow's theory. $B \cup C$ occurs exactly with the frequency predicted by Chertkoff, while $A \cup C$ and $A \cup B$ come very close to their expected frequencies.

The least support is found for the anti-competitive model. Given the distribution of capabilities, and the anti-competitive expectation that the most equal protocoalitions prefer coalitions with each other, one would have expected $A \cup B$ coalitions in Bihar, Madhya Pradesh, the Punjab, and in at least some iterations in West Bengal and Kerala. That only one $A \cup B$ coalition formed indicates that there was not a strong preference for coalitions among roughly equal protocoalitions.

Through the use of each protocoalition's legislative representation, it has been possible to account for the exclusion of the Congress Party from most winning coalitions. It has also been possible to account for the occasions when the Congress was not excluded, simply by referring to the distribution of capabilities and the hypothesized probability distribution of

Size and coalition politics

winning coalitions. Despite the support for the first hypothesis, it is possible that the relationship is spurious. Since the Congress Party happened to be the largest protocoalition during most coalition formation situations, it is possible that size is mistakenly being credited for the explanatory power possessed by an alternative variable. That alternative variable, of course, is ideology.

Ideology and coalition formation

Continuing the spatial assumption that leftists are more like each other than they are like rightists, and vice versa, it follows that the Congress Party must be ideologically closer to either the rightist or the leftist protocoalitions than those protocoalitions are to each other. If the coalitions were primarily ideological, we should expect to find cooperation between the Congress and either ideological protocoalition both in terms of pre-election electoral adjustments and in terms of post-election coalition formation.

All the coalitions that were based upon pre-election alliances were formed by ideologically similar political parties. In Orissa the coalition between the Swatantra Party and the Jan Congress – both right of the Congress Party – was formed as a consequence of a broad based agreement to avoid multiway contests in the elections. The midterm poll of 1969 in the Punjab was also fought by somewhat 'likeminded' parties that subsequently formed a coalition government. In that case, the Jana Sangh and the Akali Dal (Sant) cooperated in the election and in the coalition. Although these two parties have many serious differences among their policy preferences, they both share a traditional, religiously oriented outlook on politics (albeit, they are different traditions and different religions). In this sense, at least, their pre-election alliance was an ideologically homogeneous one. Both united fronts in 1967 in West Bengal, and the Kerala united front in 1967 were among leftist political parties. These united fronts also managed to form fairly ideologically oriented alliances after the elections. The rifts within these protocoalitions were more a consequence of differing political aspirations than differing policy preferences. There were no such pre-election alliances involving the Congress Party or involving protocoalitions from opposite ends of the ideological spectrum. In this sense, at least, the pre-election behavior of the parties was guided by ideological considerations.

The ideological guidance which played an important part during the 1967 campaign, some of the midterm campaigns, and to a lesser extent, the 1972 campaign, was all but lost once the election results were in. In those states where pre-election alliances had resulted in a legislative majority for the united fronts, ideologically based coalitions were formed.

Size and coalition politics

In those states where ideologically homogeneous groups did not secure a majority, the rightists and the leftists were successful at reaching agreement with each other. They did not reach agreements with the Congress Party.

The combination of rightists and leftists does not necessarily preclude the application of ideological considerations in the coalition formation process. Leiserson, for example, has suggested that when:

> 'an actor and his ideological allies are too weak to control the decision, he should not insist on as much similarity in attitudes as possible when forming a coalition. Instead he should form a coalition with someone with whom it is relatively easy to compromise. When is it easy to compromise? When conflicting attitudes are of greatest disparity in intensity.'[10]

By greatest disparity in intensity Leiserson means that one should examine differences in utilities for particular outcomes. Assuming that intensity can be measured without interpersonal comparisons of utility, Leiserson's formulation would lead one to expect that ideologically based coalitions might occur between a party that strongly favors an outcome and one that is indifferent to the outcome.[11] Thus, if the leftists feel indifferent about the most important policies of the rightists, and vice versa, their coalitions might satisfy Leiserson's conditions.

Applying the Leiserson hypothesis to India, one does not find evidence of ideological considerations in the coalition formation process. The rightists and the leftists in India generally have more intense policy preferences than does the Congress Party. The CPI, for example, strongly favors closer ties with the Soviet Union, while the Jana Sangh and the Swatantra Party strongly oppose such ties. The Congress Party is somewhat in favor of developing closer relationships between India and the Soviet Union. Nevertheless, until recently, there were no examples of coalitions including communists and Congressmen. The Congress and the CPI have coalesced in Kerala and in West Bengal. In these cases, however, one cannot conclude that ideology played a more important role than size. After all, the leading alternative protocoalition in both these states is another communist party – the CPI(M). It is true that there are major ideological differences between the Marxist communists and the CPI, but these differences are not as great as the ideological rift between the CPI and the Congress Party.

Non-Congressism, it will be recalled, is potentially an ideological explanation of the exclusion of the Congress Party from coalitions. It is also potentially a size-oriented explanation of the exclusion of the Congress Party. In order to determine which of these explanations makes more sense, I asked prominent political leaders from the All-India parties why

Size and coalition politics

they joined the coalitions they did. If ideology was a major consideration in the non-Congress strategy, then the desire to oust the Congress from power should be the most common response in all seven states being studied. If the proximity of the Congress Party to the size required for monopoly control over the decision-making process was a major consideration, then the desire to oust the Congress should have been less frequently expressed in those states where the Congress was farthest from monopoly control.

When asked why they had joined the coalition in their state, 25.9 per cent of the respondents ($N=85$) maintained that they wanted to oust the Congress from power. The only reason given more frequently was the desire to implement certain programs (31.8 per cent). The large percentage who indicated that they wanted to oust the Congress from power supports the contention that the Congress Party was systematically excluded from winning coalitions, but it does not reveal whether they were excluded because of their size or because of ideological considerations. As we have already seen, Lohia proposed the non-Congressism strategy for both purposes. But Lohia also declared that 'this phrase "likemindedness" must not be used any more'.[12] That is, Lohia discounted ideological considerations when they jeopardized the opposition's hopes of gaining control over the government. Does this same pattern of paying lip-service to ideological considerations while playing power politics reveal itself in the interviews?

In the two states where the Congress Party was not the largest protocoalition in 1967 (i.e., Kerala and Orissa) not even one respondent specified the desire to oust the Congress from power as either a primary or a secondary reason for joining the coalition government. Where the Congress was the largest protocoalition after the fourth general election, the desire to form non-Congress governments was frequently expressed as a primary or secondary motive for joining the particular coalition that was formed. Size appears to have been considerably more influential in limiting the Congress's access to winning coalitions than were ideological considerations. Table 4.1 summarizes the motives guiding coalition formation as they were expressed in the interviews.

Table 4.1 not only indicates the importance of size in determining who gains access to winning coalitions, it also reflects the insignificance of ideology in the coalition formation process in India. After all, the Congress Party's ideology was not markedly different in the states where it was the largest protocoalition from the states where it was not the largest protocoalition. In both sets of states, the Congress Party was the ruling party prior to the fourth general election. Yet, where the Congress did not emerge as the largest group none of the respondents indicated a preoccupation with ousting the Congress, even though they were given two oppor-

Size and coalition politics

TABLE 4.1 *Motives for joining coalitions*

Largest protocoalition in respondent's state	Oust Congress	Other
Congress (N=74)	41%	59%
Other (N=14)	0%	100%

tunities to do so. In the other states, of course, this preoccupation was commonly expressed. From this we can conclude that the coalition formation process is more attentive to size than to ideology.

Size and redistributive benefits

The second size-related hypothesis states that the parity norm is not applied to the allocation of redistributive benefits. It does not preclude the possibility that such a decision-rule is used to determine the distribution of other benefits.

In order to test the relationship between the size of parties and their coalition benefits, it is necessary to define the payoffs more precisely. The principal reward secured by coalition governments is control over the administration of resources. The specific benefits vary from relatively minor administrative positions to positions that are central to the entire operation of government. In order to examine the relative impact of these benefits, I have constructed three increasingly restrictive categories. The *ministries* variable is the percentage of all ministerial positions controlled by a political party in a coalition government. This variable includes not only cabinet portfolios, but also lower level ministerial positions, such as deputy ministries and state ministries. The *cabinet ministries* variable measures the percentage of all full cabinet ministers from each party in a coalition. The third and most restrictive category is a measure of the percentage of *important cabinet portfolios* controlled by each political party in a coalition. In order to determine which portfolios fall into this category, I asked the leaders of the All-India parties to specify the portfolios they would most like to have under their own control. The portfolios were then ranked according to the frequency with which they were named. Eight portfolios were named most often: Home, Finance, Agriculture, Education, Labour, Land and Land Revenue, Power and Irrigation, and Industries.[13] In addition to the preference expressed by the Indian politicians for these ministries, these portfolios accord well with an intuitive judgement of what constitutes the most valued cabinet positions in India. These particular positions control more patronage, more resources, and more visibility than any other state-level positions in India. They deal with

Size and coalition politics

the questions that are of greatest concern to the population, and they control the resources that allow their holders to influence the lives of virtually all the citizens in a state.

Two variables are constructed from the data related to important portfolios: *important ministries* measures the percentage of those positions controlled by each party in a coalition, the *importance ratio* measures the disproportionalities in the distribution of the important cabinet positions. This ratio equals the percentage of important ministries awarded to a party divided by the percentage of seats it contributed to the coalition.

Before turning to the relationship between these four indicators of coalitions payoffs and size, let us examine the impact each of these variables has on the subsequent performance of the parties that participated in coalitions. This will establish the validity of the categorization of some portfolios as being more important than others, and, if the categorization is validated, it will also lend support to the assumption that political parties attempt to maximize their long-term influence over the decision-making process. That is, it will provide an empirical basis for the postulated goal investigated in this study.

Four variables are used to test the redistributive effects of the coalition benefits identified earlier. The first two tests examine the correlation between each payoff and the subsequent success of each coalesced party in winning seats and winning votes in the midterm elections held between 1969 and 1971. These two tests are based on partial correlation coefficients, with the control variables being the number of seats won by each party in 1967 and the percentage of votes won by each party in 1967 respectively. The controls are introduced to facilitate the evaluation of the payoff on the growth of each party. Thus, it is the increment or decrement in influence that is of interest, rather than the initial base of influence with which each party entered coalition politics. By eliminating the pre-coalition factors that influenced the initial success of each party these controls reduce the probability that the payoffs are spuriously associated with the subsequent performance of the parties.

The second set of tests involves the change in legislative representation and the change in the percentage of votes won by each party between 1967 and the midterm elections. Both of these variables also measure the increment or decrement in influence experienced by the parties as a consequence of their coalition experiences. For these two tests it is not necessary to control the initial base of support of the parties since the use of first differences already removes any measurement advantage that an initially large base of support might give.[14] The results are reported in table 4.2.

As expected, only two variables – the importance ratio and the important ministries – are reasonably consistent in their ability to account for variations in the outcome of the midterm elections. Disproportionalities in the

Size and coalition politics

TABLE 4.2 *Coalition payoffs and electoral performance*

Variables	Midterm seats	Midterm votes	Change in seats	Change in votes
Ministries	0.20 ($N=43$)	−0.36 ($N=28$)	−0.15 ($N=43$)	−0.13 ($N=28$)
Cabinet rank	0.25 ($N=43$)	−0.24 ($N=28$)	−0.14 ($N=43$)	−0.01 ($N=28$)
Important ministries	0.59 ($N=43$)	0.36 ($N=28$)	0.26 ($N=43$)	0.32 ($N=28$)
Importance ratio	0.52 ($N=43$)	0.09 ($N=28$)	0.52 ($N=43$)	0.14 ($N=28$)

acquisition of these benefits are likely to produce a redistribution of political influence favoring those parties with the largest share of important portfolios. Is the distribution of these and other coalition benefits related to the size of each party's contingent in its winning coalitions?

If the second hypothesis is correct, the relationship between a party's size in a coalition and its acquisition of benefits should be greatest when the payoffs are of the least importance. The association should be weakest when the dependent variable is the distribution of redistributive benefits. Table 4.3 presents the percentage of variance which is accounted for in the four payoff measures as a consequence of the percentage of seats each party contributes to its coalitions. The first set of coefficients refers to the relationship just in the first round of coalitions. The second set of coefficients refers to the relationship between size and payoffs in subsequent coalitions.

As can be seen, the hypothesis is supported by the evidence. The association is strongest with the percentage of all ministries, and is weakest when the focus is on the important ministries. In fact, slightly more than 55 per cent of the variation in the distribution of important ministries is left unexplained by the size of the parties in the first coalitions, and virtually all of the variance remains unexplained in all subsequent coalitions. In the first coalitions, no variance is accounted for in terms of the importance ratio while the inclusion of subsequent iterations indicates that size tends

TABLE 4.3 *The impact of size on coalition benefits as indicated by the coefficient of determination*

Payoff in relevant coalition	Size in the first coalition	Size in subsequent coalitions
Ministries	0.59 ($N=50$)	(−)0.01 ($N=27$)
Cabinet rank	0.54 ($N=50$)	0.00 ($N=27$)
Important ministries	0.45 ($N=50$)	(−)0.01 ($N=27$)
Importance ratio	0.00 ($N=48$)	(−)0.08 ($N=27$)

Size and coalition politics

to have a slightly negative effect on the distribution of benefits. That is, larger parties tend to lose any advantage they had in terms of the allocation of redistributive benefits after their initial success in the first coalitions.

The failure to account for the variance in the importance ratio would not be surprising if the association between important ministries and size were stronger. In that case, one would expect the importance ratio to be reduced to a constant. That is, if all parties received their fair share of important portfolios, as prescribed by the parity norm, then the importance ratio would equal 1.0 for each party. In this case there would be no variance in the distribution of this benefit and, consequently, there would be no disproportionalities to explain. There is, however, a substantial amount of variation in the distribution of important benefits. The importance ratio ranges from a low of zero to a high of 7.02, with a standard deviation of 1.43, and a mean of 1.05. This indicates that some members of winning coalitions receive no important cabinet portfolios while others receive more than seven times their fair share. In the light of this large range of values, the inability of size to account for the variance in the importance ratio is an important indication that disproportionalities in the allocation of the redistributive benefits of coalitions are unrelated to the size of political parties. The random relationship indicates that such factors as 'lumpiness' on the one hand, or 'control' on the other, do not serve to benefit systematically either small parties or large parties. Regardless of a party's size, it has an opportunity to secure a disproportionately large (or small) share of redistributive benefits.

One might speculate that although the size of a party's representation in a winning coalition is not associated with its acquisition of redistributive benefits, representation operates directly to produce increases in political influence. This is conceivable given that the importance ratio only accounts for 28 per cent of the shifts in legislative representation. Of course, if the theory is correct, the percentage of seats contributed by a party to a winning coalition should not explain subsequent shifts in political influence, such as are indicated by changes in legislative representation of a party. The partial correlation between the percentage of seats contributed to a coalition and the number of seats won in the midterm elections, controlling for the number of seats the party won in the fourth general election, is only 0.05 ($N=43$). Partialing for the percentage of votes the party won in 1967, the correlation between its representation in a coalition and its subsequent acquisition of votes in the midterm elections is only 0.02 ($N=28$). With respect to the change in the number of seats a party won between the fourth general election and the midterm polls, the correlation with representation in a coalition is -0.01 ($N=43$). Substituting the change in votes, the correlation is only 0.18 ($N=24$). In short, the size of a party's contingent in a winning coalition generally does not directly or in-

Size and coalition politics

directly account for changes in its level of political influence in future legislative or electoral situations.

Before turning to a case history that highlights some of the findings reported here, let us examine the extent to which the second hypothesis is supported when state branches of only All-India parties are investigated. This will help set the stage for the remaining chapters in which only All-India parties are studied.

Size and All-India parties

An examination of the relationship between the size of the All-India parties and their acquisition of benefits in a coalition is important for several reasons. The All-India parties are much more involved with and concerned about the national implications of their behavior in state coalitions than are local political parties.[15] The local parties concentrate their efforts on establishing as much influence as they can in local politics. All-India parties attempt to maximize their influence over local and national politics. Consequently, their behavior is likely to have far-reaching importance in the unfolding of Indian politics. Second, the interviews for this study were conducted exclusively with leading members of All-India parties. The analysis of strategic and motivational predispositions which follows in the next two chapters is dependent on the interview data. Consequently, those analyses focus exclusively on All-India parties. It is important, therefore, to understand any differences in the patterns of behavior that distinguish the All-India parties from other political parties in India.

There is a somewhat stronger association between the size of an All-India party's representation in a coalition and its importance ratio than there was for all parties in general ($r=0.35$, $N=21$). The relationship is not, however, significant either in the statistical sense (at the 0.05 level) or in the substantive sense. Thus, only 12 per cent of the disproportionality in the distribution of important portfolios is accounted for by the percentage of seats that All-India parties contribute to their winning coalitions.

As with all other parties, the size of a party's representation in a coalition does not account for subsequent changes in the party's political influence. The correlation between size and the change in seats won between 1967 and the midterm polls, for example, is only 0.35 ($N=15$). Again, this is neither statistically nor substantively significant. The importance ratio, on the other hand, is modestly associated with the change in legislative representation of the All-India parties between these two elections. The correlation is 0.45 ($N=15$), which is significant at less than the 0.05 level.[16] We may conclude, therefore, that the relationship between party size in

Size and coalition politics

coalitions and the acquisition of redistributive benefits is no different for the All-India parties than it is for Indian parties in general.

Case history: Uttar Pradesh

Uttar Pradesh provides an interesting case history of the impact that important cabinet portfolios can have on the legislative strength of political parties. The initial coalition in Uttar Pradesh was formed by a group of ideologically disparate political parties. The leader of the coalition government, Charan Singh, defected from the Congress Party after the 1967 election, bringing seventeen supporters with him. Although Charan Singh and his followers did not constitute one of the larger groups within the coalition, they were pivotal, at least in the sense that a winning coalition could not be formed until their defection. Because of their pivotal position, they could be expected to command a disproportionately large share of the coalition's important benefits.[17] Charan Singh's party, the BKD, did, in fact, secure enough important portfolios to achieve an importance ratio of 7.02.

At whose expense did the BKD acquire its extra share of redistributive benefits? What consequences followed from the disproportionalities in the distribution of those benefits? The answers to these questions as they pertain to politics in Uttar Pradesh provide a dramatic example of the care parties must take in making political concessions.

No party, other than the BKD, managed to receive even a fair share of important portfolios, although many received substantial numbers of cabinet rank and lower level ministries. Table 4.4 provides a breakdown of the distribution of important portfolios (in terms of the importance ratio) as well as an examination of its consequences. Predictions are made concerning the number of seats each party would control following the 1969 midterm poll by multiplying their former strength times the importance ratio. The assumption underlying this illustrative analysis is that the importance ratio is convertible into a proportionate change in political influence comparable to the magnitude of the ratio. For example, a party with a ratio of 0.5 is expected to lose half its seats in a subsequent election, while a party with a ratio of 1.5 is expected to increase its seats by 50 per cent. A party having a ratio larger than 1 is always expected to increase in influence, while a party having a ratio less than 1 is always expected to decline in influence.

The results presented in table 4.4 leave little doubt concerning the impact of the importance ratio on politics in Uttar Pradesh. The actual change in seats is almost perfectly predicted by the importance ratio multiplied by the initial base of strength.

An examination of the situation in Uttar Pradesh suggests that the

Size and coalition politics

TABLE 4.4 *Political benefits from the Uttar Pradesh Coalition of 1967.*

Party	Seats at beginning of coalition	Importance Ratio	Predicted seats in 1969	Actual seats in 1969
Jana Sangh	98	0.384	38	49
SSP	44	0.732	32	33
Swatantra	12	0.434	5	5
RPI	10	0	0	2
PSP	11	0.255	3	2
CPI	13	0.383	5	4
BKD	18	7.02	126	99
CPM	1	0	0	1

parties in the coalition were not adequately aware of the dire consequences their ministerial concessions could have. Thus, the evidence suggests they thought they were adhering to the parity norm when in terms of redistributive benefits they were not. The distribution of all portfolios reflects the general acceptance of the parity norm, with the exception that the BKD – being in a pivotal position – was able to demand and get more than its fair share of all types of portfolios. Among the other parties, however, the distribution of portfolios followed very closely the rank ordering of their contribution to the resource pool of the alliance. Thus, the Jana Sangh, as the largest party, had seven ministers in the coalition, four of whom held full cabinet rank. The SSP, as the second largest party in the alliance, held three cabinet rank, and two lesser positions in the cabinet. The CPI held one cabinet and one lesser position, while the slightly smaller Swatantra Party and Praja Socialist Party each controlled only one cabinet rank position. The still weaker RPI had no cabinet rank ministers, although it did have two lesser members of the ministry. It is at this gross level, however, that compliance with the parity norm ends.

The Jana Sangh, despite its size in the coalition, received only one important cabinet portfolio, while Charan Singh assigned four of the most desirable portfolios to his own party, including Home and the chief ministership to himself. Despite these inequities, few leaders of the All-India parties in Uttar Pradesh believed their losses in the midterm elections stemmed from the allocation of benefits within the coalition. Instead they accounted for their losses either in terms of misperceptions by the electorate or in terms of unethical campaign practices on the part of Charan Singh and the BKD.

Two typical explanations that rely on misperceptions by the electorate are as follows:

'The BKD improved very much because of the image of Charan Singh. The problems of the peasantry for which we fought continuously – he

Size and coalition politics

somehow or other gave them the impression that he did all for the peasantry.'

'The BKD improved its position, but at the cost of the socialists. So far as the program was concerned, it was really the program of the SSP, but Charan Singh, being the chief minister, the popularity went to him on the implementation of certain programs because it was his government.'

The more common explanation, however, was that Charan Singh and the BKD used unethical campaign practices which the other parties did not feel they could apply. As a leading figure in the Samyukta Socialist Party explained to me, 'The SSP, like all the other parties, lost in the midterm election because the BKD fought the election on casteism ... We did not lose seats on account of the coalition. We lost because of our meager resources and because of casteism and because of the division of opposition votes because there were no electoral adjustments in 1969.' A leader from the PSP explained that the BKD success was based on '(*a*) huge amount of money and resources for the election – from all sectors; (*b*) BKD gave slogans to the masses completely based on caste and community ... Any socialist party rules out using caste and community.'

Curiously, most of the All-India party leaders in Uttar Pradesh did not question how the BKD secured the organization and the visibility to use its electoral tactics successfully. Their focus on caste and other external factors, of course, made it difficult for them to recognize the organizational benefits that the BKD might have obtained through the coalition. It also made it difficult for them to recognize the danger inherent in assuming that their parties were not hurt by their own behavior in the coalitions. Although such an attitude may serve to protect their self image, and their position as leaders, it cannot help restore the lost influence of their parties. The risk of failure will continue to be high for these parties until they become sufficiently introspective to recognize their own miscalculations. Identifying their own errors must be a first step toward the identification and implementation of a coalition strategy likely to lead to future success.

Summary

The relationship between size and coalition formation, on the one hand, and coalition benefits, on the other hand, was examined in this chapter. The evidence indicates, as one would expect from Chertkoff's iterative theory of coalition formation and from the law of large numbers, that minimal winning coalitions are preferred to other types of coalitions, although with time there is an increasing tendency toward intermediate-sized coalitions. The evidence indicates that once a winning coalition is formed, the size of the constituents has only a little impact on the allocation of redistributive benefits. Non-redistributive benefits are allocated in accordance with the parity norm, although even among these benefits the relationship with representation in the coalition is not very strong. The importance of size in determining the allocation of benefits was found to decline markedly after the initial round of coalition terminations.

5. Strategic behavior and political influence

Politics is the struggle for influence, but the acquisition of influence does not guarantee success in the struggles of politics. The right to win in most political situations is defined in terms of the size of the contestants' resource bases. Yet, as we have seen, one's control over decision-making does not necessarily increase with increases in size. To be sure, one *cannot* exert political influence without having an adequate resource base. Legislative representation, for example, is a necessary attribute of any political party that wishes to secure control of a government in a parliamentary democracy. Legislative representation is not, however, sufficient to insure that a party will increase its legislative representation, and its concomitant potential to influence or control the decision-making process. Furthermore, legislative representation is not sufficient to insure that a party will convert its potential influence into real influence. The concern of this chapter is to identify the associations between changes in the potential influence of political parties and their strategic behavior in coalitions. In particular, we will focus on the extent to which a preference for a mixed strategy results in the acquisition and conversion of coalition benefits into subsequent increases in electoral and legislative success.

Two sets of questions are examined. The first asks what the Indian political elites *believed* was important in determining the outcome of their coalition experiences. The second asks what *actually* influenced the distribution of benefits and losses that resulted from the coalition experiences of the All-India parties.

Elite perceptions

In the preceding chapter we learned that the size of a party's representation in a winning coalition was unimportant in accounting for the distribution of important benefits within the coalitions, and the performance of the coalition participants in subsequent elections. Although these findings are of theoretical interest, their relevance to policy formulation in India depends upon the way in which key decision-makers perceive the role of size in Indian politics. In order to establish a link between the theory and policy formulation in the coalitions, it is useful to determine the extent to which the decision-makers from the All-India parties perceived size or strategy as the most important element influencing the outcome of the coalitions.

Representatives of the six All-India parties were asked a series of questions pertaining to the source of their gains and losses in the coalitions. These open-ended questions included items such as: Did the larger or

Strategic behavior and political influence

smaller parties gain more in your experience? Why? Did your party gain or lose? Why? Did your party gain more or less than the other parties in your coalition? Why?, and so on. The responses to these questions were recoded into a single dichotomous variable. The two categories are (*a*) gains are a function of a party's size; and (*b*) gains are a function of a party's strategy. The strategy dimension includes responses such as: gains depend on the party's organizational work; gains depend on the lack of scruples of the parties; gains depend on the effective utilization of leadership positions for party ends. The size category includes responses such as: gains depend on holding the balance of power; gains depend on controlling adequate resources.

Table 5.1 reports the distribution of responses along the size and strategy dimensions. Of the forty-seven political leaders who answered the questions from which the strategy and size categories were derived, 68 per cent felt that size was less important than strategy in influencing the distribution of coalition benefits. A majority of the leaders from each party, except the CPI (M), responded that strategy was more important than size. In the case of the CPI(M), their apparent deviation from the general pattern can be explained by the very small size of the sample (a majority of the Marxist communists who were interviewed did not respond to this issue) and the observation that the CPI(M) leaders focus their strategic maneuvers on activities outside the government apparatus. They may not have considered such strategic actions relevant to questions which focused on maneuvering within the government. This difference in focus is supported by other studies of the strategic and organizational orientation of the CPI(M).[1] In any event, even with the deviation of the CPI(M), the distribution favoring strategy over size as a key determinant of coalition benefits is not significantly different from party to party. The general orientation for the six parties was to credit strategy with the derivation of benefits in the coalitions, rather than credit size.

The results reported in table 5.1 establish that the parties, in general,

TABLE 5.1 *Coalition gains depend on size or strategy*

	CPI(M)*	CPI	SSP	PSP	JS	Swatantra	Total
Strategy	0(0.0)	6(85.7)	9(64.3)	4(80.0)	7(63.6)	6(85.7)	32(68.1)
Size	3(100)	1(14.3)	5(35.7)	1(20.0)	4(36.4)	1(14.3)	15(31.9)
Total	3(100)	7(100)	14(100)	5(100)	11(100)	7(100)	47(100)

Chi square = 8.922. Not significant.

* Numbers within the parentheses refer to the percentage of respondents from a particular party falling within the specific category. Missing data cases have been deleted.

Strategic behavior and political influence

attributed greater importance to strategy than to size in explaining the distribution of gains. It is possible, however, that these results mask significant differences in the distribution of preferences based on categories other than party membership. For instance, leaders from small parties might be disproportionately inclined to minimize the significance of party size in acquiring coalition benefits. Of course, if they were unsuccessful in the coalition, they might be disproportionately inclined to minimize the importance of their strategic behavior, discounting their failures by blaming them on the party's inadequate size. In order to ascertain if perceptions concerning the distribution of coalition benefits depended on the size of the respondent's party, I divided the state branches of the All-India parties into large and small political parties. Since the concern here is with the organizational size of the parties and the accompanying ability to deliver organizational resources needed to convert benefits into future political influence, the dichotomization is based on the percentage of votes won by each party in the 1967 state assembly elections. Those parties that were above the mean were classified as large, while those below the mean were classified as small. Eliminating all of the exclusively national leaders from the All-India parties, seventy-six leaders of state branches of All-India parties remain. Of those, thirty-three from large parties, and twelve from small parties responded to the questions related to the distribution of coalition benefits.

The percentage of respondents in each category who claimed that strategic behavior was more important than size in determining the distribution of benefits is about two-thirds. This is almost identical to the percentage favoring strategy, when the respondents were categorized according to their party membership. More importantly, there is not a significant difference in the distribution of responses among the large party elites and the small party elites. The results of this analysis, reported in table 5.2, reinforce the observation that all leaders were equally likely to perceive that strategy is more significant than size in coalition politics.

It is clear that the leaders perceived strategy to be more important than size in determining the distribution of benefits. It does not necessarily follow, however, that they perceived that strategy was more important than size with respect to the gains of their own party. Although one would ex-

TABLE 5.2 *Party size and leader perceptions concerning coalition benefits*

	Party size	
	Large	Small
Strategy	20(64.5%)	8(66.7)
Size	11(35.5)	4(33.3)

pect their perceptions to be guided primarily by their own experiences, this linkage should be established before we turn to the actual effect of strategy on the redistribution of political influence. Two questions were asked that focus on the actual success the leaders believed their party had in the coalitions. In one question they were asked whether the coalition experience had an impact on the organizational strength and cohesion of their party. The other question asked whether they believed their party gained as much as they expected it to from the coalition experience.

Dichotomizing the parties on the basis of their size as before, we find in table 5.3 that there is not a significant difference in the perceived impact of the coalitions on the strength and cohesiveness of party organizations as a function of each party's initial size.

TABLE 5.3 *Size and organizational development*

Party size	Great growth	Some growth	No change	Some loss	Great loss
Large	5(9.8%)	18(35.3)	12(23.5)	10(19.6)	6(11.8)
Small	0(0%)	9(47.4)	3(15.8)	5(26.3)	2(10.5)

$N=70$. Chi square$=3.082$. Not significant.

Using the same dichotomy, table 5.4 reports the relationship between party size and the degree to which the leaders felt their expectations were satisfied in the coalitions. Once again, the results indicate that size fails to lead to a meaningful difference in the perceived performance of the parties. This is especially interesting when we note that in response to another question, it was found that elites from large parties did not have significantly different expectations from the small party elites. What is more, when the leaders were asked if their parties had actually gained more or less than the other parties in the coalitions, the responses were not significantly different when compared on the basis of party size.

With the perceptual importance of strategy clearly established, it is possible to turn to the actual association between strategic preferences and political outcomes.

TABLE 5.4 *Did the gains equal your expectations?*

Party size	Response			
	No	Somewhat	Yes	We did even better
Large	20(43.5%)	5(10.9)	19(41.3)	2(4.3)
Small	9(50.0)	4(22.2)	5(27.8)	0(0.0)

$N=64$. Chi square$=2.721$. Not significant.

Strategic behavior and political influence

The meaning of strategic preferences

The third hypothesis states that the greater the preference of a party's leaders for a mixed strategy, the greater the party's success in acquiring redistributive coalition benefits and converting them into increased political influence. The evaluation of this hypothesis depends upon the operationalization of strategic preferences. The needed operational indicators are developed in this section.

The operationalization of strategic preferences could have followed either of two paths. We might undertake an in depth examination of the reported behavior of each political party in each of its coalitions, or we might measure the strategic predispositions of the leaders of each relevant party. The first approach would result in the compilation of actual events, and the coding of those events into cooperative and competitive actions.[2] Two serious problems led me to rule out this approach.

The collection of events data concerning strategic behavior is extremely unreliable, especially when even the most reliable news sources in India – the *Hindustan Times*, the *Times of India*, and the *Statesman* – are not likely to give the necessary in depth coverage to the events in each state coalition on each day. What is more, many moderately competitive demands within a coalition are unlikely to be reported in the media. Instead, attention is drawn to extreme behavior. A focus on extreme behavior alone would result in a misrepresentation of the actual distribution of events.

Even if the problems involved in reportage could be solved – and they cannot be – the problems of intercoder reliability would remain. Judgements concerning the cooperativeness or competitiveness of behavior are extremely subjective. For instance, would one classify Ajoy Mukherjee's decision to embark on a strike against the West Bengal united front as a cooperative or a competitive act? Ajoy Mukherjee, who was then chief minister in West Bengal, launched the strike to protest the behavior of the CPI(M), and especially the behavior of his Home minister, Jyoti Basu. This was certainly a competitive act from the perspective of the CPI(M). On the other hand, its purpose allegedly was to restore the coalition to its agreed-upon program. This is, by definition, a cooperative action. Of course, the CPI(M) believed that it was Ajoy Mukherjee and his followers who had wandered from the minimum program. Consequently, one who agreed with the CPI(M) position would have classified their behavior as cooperative (remembering that cooperativeness refers to promoting the policy goals of the coalition), while one who sympathized with Ajoy Mukherjee would have classified his behavior as cooperative. There is no correct interpretation of the strategic maneuvering in the first and second united fronts in West Bengal, simply because certain shared policy goals served the political interests of some parties more than others, while other shared policy goals served the political interests of still other parties.

Since the events data approach does not seem feasible, I have focused my efforts on measuring the *strategic predispositions* of the leaders of the All-India parties. This approach has several advantages. First, it is easier to construct questions that measure the strategic orientations of the leaders than it is to measure their actual behavior. Second, the definitional conditions differentiating competitiveness and cooperativeness can be precisely assessed by constructing projective questions specifically concerned with operationalizing those conditions. Thus, strategic predispositions can be measured exactly in the terms specified in the theoretical development of hypothesis 3. Third, by measuring strategic predispositions, the utility of the data is extended well beyond any individual researcher's access to 'inside' information concerning actual events. So long as the leadership of a given party remains fairly constant, the predispositional data should be an accurate measure of the party's strategic orientation. This means that the data can be used for actual predictions of future performance, as well as for the explanation of earlier party successes and failures.

The predispositional approach would be especially helpful in political systems marked by low levels of turnover in political leaders. Unfortunately, elite turnover is not very low in the Indian parties studied here. Since the research for this project was completed, for example, two parties – the Samyukta Socialist Party and the Praja Socialist Party – have merged into a single party, resulting in substantial changes in leadership personnel. Nevertheless, even in India there is sufficient elite stability to lead to the expectation that the predispositional approach to strategic preferences should facilitate the evaluation of future electoral outcomes.

It will be recalled that cooperative behavior was defined as behavior that is primarily oriented toward satisfying the collective policy goals of a coalition. Competitive behavior was defined as behavior primarily oriented toward satisfying the private political goals of an individual leader or party. In order to measure the strategic predispositions of the leaders of the All-India parties I developed several hypothetical questions that asked them to choose between promoting collective policy benefits or private political benefits. All of the questions were open-ended so that the respondents could elaborate on the problem-solving techniques they would employ in the situations described by the questions. The actual questions that I used can be found in appendix III.

Responses that indicated a preference for actions that would aid the respondent's party at the expense of the other members of the coalition were judged competitive. Responses that indicated that the respondent was willing to sacrifice some benefit that his party might have acquired in

Strategic behavior and political influence

order to protect the interests of the coalition were judged cooperative. Eight questions were used to evaluate each leader's strategic predisposition. Each time a leader responded cooperatively he was assigned a score of −1.00. Each time he responded competitively, the leader was assigned a score of +1.00. If the response was neither cooperative nor competitive, the respondent was assigned a score of 0.00. To be included in the subsequent analyses of strategic predispositions, the respondent had to give a cooperative or a competitive response on at least one of the eight questions in this series. Only two respondents failed to meet this requirement. From the raw scores, two indices of strategic predispositions were constructed for each state branch of each All-India party that participated in a coalition government between 1967 and 1970.

One index is concerned with the overall average strategic orientation of the leaders. It is computed by summing all of the cooperative and all of the competitive responses given by each leader of each party in each state, and then dividing by the number of responses given by those leaders. This variable, called the *average strategy*, has a potential range from −1.00 to +1.00. A score of −1.00, of course, indicates that all the responses by all the leaders of the state branch of a party were cooperative. A score of +1.00 indicates that all the responses were competitive.

The other index, called the *mixed strategy*, measures the extent to which the strategic predispositions of the leaders of a party tend toward a mixture of competitiveness and cooperativeness. Using the raw scores for each leader, the mixed strategy is computed as follows:

$$\text{Mix} = 1 - \left| \frac{f_i - f_j}{f_i + f_j} \right|$$

f_i is equal to the frequency of competitive responses for the leaders of any single party, and f_j equals the frequency of their cooperative responses. The mixed strategy index assesses the extent to which a party deviates from a purely cooperative or a purely competitive strategy, without regard for the direction of the deviation. Thus, a score of 0.00 indicates that all the leaders in a party are predisposed to pursue either a purely cooperative or a purely competitive strategy. A score of 1.00 indicates that the number of competitive and cooperative responses given by the leaders of a party were equal.

Table 5.5 presents the average strategy and the mixed strategy scores for each relevant state branch of the All-India parties. The mean score for the average strategy index is −0.22, with a standard deviation of 0.314. The mean score for the mixed strategy index is 0.70, with a standard deviation of 0.227. Each index is based on two assumptions concerning individual strategic predispositions and political party actions. First, I

Strategic behavior and political influence

assume that a party's strategic predisposition is equivalent to the average strategic orientation of its key leaders.[3] The second assumption is that the strategic decisions made by party leaders are highly correlated with their strategic predispositions. This assumption facilitates inferences from the analyses that follow, but it is not essential to test the theory.

TABLE 5.5 *Strategy scores for state branches of All-India parties*

Party	State	Average strategy	Mixed strategy
Jana Sangh	Punjab	+0.500	0.500
CPI	Punjab	−0.500	0.500
Jana Sangh	Uttar Pradesh	−0.500	0.500
SSP	Uttar Pradesh	−0.160	0.840
Swatantra	Uttar Pradesh	−0.500	0.500
PSP	Uttar Pradesh	−0.500	0.500
CPI	Uttar Pradesh	−0.330	0.670
SSP	Bihar	+0.160	0 840
Jana Sangh	Bihar	+0.200	0.800
PSP	Bihar	−0.500	0.500
CPI	Bihar	−0.250	0.750
CPI (M)	West Bengal	0.000	1.000
CPI	West Bengal	0.000	1.000
SSP	West Bengal	0.000	1.000
PSP	West Bengal	0.000	1.000
Swatantra	Orissa	−0.646	0.354
Jana Sangh	Madhya Pradesh	+0.055	0.945
SSP	Madhya Pradesh	−0.065	0.935
CPI (M)	Kerala	−0.600	0.400
CPI	Kerala	−0.395	0.605
SSP	Kerala	−0.500	0.500

Strategy and coalition benefits

Hypothesis 3 may be divided into two propositions. The first states that parties whose leaders are predisposed to follow a mixed strategy receive a disproportionately large share of the most valued coalition benefits. The second proposition indicates that the same parties are most effective at converting their redistributive coalition benefits into increased success in subsequent elections. The empirical evidence for the first proposition is investigated in this section.

The theoretical argument from which the relationship between the mixed strategy and the allocation of redistributive benefits was derived assumed that the degree of cooperativeness or competitiveness of a party would be influenced by the location of the tolerance limits of one's partners. In the analyses that follow I do not attempt to measure the location of those limits, but rather I continue to apply the assumption that

Strategic behavior and political influence

the ideal strategy is a fifty-fifty mix of competitive and cooperative orientations. It will be recalled that this assumption is consistent with the experimental literature on iterative games and also with the operational definition of the mixed strategy. Thus, the mixed strategy indicator achieves its maximum value when there is an equal mix of competitive and cooperative responses.

The correlation between the mixed strategy and the importance ratio – the most redistributive coalition benefit – is 0.21. The relationship between the importance ratio and the average strategy is 0.02. Although a correlation of 0.21 is rather modest, the results support the proposition at least to the extent that the average strategy, which reflects competitiveness, is completely unassociated with the importance ratio while the mixed strategy is somewhat associated with it. What is more, the weakness of the association between the mixed strategy and the importance ratio is not inconsistent with the expectations that follow from the theory. It will be recalled that the last hypothesis developed in chapter 2 states that the predisposition to pursue a mixed strategy must be accompanied by sufficient organizational capabilities to convert intentions into effective behavior. An examination of this hypothesis is postponed until the next chapter. In the meantime, it should be borne in mind that the present analyses do not include any attempt to place the strategic predispositions within the framework of the organizational constraints of the parties.

Strategy and electoral success

The first proposition of hypothesis 3 is only modestly supported by the evidence. This may indicate at least one of two things: either the set of portfolios included in the importance ratio is too broad and includes some benefits which are not redistributive, or strategic predispositions are less important than the theory suggests. If the set of important ministries is too broadly defined, then the inclusion of non-redistributive benefits within that category may be responsible for the weak association between the importance ratio and the mixed strategy. If that is the case, then the mixed strategy should be substantially correlated with several measures of the conversion of coalition benefits into political influence. On the other hand, if the strategic predispositions of political parties are not crucial to their performance in elections and coalitions, then the mixed strategy variable should not be substantially correlated with the indicators of changes in political influence. That is, if the weak association between the mixed strategy index and the importance ratio reflects a weakness in the theory, then proposition 2 of hypothesis 3 should not be supported by the evidence.

In order to test proposition 2, several indicators of electoral success are

Strategic behavior and political influence

constructed. These indicators are intended to reflect changes in the base of support of the All-India parties. The underlying assumption continues to be that a substantial resource base is a necessary condition for political influence. The indicators are (*a*) the number of state legislative assembly (i.e. Vidhan Sabha) seats won by each party in the midterm elections conducted between 1969 and 1971; (*b*) the percentage of votes won by each party during the midterm elections; (*c*) the number of national parliamentary (i.e. Lok Sabha) seats won by each party in the 1971 Lok Sabha elections; (*d*) the percentage of votes won in the 1971 Lok Sabha elections; (*e*) the change in the number of state assembly seats won between the fourth general election (which preceded the coalitions) and the midterm polls (which followed the first round of coalitions in the states); (*f*) the change in the percentage of votes won between 1967 and the midterm polls; (*g*) the change in the number of Lok Sabha seats won between 1967 and 1971; (*h*) the change in the percentage of votes won for the Lok Sabha between 1967 and 1971; (*i*) the percentage change in the number of state assembly seats won between 1967 and the midterm polls; (*j*) the percentage change in the percentage of votes won in the state assembly contests between 1967 and the midterm polls; (*k*) the percentage change in the number of Lok Sabha seats won between 1967 and 1971; and (*l*) the percentage change in the percentage of votes won for the Lok Sabha between 1967 and 1971. Variables (*e*), (*f*), (*g*), and (*h*) differ from variables (*i*), (*j*), (*k*) and (*l*) in that the first set are simple first differences, while the latter set reflects rates of change. Thus, the latter set is computed by dividing the difference in seats or votes won across the two elections by the number of seats or percentage of votes won in 1967. By doing so, the change is adjusted to reflect the proportionate growth or decline of the parties.

Of these twelve indicators, the most interesting ones, from the perspective of the theory, are those concerned with change. Thus, the first four reflect the absolute magnitude of the resources of each party after the coalitions. They do not indicate the extent to which the absolute resource bases have been increased, decreased or remained the same. The eight change variables, on the other hand, indicate the degree to which a party improved its resource base and its electoral appeal. It is these latter eight indicators, therefore, that reveal the most in terms of the conversion of strategic predispositions into real political influence.

Table 5.6 contains the bivariate correlations between the mixed strategy, the average strategy, and the twelve indicators of electoral success. The results indicate support for the hypothesis in several ways. First, and most important, almost all the coefficients are in the predicted direction. Second, the correlations between benefits and the mixed strategy are stronger in most cases than are the correlations with the average strategy, though many of the associations with the average strategy are fairly substantial.

Strategic behavior and political influence

This is important for two reasons. First, it indicates that a predisposition to pursue a mixed strategy results in greater success than a predisposition to behave competitively. Secondly, it indicates that competitiveness generally is more beneficial than cooperativeness in iterative, redistributive coalitions. Accordingly while the mixed strategy indicator reveals that moderate behavior is more effective than either extreme, the average strategy indicator contrasts the impact of cooperativeness with the effectiveness of competitiveness. As suggested by the theory, the most effective strategy is the mixed strategy, and the second most effective strategy, in terms of acquiring increased influence, is the competitive strategy.

The results support the contention that shifts in the resources of parties are affected by the strategic predispositions of their leaders. Thus, the largest coefficients are associated with the change in legislative representation of the parties, rather than with their absolute size. In fact, if significance tests were used, they would indicate that most of the correlations between the mixed strategy and the measures of change in influence are large enough that they would have occurred fewer than five times in one hundred by chance alone. These results hold both for state assembly elections and for national parliamentary elections. That is, the strategic predispositions of the key leaders of the All-India parties during the coalition period after the fourth general election have played an important role in altering the future political influence of their parties.

Before turning to a case history which will help illuminate the workings

TABLE 5.6 *Strategy and post-coalition performance*

Performance	Mixed strategy	Average strategy	N
Vidhan Sabha seats, midterm	0.32	0.22	19
Vidhan Sabha votes, midterm	0.15	0.31	15
Lok Sabha seats, 1971	0.37	0.17	21
Lok Sabha votes, 1971	0.07	−0.24	12
Change in Vidhan Sabha seats, 1967–midterm	0.59**	0.48*	19
Change in Vidhan Sabha votes, 1967–midterm	0.38	0.35	15
Change in Lok Sabha seats	0.42*	0.34	21
Change in Lok Sabha votes	0.58*	0.21	12
Percentage change in Vidhan Sabha seats	0.70**	0.57**	19
Percentage change in Vidhan Sabha votes	0.35	0.40	15
Percentage change in Lok Sabha seats	0.45*	0.30	19
Percentage change in Lok Sabha votes	0.28	−0.04	12

** Significant at the 0.01 level or better.
* Significant at the 0.05 level or better.

Strategic behavior and political influence

of the mixed strategy, let us examine a few multivariate relationships concerned with the convertibility of coalition benefits. In particular, let us focus our attention on changes in the legislative representation of the All-India parties. The four variables associated with such changes are, perhaps, the most important measures of long-term benefits in this study. They not only indicate changes in each party's appeal in the elections; they also indicate the extent to which each party has increased its potential influence over the decision-making process within the legislature. In addition to the four dependent variables – change in Vidhan Sabha seats, percentage change in Vidhan Sabha seats, change in Lok Sabha seats, and percentage change in Lok Sabha seats – the analyses will include the importance ratio and either the mixed strategy or the average strategy.

A comparison of tables 5.7 and 5.8 indicates that the combined effect of the mixed strategy and the importance ratio is always greater than the combined effect of the average strategy and the importance ratio. Although the importance ratio is far from any conventional view of statistical significance in most of the regression analyses, its impact on subsequent electoral performance is almost always greater when it is accompanied by the mixed strategy indicator than when it is accompanied by the average strategy indicator. That is, a predisposition to pursue a mixed strategy and the acquisition of a disproportionately large share of important ministerial positions leads to growth in legislative influence. This is especially evident in terms of changes in representation in the state legislative assemblies.

TABLE 5.7 *The mixed strategy, the importance ratio and changes in legislative influence*

Variable	Change in Vidhan Sabha seats	Percentage change in VS seats	Change in Lok Sabha seats	Percentage change in LS seats
Intercept	−42.26	−1.64	−9.46	−1.93
Mixed strategy				
Partial	0.62	0.76	0.47	0.49
Reg. coefficient	46.46	1.61	10.13	2.12
Std error	15.09	0.35	4.90	0.96
Importance ratio				
Partial	0.26	0.46	0.15	0.12
Reg. coefficient	8.46	0.56	1.45	0.19
Std error	10.41	0.27	3.49	0.68
R^2	0.37	0.60	0.21	0.24
Std error	14.08	0.32	4.63	0.90
F	4.78	11.82	2.13	2.47
Significance	0.05	0.01	n.s.	n.s.
N	19	19	19	19

Strategic behavior and political influence

TABLE 5.8 *The average strategy, the importance ratio and changes in legislative influence*

Variable	Change in Vidhan Sabha seats	Percentage change in VS seats	Change in Lok Sabha seats	Percentage change in LS seats
Intercept	−1.19	−0.10	—0.40	—0.07
Average strategy				
Partial	0.48	0.58	0.34	0.30
Reg. coefficient	24.81	0.85	5.16	0.91
Std. error	11.43	0.30	3.59	0.72
Importance ratio				
Partial	0.13	0.26	0.06	0.02
Reg. coefficient	2.27	0.18	2.07	−0.11
Std. error	11.38	0.30	3.62	0.73
R^2	0.23	0.34	0.11	0.09
Std. error	15.62	0.41	4.91	0.98
F	2.39	4.20	1.03	0.82
Significance	n.s.	0.05	n.s.	n.s.
N	19	19	19	19

That the results should be stronger here than with the Lok Sabha elections is not surprising. After all, the elites interviewed for this study were selected primarily on the basis of their importance to the decision-making process within their state governments. Consequently, their strategic predispositions are expected to have a greater impact on state politics than on national politics.

To summarize the evidence for hypothesis 3, we may say that a predisposition to pursue a mixed strategy is very substantially related to increases in legislative representation, especially in the state legislative assemblies. Less associated with success, though still beneficial as a strategic predisposition, is an orientation toward competitive behavior. The least beneficial strategy, from the perspective of increased potential political influence, is an orientation to cooperate.

Case history: the Jana Sangh

A comparison of the behavior of the Jana Sangh in the coalitions in Bihar and Uttar Pradesh highlights the difference between the implementation of a mixed strategy and a cooperative strategy. It underscores the relative importance of the focus on political outcomes as compared to policy outcomes. What is more, by comparing a single political party in two states, the importance of strategic differences is underscored while the relevance of ideological differences is controlled.

Strategic behavior and political influence

The Jana Sangh leaders in Uttar Pradesh in 1970 were predisposed to be fairly cooperative in their political dealings. Their score on the average strategy index was -0.500, while their score on the mixed strategy index was 0.500. In Bihar, on the other hand, the Jana Sangh leaders were predisposed to combine cooperative actions with competitive actions. They leaned slightly toward a preference for competitive actions. Their score on the average strategy was $+0.200$, while their score on the mixed strategy index was 0.800. Are these scores indicative of their actual behavior?

As noted earlier, it is all but impossible to assess precisely the extent to which a party did or did not make competitive demands. Consequently, the discussion that follows is intended to be an illustrative account rather than a definitive account of differences in Jana Sangh behavior in Uttar Pradesh and Bihar. The events are derived from an examination of relevant newspaper reports and from conversations with leaders of the All-India parties in those states.

On the surface there are many similarities in the behavior of the Jana Sangh leaders in Bihar and Uttar Pradesh. In both states they felt compelled to resist policies of the chief minister and to threaten to withdraw their support if their grievances were not repressed. The important difference between the strategic behavior of the Jana Sangh leaders in Bihar and in Uttar Pradesh resides in the nature of their grievances, rather than in the frequency or severity with which they expressed those grievances.

In Uttar Pradesh, the Jana Sangh was confronted with three important decisions in terms of its ability to promote its own interests. The first arose over the distribution of cabinet portfolios. The Jana Sangh, as noted in the preceding chapter, received a substantial number of cabinet level, and lesser positions in the Uttar Pradesh ministry. Despite the number of positions they were awarded, the Jana Sangh was deprived of a fair share of important portfolios. The leadership chose to accept this state of affairs, and to cooperate with the demands of Charan Singh and the Bharatiya Kranti Dal.

The second important decision revolved around the threatened resignation of the Samyukta Socialist Party from the coalition government. The SSP was concerned that the government was not implementing the minimum program on which the coalition was based. In particular, the SSP claimed that the government was not living up to its agreement to eliminate land revenue on uneconomic holdings. The two parties most opposed to the SSP demand were the Swatantra Party and the Jana Sangh. Once again the Jana Sangh agreed to compromise on this issue. In this case, the compromise meant conceding a policy position which was not central to the Jana Sangh's political aspirations. The concession was, on the other hand, central to the political aspirations of the SSP. Consequently, the Jana

Strategic behavior and political influence

Sangh compromise on the land revenue issue may have yielded additional redistributive benefits to the SSP.

The third, and most interesting decision, concerns the Jana Sangh's response to the threatened resignation of the CPI. The communists threatened to resign from the coalition cabinet because of the application of the Preventive Detention Act against trade unionists. The CPI, of course, had an important political investment in the trade unionists. Had they failed to have the Preventive Detention Act withdrawn, the communists might have lost considerable support among the trade unionists. This would have been contrary to their political interests, but could easily have benefited the political interests of the Jana Sangh. It is true that the resignation of the CPI might have resulted in the downfall of the coalition government in Uttar Pradesh, but it is not necessarily true that such a downfall would have been contrary to the interests of the Jana Sangh. Terminating the coalition at that point might have proven more beneficial for the Jana Sangh than permitting it to be terminated by Charan Singh just a few weeks later. By permitting Charan Singh the opportunity to take the initiative, the Jana Sangh, as well as the other parties, permitted him to maximize his exposure in the media. Through that exposure, Charan Singh was able to project the impression that obstructive policies by the other parties led to the downfall of the government. The other parties were left standing by with little opportunity to present their case against Charan Singh. The Jana Sangh leadership did not choose to terminate the coalition at the time the CPI threatened to resign. Quite the contrary. They chose to support the CPI position, even to the extent of threatening to resign themselves if Charan Singh did not withdraw the applications of the Preventive Detention Act. That is, the Jana Sangh used a competitive threat to preserve the coalition and to promote the political interests of their arch rival – the Communist Party of India.

To summarize the behavior of the Jana Sangh, their cooperative actions and their one major competitive action focused on policy issues that helped benefit other parties. Their actions were not focused on political decisions that were likely to result in substantial benefits for the Jana Sangh. Not surprisingly, the Jana Sangh proved very unsuccessful in the subsequent election, losing 50 per cent of its seats in the state assembly.

In Bihar, the Jana Sangh joined a coalition government at least as ideologically diverse as the coalition in Uttar Pradesh. The first coalition in Bihar, in fact, was confronted with many of the same issues as the coalition in Bihar. There were trade union difficulties, concern over the abolition of land revenue on uneconomic holdings, threats of resignation from important constituents in the coalition, and so on. The Jana Sangh response to these conditions, however, was in sharp contrast to their responses in Uttar Pradesh.

Strategic behavior and political influence

The Jana Sangh remained aloof from most policy disputes in Bihar. Although it was not derelict in its concern over policy questions, the Jana Sangh chose not to become actively involved in policy disputes unless it could clearly derive political gains from the outcome. Thus when the Praja Socialist Party threatened to resign unless the government intervened to aid the workers at the Rohtos Sugar plant, the Jana Sangh apparently did not play an active role in convincing the chief minister to redress the grievances of the workers. On the other hand, when the Samyukta Socialist Party proposed that Urdu be made an official language in Bihar – a policy directly in conflict with the Jana Sangh's pro-Hindi stance – the Jana Sangh took a very active part in campaigning for the defeat of the proposal. In this case, the policy issue was of direct concern to the Jana Sangh, not only because of its policy preferences, but because of the characteristics of the Jana Sangh's base of political strength. Urdu is, of course, the language of the Muslim community. Since the Jana Sangh's organizational strength and electoral support comes from the Hindu community, passage of the SSP proposal would have had undesired political consequences for the Jana Sangh.

The issue over which the Jana Sangh most frequently expressed competitive demands within the Bihari coalitions concerned the appointment of political defectors to important cabinet positions. The Jana Sangh repeatedly demanded restraint in appointing defectors to high level cabinet posts. After the formation of the second coalition government involving the Jana Sangh in Bihar, the Jana Sangh leaders went so far as to suggest that the chief minister and other defectors resign and subject themselves to new elections to demonstrate their legitimacy as legislators. Such competitive behavior was not likely to win friends among their coalition partners, but it was likely to project an image of the Jana Sangh as a party with integrity. Thus, since there was widespread disenchantment with defector politics in Bihar, both informed public opinion and editorial opinions in the press were likely to support the Jana Sangh position with regard to the defectors. This had considerable potential value as a political asset.

The Jana Sangh made a major concession in only one area. It held a substantially smaller share of important cabinet positions than its fair share would have dictated. Although this probably hurt the party to some extent, the ability to focus their competitive demands on issues that were popular with the electorate probably helped to compensate for their cooperativeness with respect to cabinet portfolios. Thus, during the 1969 midterm election in Bihar the Jana Sangh increased its legislative representation by 31 per cent.

Although this case history of the Jana Sangh in two states is only intended to be illustrative, it does point out the potential benefits that are associated with focusing competitive demands on politically beneficial

Strategic behavior and political influence

issues. At the same time, it highlights the risks inherent in making competitive demands that serve the political interests of one's opponents. Finally, it underscores the consequences of cooperating with the competitive demands of one's allies. Concessions are always risky when they provide greater political benefits for one's opponents than they provide for oneself.

Summary

In this chapter, we examined the relationship between strategic predispositions and the allocation of redistributive benefits from coalitions. The Indian elites were found to perceive that strategic considerations were much more important than size in determining the distributions of coalition benefits. Their perceptions were found to be in accord with the actual events surrounding the coalitions in India. A predisposition to pursue a mixed strategy was found to be substantially associated with the outcome of state assembly and national parliamentary elections. In fact, the results indicated that the mixed strategy was the most effective strategic orientation for parties that seek an increase in their potential political influence. As suggested in the theoretical discussion, the mixed strategy is followed in effectiveness by the competitive strategy. The least effective strategic predisposition in terms of performance in post-coalition elections proved to be the cooperative strategy.

6. Need for achievement, risk and success

Why are some political leaders more likely to prefer the mixed strategy than are others? In particular, what relationship does need for achievement have with the selection and implementation of the cooperative, competitive, and mixed strategies? Theoretical responses to these questions were provided in chapter 2. Now we may examine the empirical accuracy of those responses in terms of the three remaining hypotheses of this study. Those hypotheses indicate that individuals with high need for achievement (*a*) prefer the mixed strategy to the competitive or the cooperative strategy; (*b*) secure a disproportionately large share of the redistributive benefits available in a coalition; and (*c*) convert a substantial portion of those benefits into subsequent electoral success, especially if they have the organizational capabilities to implement their preferred strategy.

Measuring need for achievement

An investigation of the remaining portions of the theory requires that an operational procedure is established to measure need for achievement.

Since the late 1940s social psychologists have given considerable attention to the measurement and interpretation of need for achievement.[1] Most of the research in this area has used projective tests as the source of information on the need for achievement of experimental subjects. Most commonly, subjects are shown pictures as part of a Thematic Apperception Test (TAT), and asked to write brief stories about what they see. The resultant stories are then coded in terms of several achievement-related categories; the most important of which is the presence or absence of achievement imagery. Achievement imagery is defined as a desire to compete with a standard of excellence, to achieve a unique accomplishment, or to pursue a long-range achievement goal.[2]

For many research problems, the attributes associated with achievement imagery are of considerable interest. In studying economic development, for example, many scholars have been concerned with the importance of need for achievement, though their research has not always been able to derive data from the use of a thematic apperception test.[3] It is impossible, for instance, to use direct experimental methods to evaluate the need for achievement of ancient civilizations. In response to this difficulty, David McClelland and other social psychologists have developed alternative indicators of need for achievement. In *The Achieving Society* McClelland made use of school primers and children's stories to evaluate the need for achievement of entire societies. He also made use of a variety of other

Need for achievement, risk and success

indicators that are suspected of being correlated with need for achievement.[4] Other researchers have extended McClelland's techniques to include the content analysis of documents such as presidential inaugural addresses to measure need for achievement.[5]

The studies by McClelland and others are particularly important because they demonstrate that it is possible to measure need for achievement without placing subjects in the very artificial setting of a thematic apperception test. Moving out of the laboratory facilitates the investigation of the impact of need for achievement on a much broader variety of phenomena than was possible before. These new approaches may be applied with some confidence since the research to date that uses these inobtrusive measures of need for achievement reveal the same pattern of associations as was found when n-achievement was measured from thematic apperception tests.

Recently, interest has grown in the possibility of measuring need for achievement from responses to interview questions. In conjunction with this interest, Joel Raynor has developed a modified coding manual to measure need for achievement, need for affiliation, and need for power from interview data.[6] Raynor's modifications of the traditional n-achievement coding manual include (a) coding only achievement imagery; (b) eliminating questions answered fewer than 10 per cent or more than 90 per cent of the time with achievement imagery present; and (c) controlling for the length of a response. Although there are no earlier applications of interview data, or of the Raynor manual, in the measurement of need for achievement, I use his procedure here.[7] Therefore, the validity of the method must rest on the degree to which support for the hypotheses reveals the patterns expected with more conventional measures of need for achievement. Should the hypotheses not be confirmed, then the question remains whether this is due to an error in the theory or an inadequacy in the coding rules.

In order to measure each respondent's need for achievement I asked a series of open-ended, projective questions concerned with the individual's personal political aspirations and the individual's aspirations for his political party. The specific questions used to measure need for achievement can be found in appendix III. In order for this procedure to yield meaningful results it must be the case that the individual is 'aroused' by the questions. That is, the respondent must care about the outcome of the situations posed by the interview instrument. It seems reasonable to assume that political leaders are concerned about their political future and the future of their party, with which they are most closely identified.

An inspection of the responses to the relevant questions in each interview results in a need for achievement score for each political leader interviewed in conjunction with this study. These scores must then be converted into a measure of the general level of need for achievement for each of the parties. This was done by first computing the arithmetic mean of the achievement scores of the leaders within each party. Although this computation probably oversimplifies the true relationship between the achievement motive of each leader in a party and the overall achievement level within the party, the experimental literature does lend some support to this procedure.[8] In addition, such an assumption is consistent with the approach taken earlier in determining the strategic orientation of each state branch of the All-India parties.

After the need for achievement level was computed for each state party unit, an index of the relative need for achievement of the parties was computed using the following procedure:

$$n\text{-achievement} = X_{ij} / \sum_{i=1}^{N} X_{ij} - 1/N$$

where X_{ij} is the need for achievement level of party i in state j and N is the number of national parties that participated in at least one coalition with i in state j.[9]

The n-achievement index reflects the extent to which a party's leaders need for achievement was above or below the expected share *in its state*. A positive score on the index indicates a party whose leaders were high in the need to achieve, while a negative sign indicates a party whose leaders were low in the need to achieve. This indicator is more meaningful than the raw need for achievement scores of the party's leaders in that it reflects the strength of a party's achievement motive relative only to those parties against which it must actually compete. The raw scores, on the other hand, reflect the distribution of need for achievement across parties that are not necessarily involved in competition with each other.

Before concluding this section, I should mention that there are a host of potential sources of measurement error in the need for achievement variable. Some result from linguistic problems, some from the situational context, and still others from our virtually complete ignorance of the reliability of interview data for coding achievement imagery.

Any measurement technique that relies on content analysis for the derivation of indicators must be sensitive to the impact of linguistic problems between the subject and the analyst. When the measurement technique is concerned primarily with the use of imagery and not the substance of responses, language problems are magnified even further. The coding rules for need for achievement involve all of these difficulties. The problem has been circumvented to a limited degree. Thus, those interviews not conducted in English were excluded from the analysis of motivation. Still, among the remaining eighty-three respondents, few spoke English as their first language. Of course, none of them spoke idiomatic American English,

Need for achievement, risk and success

while this researcher does not speak idiomatic Indian English. Consequently, I cannot be certain that the imagery has been correctly interpreted in every case.

Even if the imagery has been coded properly, there is no way to be certain that the temporal and spatial setting within which each interview was conducted did not alter the comparability of stimuli across subjects. When need for achievement is coded from a thematic apperception test, the experimental design generally controls most external stimuli by subjecting all respondents to the same stimuli at the same time. Simultaneity maximizes the probability that all subjects are being exposed to identical conditions. This is particularly important when measuring need for achievement because the degree of arousal has a marked effect on the stability of an individual's need for achievement. Simultaneity is not possible, nor is it desirable (for other reasons), when the subjects are political elites. Thus, the external conditions surrounding the interviews have not been controlled. This may threaten the comparability of the conditions under which need for achievement was assessed.

The problems outlined above are likely to lead to random measurement error. As is well known, such error tends to reduce associations rather than increase them. Systematic bias, on the other hand, could result in artificially inflated correlations. Fortunately, this is unlikely to be a problem here. The significance of this point with respect to need for achievement is important enough to warrant further discussion.

Many social scientists unfamiliar with the motivation literature are naturally suspicious of predispositional measures. In particular, it seems common to suspect that need for measurement scores are contaminated by the prior success of respondents. That is, it is often suspected that political or economic success leads one to talk like an achiever rather than the other way around. Fortunately, the available evidence indicates that this suspicion is unwarranted. Need for achievement is a very stable personality attribute which, in several long-term panel studies, has not been found to fluctuate with the waxing and waning of personal success. Instead, each individual's score remains essentially constant across time and across life's experiences.[10] Many successful people have low need for achievement, while many unsuccessful people are high in the need to achieve. Indeed, a study of Nobel laureates indicates that they have an average level of need for achievement.[11] This should not be surprising when we consider that some endeavors do not reward the risk-taking orientation of high need for achievers. It is only in those endeavors that do reward moderate risks that high need for achievers are expected to outperform low need for achievers.

These caveats should be borne in mind while examining the analyses of the achievement related hypotheses. Before turning to those analyses, let us examine the distribution of need for achievement among the All-India

Need for achievement, risk and success

TABLE 6.1 *Need for achievement by party and controlling for state*

Party	State	Raw Score	n-Achievement Index
Jana Sangh	Punjab	Missing data	Missing data
CPI	Punjab	Missing data	Missing data
Jana Sangh	Uttar Pradesh	4.83	0.040
SSP	Uttar Pradesh	3.00	−0.051
Swatantra	Uttar Pradesh	4.00	−0.002
PSP	Uttar Pradesh	4.00	−0.002
CPI	Uttar Pradesh	4.33	0.015
SSP	Bihar	2.43	−0.096
Jana Sangh	Bihar	6.00	0.130
PSP	Bihar	2.67	−0.081
CPI	Bihar	4.67	0.046
Swatantra	Orissa	2.00	Not applicable
CPI (M)	West Bengal	2.75	0.006
CPI	West Bengal	0.00	−0.250
SSP	West Bengal	4.00	0.122
PSP	West Bengal	4.00	0.122
Jana Sangh	Madhya Pradesh	3.83	0.023
SSP	Madhya Pradesh	3.50	−0.023
CPI (M)	Kerala	1.50	−0.061
CPI	Kerala	2.00	0.030
SSP	Kerala	2.00	0.030

parties. Table 6.1 reports the raw scores and the n-achievement index used in the analyses. The mean raw score is 3.31, with a standard deviation of 1.42. The mean for the n-achievement index is 0.00, while the standard deviation is 0.090. Where the analyses require the dichotomization of the n-achievement index, the parties are grouped on the basis of whether they have a score above or below the median. Consequently, the Jana Sangh and the CPI in Uttar Pradesh, the Jana Sangh and the CPI in Bihar, the SSP and PSP in West Bengal, the Jana Sangh in Madhya Pradesh, and the CPI and SSP in Kerala constitute the high need for achievement group. The remaining parties constitute the low need for achievement group. The Swatantra Party in Orissa is excluded from the analyses since the n-achievement index is not meaningful when there is only one relevant party in a state.

Need for achievement and strategic preferences

Political parties with leaders who are high in the need to achieve are expected to prefer the mixed strategy to the competitive or the cooperative strategy. It will be recalled that this hypothesized relationship stems from the preference for activities involving uncertainty among decision-makers with high need for achievement. In order to test the relationship, two types of data are used. First, the association between need for achievement and the mixed strategy index is examined. If the hypothesis is correct, this relationship should be weak, but positive. The weakness of the relationship stems from the theoretical discussion reported in table 2.3. In that discussion it was observed that individuals with high need for achievement have a strong preference for the mixed strategy, but individuals with low need for achievement have varied preferences depending on unspecified variables. Thus, some decision-makers with low need for achievement might prefer the cooperative strategy, some might prefer the competitive strategy, and still others might prefer (or at least behave as if they prefer) the mixed strategy. As a result of the expected distribution among decision-makers with low need for achievement, the overall association between strategic preferences and n-achievement is expected to be weak.

Second, the association between need for achievement and actual participation in situations with varying degrees of uncertainty is examined. The specific situations which are examined involve the decisions by political party leaders to enter candidates in electoral contests. The choice of constituencies in which to enter candidates is interesting because leaders are likely to have a reasonably accurate idea of their candidates' chances of winning. Of course, no political party would willingly forgo the opportunity to contest a constituency it is almost certain to win. Thus, no variance is expected in the probability of contesting sure constituencies because of differences in need for achievement. Political party leaders must frequently choose, however, between committing their resources to contests they expect to be close or channeling some of those resources into constituencies where they have a low probability of winning. In a close constituency the probability of success approaches the 50:50 level. That is, a party's leaders are faced with an uncertain outcome. Selecting such constituencies involves the moderate risks and the uncertainty preferred by individuals with high need for achievement. Selecting remote constituencies, on the other hand, involves a high degree of certainty concerning the outcome. A party's candidate is almost certain to lose in such a constituency. This degree of certainty is expected to appeal to decision-makers with low need for achievement.

Why would any party, regardless of its risk-taking predisposition, commit resources to remote constituencies? First of all, success in such contests is an indication that the resource base, and especially the organizational base, of the party is expanding. A good showing in a remote constituency helps to increase the overall visibility of a party. A poor performance in a remote constituency, on the other hand, is not unexpected and so probably does not detract significantly from the party's image or its base of support. Thus, little support is lost by failure, and some support may be gained by success in remote constituencies. The decision, however, to commit resources to losing campaigns does incur costs. Even if a party contests all of its potentially close constituencies, some of its resources are diverted if it also campaigns in remote constituencies. The failure to concentrate its efforts in close constituencies may have serious repercussions for the future growth of the party. These repercussions may outweigh the gains derived from scattered successes in remote constituencies. Consequently, parties whose leaders have low need for achievement are likely to suffer greater setbacks in the long run than parties whose leaders have high need for achievement.

The first proposition of hypothesis 4 does not appear to be supported by the evidence. Using the n-achievement index, the correlation between risk-taking and the mixed strategy index is only 0.04 ($N=18$). This coefficient indicates essentially no relationship at all. The weakness of the association of course raises questions as to whether the theoretical argument is incorrect or this particular test which assumes a linear relationship is too stringent given the expectation of a weak association. One way to evaluate the merits of each of these interpretations is to perform a one-way analysis of variance. In this test, the mean strategic preference of the high need for achievement group is compared to the mean strategic preference of the low need for achievement group. No linearity is assumed since n-achievement is not assumed to be a continuous variable in this test. If the hypothesis is correct, the high n-achievement parties should, on average, prefer the mixed strategy more often than the low n-achievement parties. In addition, according to table 2.3, the high n-achievement parties should have a smaller amount of overall variance than the low n-achievement parties.[12] Table 6.2 reports the results of the analysis of variance. The parties whose leaders were high on the need to achieve did, in fact, have a strong enough preference for the mixed strategy that the difference in the mean for the high n-achievement group compared to the low n-achievement group would have occurred only three times in one hundred by chance alone. As further support of the theoretical argument, we can observe that the total variance in the low n-achievement group is somewhat greater than in the high n-achievement group. This difference is not, however, large enough to be considered statistically significant.

The second proposition of hypothesis 4 indicates that the degree of preference for moderate risks should be observable in the constituency selection process. That is, political parties with leaders who have high need for achievement should prefer close constituencies, while parties with leaders who have low need for achievement should prefer remote constituencies.

In order to operationalize the risk-taking propensities of the leaders of the All-India parties I rely on an official report of the Indian government.

Need for achievement, risk and success

TABLE 6.2 *Need for achievement and the mixed strategy*

n-achievement	Mean strategic preference	Variance	N
Low	0.632	0.043	9
High	0.844	0.031	9
Total	0.738		

$F = 5.46$. Probability <0.03.

That report indicates that the Indian Election Commission, in 1967, defined a state assembly constituency as being close for a party if it won or lost by 5,000 or fewer votes. Constituencies which were won or lost by more than 15,000 votes were defined as remote. Fair constituencies were defined as those won or lost by more than 5,000 but fewer than 15,000 votes. Constituencies won by more than 15,000 votes are ignored since I assume political parties always put up candidates where they are almost certain to win. Constituencies lost by that margin are assumed to have involved a high degree of certainty of failure. Constituencies won or lost by 5,000 or fewer votes are assumed to have involved a high degree of uncertainty. Constituencies that fell between these extremes are excluded from the present analysis. This is done for reasons which are explained shortly.

The risk-taking indicator does not, strictly speaking, reflect the subjective probability of success as perceived by each party's leaders. Rather, it reflects the *post hoc* probability of success. One might argue that this indicator should not be used as an expression of each party's leaders' awareness of the likelihood that their candidates would win or lose. This argument, however, is probably incorrect. I have incorporated in the analyses only those constituencies where the outcome indicated either a severe defeat or a marginal victory or a marginal defeat. I have excluded the constituencies where the outcome fell between the extremes. These excluded constituencies, rather than the extreme cases I have selected, are likely to have been the most difficult for the leaders to formulate reasonable expectations about. It is unlikely that experienced political leaders would systematically assess their party's chances as being good across the set of constituencies where their candidates were severely defeated. Similarly, it is unlikely that they would systematically evaluate close constituencies as being highly risky. Therefore, I assume that the leaders correctly perceived the probable outcome in the close constituencies and the remote constituencies.

As in the investigation of the first proposition of hypothesis 4, the expectation is that there is a weak, positive association between each party's

Need for achievement, risk and success

level of need for achievement and their propensity to contest close constituencies. Focusing our attention on the close constituencies and the constituencies where a party's candidates were severely defeated, we find a correlation of 0.26 ($N=18$) between the percentage of the party's constituencies that were close and the party's level of need for achievement. That is, as expected, the higher a party's score on the achievement index, the larger the proportion of close constituencies that is contested. On average, the parties whose leaders have low need for achievement contested 11 per cent more remote constituencies than the parties whose leaders have high need for achievement. Thus, hypothesis 4 is supported both by the strategic predispositions and by the strategic behavior of the leaders of the All-India parties.

Need for achievement and redistributive benefits

The importance of need for achievement, and risk-taking orientations in general, does not reside in its association with strategic preferences. Instead, the importance of the achievement index resides in its ability to account for the effective application of the mixed strategy. Thus, high need for achievement is expected to lead political leaders to optimize the application of the mixed strategy, while low need for achievement is expected to result in the misapplication or incorrect sequencing of competitive and cooperative actions. In order to evaluate this aspect of the achievement motive, it is necessary to analyze the relationship between each party's leaders' need for achievement and the performance of the parties in the coalitions and the elections. That is, it is necessary to turn our attention to the fifth hypothesis of this study.

Within the coalition setting, the two best indicators of redistributive benefits are the importance ratio and the percentage of important ministries received by each party. Both of these variables have already been shown to have a substantial relationship with the performance of the All-India parties in subsequent elections. Consequently, they are used to evaluate the effects of need for achievement on the allocation of redistributive benefits within coalitions.

Political parties whose leaders have high need for achievement do, as expected, receive more important cabinet portfolios than parties with leaders who have low need for achievement. The analysis of variance presented in table 6.3 indicates that there is a modest tendency for high n-achievement parties to receive a disproportionately large share of important portfolios. The analysis of variance reported in table 6.4 reveals that need for achievement has a substantially greater impact on the percentage of important portfolios received by each of the All-India parties. In other words, the parties with leaders who have high need for achieve-

Need for achievement, risk and success

ment controlled more important cabinet portfolios, both in an absolute and in a relative sense. This control, in turn, was likely to give those parties access to patronage, publicity, and greater contact with the electorate – all of which are likely to lead to future electoral success.

TABLE 6.3 *Need for achievement and the importance ratio*

n-achievement	Importance ratio		
	Mean	Variance	N
High n-ach parties	1.03	0.075	7
Low n-ach parties	0.87	0.070	8
Total	0.95		

Probability <0.30.

TABLE 6.4 *Need for achievement and the percentage distribution of important ministries*

n-achievement	Percentage of important ministries		
	Mean	Variance	N
High n-ach parties	0.178	0.008	7
Low n-ach parties	0.040	0.001	8
Total	0.105		

Probability <0.01.

Need for achievement has proved to be a good indicator of risk-taking preferences and of success within redistributive coalitions. It remains to be seen if the coalition successes of parties with leaders who have high need for achievement are converted to success in subsequent elections. Indeed, it remains to be seen if need for achievement affects the outcome of elections even when there have been no coalitions. In order to establish the relationship between need for achievement and electoral success, analyses of variance are reported for fourteen separate indicators of electoral success. In each case, of course, the independent variable is the dichotomized version of the achievement index. The indicators of electoral success include the number of state legislative assembly seats won (1) in 1967 and (2) during the midterm polls; the number of Lok Sabha seats won (3) in 1967 and (4) in 1971; the percentage of votes secured for the legislative assembly (5) in 1967 and (6) during the midterm polls; the percentage of votes secured for the Lok Sabha (7) in 1967 and (8) in 1971; (9)

Need for achievement, risk and success

the change in the number of seats won in the state assembly contests between 1967 and the midterm polls; (10) the percentage change in the number of seats won in the state assembly contests between 1967 and the midterm polls; (11) the change in the number of Lok Sabha seats won between 1967 and 1971; (12) the change in the percentage of votes won in the state assembly elections between 1967 and the midterm polls; (13) the percentage change in the percentage of votes won in the state assembly elections between 1967 and the midterm polls; and (14) the change in the percentage of votes won for the Lok Sabha between 1967 and 1971.

Variables (1), (3), (5), and (7) measure the relationship between need for achievement and electoral success prior to the coalitions. The remaining variables measure the impact of need for achievement in conjunction with coalition experience. The other variables are the same as those reported in table 5.6.

As can be seen from the analyses of variance reported in table 6.5, thirteen of the fourteen analyses are in the predicted direction. Only in the analysis of the change in the number of Lok Sabha seats won between 1967 and 1971 did the low need for achievement parties have a higher average level of performance than did the high need for achievement parties. In that one case, the difference between the two group means is negligible. Of the remaining thirteen analyses of variance in which the parties with high need for achievement did out-perform the parties with low need for achievement, seven of the differences in mean performance are substantial enough to be significant at the 0.05 level. Six of these seven are significant at the 0.01 level, and four of these six are significant at the 0.001 level or better. In other words, need for achievement has a substantial impact on the relative ability of political parties to increase their political influence. The parties with leaders who have high need for achievement clearly out-performed the parties with leaders who have low need for achievement in pre- and post-coalition electoral situations. What is more, they apparently used the advantages they gained during the tenure of the coalitions to expand their legislative representation disproportionately and likewise to increase their vote-getting ability disproportionately. Thus, parties, like the Jana Sangh in Bihar, that have leaders with a high need to achieve and that have leaders predisposed to follow the mixed strategy, have greatly increased their political influence. Parties like the Swatantra Party in Uttar Pradesh and Orissa, on the other hand, have leaders predisposed to behave cooperatively and with below average levels of need for achievement. These parties have experienced dramatic declines in their political influence. Some low n-achievement parties have lost so much influence that they no longer satisfy the definitional requirements of an All-India party.

Need for achievement, risk and success

TABLE 6.5 *Electoral success and the need to achieve*

Variable	n-ach	Mean	Variance	N	Significance
Vidhan Sabha	High	53.29	858.90	7	<0.01
seats (1967)	Low	12.75	33.07	8	
Vidhan Sabha	High	46.33	353.87	6	<0.001
seats (midterm)	Low	9.71	73.24	7	
Lok Sabha	High	6.86	13.14	7	<0.01
seats (1967)	Low	2.00	3.71	8	
Lok Sabha	High	6.00	50.33	7	<0.10
seats (1971)	Low	1.38	3.98	8	
Vidhan Sabha	High	16.09	58.05	7	<0.001
vote (1967)	Low	4.40	3.85	8	
Vidhan Sabha	High	13.68	28.21	6	<0.001
vote (midterm)	Low	3.57	10.74	7	
Lok Sabha	High	16.41	55.63	7	<0.001
vote (1967)	Low	4.24	9.32	8	
Lok Sabha	High	26.25	103.07	3	<0.05
vote (1971)	Low	1.25	0.13	3	
Change in VS	High	−2.83	871.77	6	<0.96
seats	Low	−3.43	22.95	7	
Percent change	High	0.18	0.36	6	<0.15
in VS seats	Low	−0.29	0.18	7	
Change in LS	High	−0.86	63.14	7	<0.94
seats	Low	−0.63	0.84	8	
Change in VS	High	−0.37	13.13	6	<0.84
vote	Low	−0.70	4.49	7	
Percent change	High	0.01	0.08	6	<0.30
in VS vote	Low	−0.21	0.16	7	
Change in LS	High	8.19	88.24	3	<0.20
vote	Low	−1.05	0.89	3	

Organization, motivation, strategy, and political success

Thus far, I have demonstrated that a party's size is important in securing membership in a coalition, but is unimportant in effecting subsequent changes in its representation or even in its acquisition of important coalition benefits. The strategic predisposition of party leaders, and their level of need for achievement, have proven to be important indicators of political success within coalitions and elections. I have not yet examined

Need for achievement, risk and success

the combined effects of both high need for achievement and a predisposition to pursue a mixed strategy. In addition, I have not yet investigated the impact that a party's organizational capabilities has on its subsequent success in elections. The examination of these multivariate relationships will complete the empirical portion of this study.

The sixth and final hypothesis states that a predisposition to pursue a mixed strategy, high need for achievement, and substantial organizational capabilities results in increases in the political influence of political parties. In order to test this hypothesis, I make use of two indicators of organizational capabilities. Before operationalizing organizational capabilities, however, let us examine the combined effects of need for achievement and strategic predispositions. Then, having illuminated their combined effects, we can turn to the more complex relationships stipulated by hypothesis 6.

Using multiple regression analysis, the sixth hypothesis is tested by focusing on the absolute change and the percentage change in the number of Vidhan Sabha seats won by the All-India parties between the fourth general election and the midterm elections which were conducted between 1969 and 1971. I chose these dependent variables because they reflect the dynamic, longitudinal impact of the model's variables on party representation. These two variables are reliable indicators of the expansion or contraction of a party's legislative base. Thus, although measures of change in voting percentages, or measures of absolute strength at a single time are interesting, they are not as informative for party leaders nor are they as indicative of the future potential of a party as are the two variables I have selected. If the model succeeds in predicting changes in legislative representation, then it provides a useful supplement to the intensive investigation of the idiosyncratic aspects of Indian politics.

Positive findings in the multivariate analyses would suggest that further explorations of risk-taking dynamics among political leaders can prove helpful in explaining political behavior. The success of the multivariate analyses would also suggest that the overall performance of political parties is very much influenced by factors that can be directly controlled by the party. That is, success in these analyses would indicate that parties are somewhat less subject to the whims of the electorate than may have been thought previously. Such a finding would be theoretically interesting to social scientists and policy relevant to political party leaders. Along with several other studies,[13] it would suggest that when elites are recruited on the basis of their political style, and other psychological attributes, handsome electoral gains may result. That is, the regression analyses will help identify the parameters within which parties may manipulate their electoral success by recruiting leaders with particular strategic predispositions and achievement orientations.

Need for achievement, risk and success

First, the percentage change in Vidhan Sabha seats won between 1967 and the midterm polls is estimated as a function of the mixed strategy index and the n-achievement index. The results are presented in table 6.6. The regression coefficients indicate the sizable benefits enjoyed by All-India parties with leaders who have high need for achievement and are predisposed to pursue a mixed strategy. Thus, on average, a hypothetical All-India party completely predisposed to pursue a mixed strategy, and having within its ranks all the political leaders in its state who have high need for achievement, would have doubled its legislative representation. These estimates are sufficiently accurate that they account for nearly two-thirds of the variance in the percentage change in representation in the state legislative assemblies.

TABLE 6.6 *Percentage change in Vidhan Sabha seats won between 1967 and the midterm polls as a function of the mixed strategy index and need for achievement*

Variable	Coefficient	Standard error	T-statistic	Significance
Intercept	−1.31	0.301	−4.301	<0.001
Mix	1.64	0.405	4.043	<0.001
n-ach	1.71	0.873	1.959	<0.07

$R^2 = 0.63$. Multiple $R = 0.80$. Std Error $= 0.34$. $F = 10.93$. Significance <0.005. Number of parties $= 16$.

Party leaders, of course, are interested in the actual number of seats they can expect to win or lose rather than in percentage changes in their representation. To estimate the absolute changes in legislative representation it is necessary to add an additional variable in order to take into account the initial base of strength from which each party contests subsequent elections. The number of Vidhan Sabha seats won by each party in 1967 is used to assess the base of strength. The other independent variables are, again, the mixed strategy index and the n-achievement index. These three variables account for 72 per cent of the variance in the change in the number of seats won between 1967 and the midterm polls. Table 6.7 presents the regression analysis. The coefficients in this analysis indicate the number of seats a party could expect to gain or lose as a function of its score on each of the three predictor variables, when the influence of the other variables is controlled. Thus, the larger a party was in 1967, the more it could expect to lose during the midterm elections, while the higher the need for achievement of its leaders and the greater their predisposition to pursue a mixed strategy, the more seats it could expect to win. These findings support the theoretical argument not only in terms of the need to achieve and the mixed strategy, but also in terms of the tendency for large

Need for achievement, risk and success

parties to lose access to redistributive benefits. That is, the negative coefficient associated with each party's initial size indicates the potential harm that can arise from becoming too large too soon.

TABLE 6.7 *Changes in Vidhan Sabha seats won between 1967 and the midterm polls as a function of the number of seats won in 1967, strategic predisposition, and* n-*achievement*

Variable	Coefficient	Standard error	T-statistic	Significance
Intercept	−18.91	11.43	−1.654	<0.12
Number of seats won in 1967	−0.47	0.13	−3.690	<0.005
Mix	39.31	13.40	2.934	<0.01
n-ach	75.12	31.82	2.360	<0.05

$R^2 = 0.72$. Multiple $R = 0.85$. Std Error $= 10.91$. $F = 10.07$. Significance <0.005. Number of parties $= 16$.

It is evident that need for achievement and the mixed strategy account for a very substantial portion of the variance in changes in legislative representation, even when organizational capabilities are not specified. We can expect, therefore, that the addition of indicators of organizational capabilities will add considerable precision to what are already very accurate explanations of the changes in representation. The organizational capabilities of political parties are very difficult to measure. Party membership might be a good indicator, except that membership criteria differ dramatically from party to party. Thus, membership in the Jana Sangh is open to almost anyone willing to pay a small membership fee, while membership in the Communist Party of India (Marxist) is extremely restrictive. A state by state breakdown of party finances might indicate the scope and effectiveness of a party's organization, but such data would be insensitive to differences in party reliance on volunteers, media, and so on. In addition, such financial breakdowns are all but impossible to obtain. Because of these difficulties, I am forced to use a poor indicator of party organization. The indicator is the percentage of votes won in each state by each party in the 1967 legislative assembly elections. The indicator is poor because of its close association with the dependent variables. It is not poor in terms of its ability to indicate each party's organizational capabilities. The percentage of votes received by a party is, after all, dependent on the party's ability to mobilize support within the constituencies. A direct link between grass roots organizations and the percentage of votes received by parties has been identified for elections in the United States where the electorate has the opportunity to receive information about

Need for achievement, risk and success

parties and candidates from a broad spectrum of sources other than grass roots political organizations.[14] If this relationship exists in the United States, it seems reasonable to presume that it plays a role in Indian politics as well. Indeed, there is some evidence to indicate that grass roots organizations play a much more important role in winning votes in India than they do in the United States.[15] The Indian electorate in general is swayed by the influence of relatively few key men in the villages and towns. These men, who influence vote banks, seem to determine their votes on the basis of several criteria, including contacts with organizational leaders from the various parties. They often make their decisions on the basis of caste or other peculiarly Indian considerations, but when competing parties nominate candidates with generally equal ascriptive appeal (and they usually do), then organizational contacts become increasingly important.[16] Since there appears to be a close association between the organizational capabilities of a party and its success at winning votes, I treat the percentage of votes won by the parties in 1967 as an indicator, albeit not a very good one, of organizational capabilities.

In addition to the percentage of votes won, I use the importance ratio as an indicator of organizational capabilities. While votes reflect organizational capabilities during the elections, the importance ratio indicates the organizational skills of a party within a coalition. Thus, the greater the organizational capabilities of a party, the more credible its demands and, therefore, the more likely it is to receive extra important cabinet portfolios.

The impact of organizational capabilities on the redistribution of political influence may be manifested in one of two ways. Either organizational capabilities may have a separate effect on electoral outcomes, or they may interact with the mixed strategy and/or need for achievement to magnify the effects of those variables. The former possibility is tested through the use of an additive regression equation, while the latter possibility is tested by constructing variables that reflect interactive effects. In order to do this and still preserve the ability to observe the magnitude of the effect of each variable, I transform the mixed strategy, need for achievement, the percentage of votes, and the importance ratio into their logarithm to the base e.[17] The regression equations using these logarithmic transformations approximate the results that would be obtained by simply multiplying the variables times each other. Of course, if that approach were taken, the interaction effect would be obtained at the cost of knowing the magnitude of the separate effects of the individual variables. The logarithmic equations assume the following form:

$$Y = b_0 + b_1(\log X_1) + b_2(\log X_2)$$

and are equivalent to the following untransformed equation:

$$Y = b_0 + (X_1^{b_1})(X_2^{b_2})$$

The interaction equations should be interpreted as indicating the joint effects of the interactive variables under the assumption that neither is sufficient, by itself, to produce an effect on the dependent variable. The interactive, or multiplicative, equations assume that all the interacting variables are necessary to produce an effect on the dependent variable. These equations also assume that the combined effect of the interactive variables is sufficient to produce an effect on the dependent variable. The additive regression equations, by contrast, assume that any individual variable can produce an effect by itself.

With respect to the percentage change in the number of Vidhan Sabha seats won by each party between 1967 and the midterm elections, the introduction of variables that take organizational capabilities into account does not add appreciably to the variance accounted for by the mixed strategy and the need to achieve. When the importance ratio is added to the equation as an additive component, the coefficient of determination increases from 0.63 to 0.69, but the n-achievement index is reduced to an insignificant component of the equation. That is, a predisposition to pursue the mixed strategy coupled with either a high importance ratio or a high score on the n-achievement index results in an increase in the legislative representation of the All-India parties.

The introduction of indicators of organizational capabilities has a substantial effect on the success with which the theory explains variance in the change in legislative seats won between 1967 and the midterm elections. With the introduction of the votes interaction term, need for achievement is reduced to an insignificant level. That is, political parties are able to increase their political influence by combining a predisposition to pursue a mixed strategy with the organizational capabilities to make their strategic actions credible. Thus, the risk-taking orientations of political party leaders appear to be adequately accounted for by the mixed strategy index, even when need for achievement levels are unspecified. Table 6.8 reports the regression analysis while table 6.9 provides a list of the actual changes in legislative representation compared to the changes in representation predicted by the regression model. As is evident from the fact that 82 per cent of the variance is explained, the regression model is an excellent predictor of the electoral success of the All-India parties.

Several interesting observations may be made about these results. First, it should be noted that less variance is accounted for when the noninteractive form of this equation is calculated. That is, the individual effect of the votes variable is diminished when it is treated as an additive component of the model. Second, the theoretical significance of these results is highlighted by the stability of the coefficients. Thus, even removing the extreme

Need for achievement, risk and success

TABLE 6.8 *The change in legislative assembly representation as a function of strategy, organization, and base of strength*

Variable	Coefficient	Standard error	T-statistic	Significance
Intercept	−9.51			
log (Mix)	36.90	6.03	6.12	0.001
log (Vote)	21.60	4.28	5.05	0.001
Vidhan Sabha seats, 1967	−0.83	0.12	−6.69	0.001

$R^2 = 0.82$. Multiple $R = 0.91$. Std Error $= 7.69$. $F = 23.57$. Significance < 0.001. Number of parties $= 19$.

TABLE 6.9 *Actual and estimated changes in legislative representation*

Party	State	Actual change	Predicted change	Error of estimate
Jana Sangh	Punjab	−1	+7	−8
CPI	Punjab	−1	−4	+3
Jana Sangh	Uttar Pradesh	−49	−50	+1
SSP	Uttar Pradesh	−11	−3	−8
Swatantra	Uttar Pradesh	−7	−12	+5
PSP	Uttar Pradesh	−9	−14	+5
CPI	Uttar Pradesh	−9	−10	+1
SSP	Bihar	−16	−10	−6
Jana Sangh	Bihar	+8	+11	−3
PSP	Bihar	0	−8	+8
CPI	Bihar	+1	+2	−1
CPI (M)	West Bengal	+37	+17	+20
CPI	West Bengal	+14	+18	+4
SSP	West Bengal	+2	+1	+1
PSP	West Bengal	−2	−1	−1
Swatantra	Orissa	−13	−21	+8
CPI (M)	Kerala	−24	−18	−6
CPI	Kerala	−3	+3	−6
SSP	Kerala	−13	−5	−8

case of the Jana Sangh in Uttar Pradesh, the regression model results in the estimation of almost the identical line.[18] That is, the function is not unduly influenced by a few extreme values. As evidence of this observation note the linearity of the fit as represented in the scatterplot reported in figure 1. Third, the great importance of the mixed strategy index should be noted. This variable, more than any other component of the theory tested here, has proven to have a consistent and substantial impact on the ability of political parties to increase their potential political influence in the legislatures of India.

Need for achievement, risk and success

Need for achievement appears to play a somewhat lesser role than does a party's strategic predispositions. On the other hand, need for achievement has proven to be an important indicator of the percentage change in legislative representation and of shifts in a party's mass appeal. Thus, need for achievement and the importance ratio together account for 45

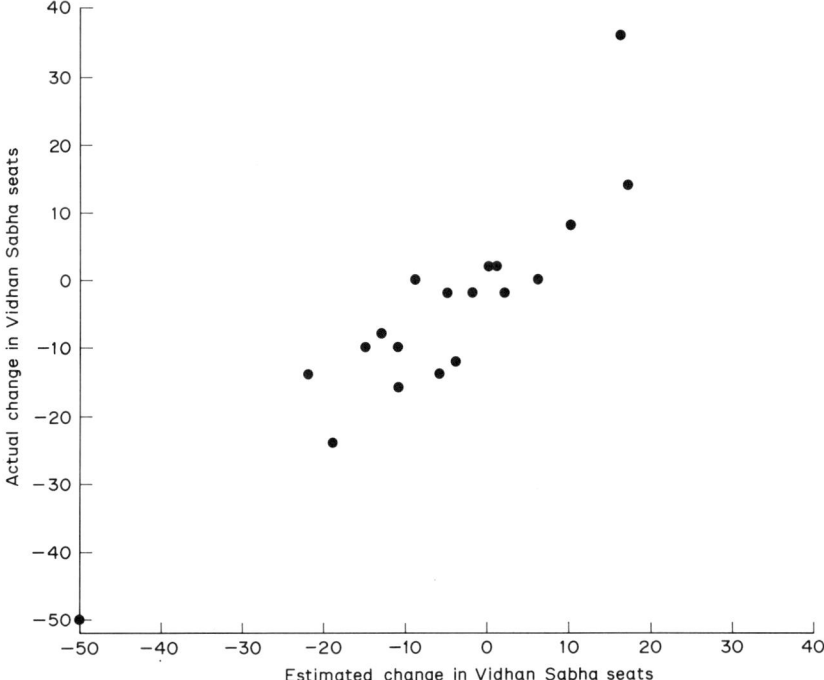

Figure 1. Vidhan Sabha seat changes estimated by the interaction of strategy and organizational capabilities

per cent of the variance in the change in the percentage of votes won by the All-India parties between 1967 and the midterm elections. In this analysis, the n-achievement indicator is significant and so is the importance ratio. That is, depending on the particular aspect of electoral performance on which our attention is focused, each of the components of the theory can be shown to play an important role in altering the potential influence of the All-India parties.

Before summarizing the results reported in this chapter, I turn briefly to a case history that highlights the significance of the elements considered in this chapter.

Need for achievement, risk and success

Case history: Bihar

We have already seen the effect that the Jana Sangh's strategic orientation has had on its success in Bihar. I would now like to compare the success of the Jana Sangh in Bihar to the failures of the SSP in Bihar. The comparison of these two parties is particularly interesting for several reasons. First, these two parties were the largest opposition parties in Bihar after the 1967 election. The SSP won fifty-eight Vidhan Sabha seats in 1967, while the Jana Sangh won twenty-six. Second, both parties were substantially oriented toward the pursuit of a mixed strategy. The SSP score on the mixed strategy index was 0.840, while the Jana Sangh score was 0.800. On the basis of these similarities, one might have expected them to experience similar changes in representation as a result of their coalition experiences, but this was not the case. The SSP lost 24 per cent of its seats and about the same percentage of its votes while the Jana Sangh gained about 33 per cent more seats and 50 per cent more votes between 1967 and 1969. When we examine the difference in the levels of need for achievement and the actual risk-taking behavior of the SSP and Jana Sangh in Bihar these differences are not surprising.

The Jana Sangh leadership in Bihar had the highest score (0.130) of any party's leadership on the n-achievement index, placing them nearly one and one-half standard deviations above the mean. The SSP leadership, on the other hand, had one of the lowest scores on the n-achievement index: -0.096, or more than one standard deviation below the mean. This difference is clearly manifested in their political behavior, and their political attitudes.

Jana Sangh leaders in Bihar continually emphasized in my interviews with them that the party's performance in the midterm election was even better than the results indicate. They called attention to the fact that the party's share of the vote had increased 50 per cent over their share in 1967, and that they lost a large number of constituencies by a very narrow margin. They did, in fact, lose many constituencies by fewer than 1500 votes. In explaining their success, Jana Sangh leaders emphasized the cohesiveness of the party's organization and their use of the coalition to enhance the party's image and organizational capabilities. As one leader of the party explained to me:

> 'Being a political party it is our aim that we should run the government. In a coalition we get the chance to work in the government, therefore, coalitions give us a better chance to prove ourselves worthy of the task for which we are working ... We are always dedicated to our organization, not to the government. Our sincerities are for the organization through which we get chances to serve the people. Therefore, our main

objective is to strengthen the organization and all legislators work in that spirit.'

It is quite evident that this attitude is one of taking risks to aggrandize the party while it participates in a coalition government. Thus, this Jana Sangh leader was willing to use the benefits derived by the coalition to enhance the organizational strength of the Jana Sangh, particularly to use patronage obtained in his capacity as a cabinet minister as a means to attract supporters to the Jana Sangh. In fact, he noted that the Jana Sangh view of patronage, as he understood it, was 'patronage is always effective. We are clear that patronage is not a separate thing from all activities of the party workers.'

While the Jana Sangh leadership was very explicitly willing to take risks to benefit the party's organizational base and its electoral appeal, the SSP leadership was taking quite a different position. From the perspective of one SSP leader, for example, the Jana Sangh success in the elections was a consequence of luck, rather than their hard work in building a solid organization. Thus, he claimed that the Jana Sangh won extra seats in Bihar because 'they fought the largest number of seats during the midterm poll . . . The SSP fought only about 200 seats whereas the Jana Sangh fought more than 300 seats and when any political party fights that large a number of seats, some are won accidentally . . . Had the SSP fought all the seats in Bihar, it must have won more than 100 seats.' If his assessment was correct, then the SSP's aversion to contesting seats cost it 48 positions in the state assembly. Of course, this is almost certainly not true. Instead, it is a typical rationalization of a risk-averse decision-maker. Thus, as is common among low need for achievers, this leader explained the Jana Sangh success in terms of luck rather than skill, while attributing his party's own failure to its unwillingness to take risks. This individual went on to explain that the SSP does not use patronage because it alienates as many voters as it attracts. Yet, a few minutes later he reported that the Jana Sangh success arose out of its use of patronage, while claiming that the SSP's only benefit from the coalition was to convince some of its partners to implement certain programs. Such policy-oriented successes are, of course, important, but they are not likely to provide a strong basis for future political or policy successes for the SSP.

The SSP attitude in favor of policy work and against political uses of the coalitions was manifested in their behavior as well as in their statements. Thus, when given the opportunity to head a coalition government that was to include the somewhat right of center Congress (O), the Bihari leaders of the Samyukta Socialist Party refused to participate. Their refusal cost them the chief ministership of the state and the concomitant ability to attract attention and support to the SSP. The Jana Sangh, on the

Need for achievement, risk and success

other hand, did not refuse to participate in any coalition in Bihar as a consequence of ideological differences. Instead, they were willing to take some risks by joining coalitions with the CPI. They explained their coalition membership strategy in terms of its ability to advance the political fortunes of the Jana Sangh. As one leader explained: 'In competition with other parties, those who have got an organizational base can flourish and the rest will fade away . . . Certainly we have a coalition strategy. We always like to give a setback to anti-nationalist forces and this is the basis of our coalition strategy.' That is, the Jana Sangh orientation was that they could use their strong organization and the benefits of the coalition to enhance the party's position at the expense of parties such as the CPI. At the same time they recognized the sophistication of the organizational workers of the CPI and the risks inherent in joining a coalition with them. The Jana Sangh leaders also recognized that the CPI intended to use the coalition to enhance their political fortunes. The unsuccessful SSP expressed no interest, and manifested little interest, in using the coalitions to benefit themselves.

Summary

Three hypotheses were tested in this chapter. The results of those tests indicate that need for achievement is, as expected, associated with the predisposition to pursue a mixed strategy and with the success political parties experience in coalitions and elections. Organizational capabilities coupled with a predisposition to pursue a mixed strategy were found to have the greatest effect on the absolute growth of the All-India parties, while need for achievement and intracoalition organizational capabilities were found to have the greatest impact on the relative growth of the All-India parties.

7. Conclusions

The principal concern of my theory of coalition behavior is the importance of strategic predispositions and risk-taking preferences in influencing changes in the distribution of political influence. The theory suggests several implications about the coalition process in general and about political party politics in India in particular. In this final chapter I examine those implications and attempt to place them in the broader context of the study of political development.

Coalition politics

The following propositions summarize the theory investigated in this volume:

(*a*) The political resources that determine political influence may be redistributed as a consequence of participation in political coalitions.

(*b*) Participants in coalitions are aware of the opportunity they have to increase their political influence.

(*c*) Because of the awareness of politicians concerning the redistributive consequences of coalitions, members of political coalitions often compete with each other over the allocation of redistributive benefits.

(*d*) The competition among coalition partners is restricted by the degree to which each partner is willing to tolerate competitive demands on the part of its allies.

(*e*) Where tolerance is very high, competitiveness is rewarded with disproportionately large increases in political influence. Where tolerance is limited, a mixture of competitive demands for politically useful benefits and cooperative pressures for the fulfillment of collective policy goals results in a greater long-term increase in political influence than does a single-minded commitment to either private political benefits or collective policy benefits.

(*f*) The preference for a cooperative, competitive, or mixed strategy is unrelated to the size of political parties.[1] Consequently, size does not substantially influence the allocation of redistributive coalition benefits.

(*g*) A preference for the mixed strategy is encouraged if a party's leaders have high need for achievement.

(*h*) The successful implementation of the mixed strategy preference is encouraged by the possession and utilization of the organizational capabilities needed to make threats credible.

(*i*) Therefore, political parties with leaders who are predisposed to follow a mixed strategy, with leaders who have high need for achievement, and

Conclusions

with substantial organizational capabilities are most likely to increase their political influence in the long run.

All of the important hypotheses of the theory, as well as most of the minor corollaries of those hypotheses, were supported by the evidence presented in this volume. There are, nevertheless, linkages among some variables that are less clear than they ought to be. It is not clear, for instance, which unspecified variables influence the strategic preferences of decision-makers with low need for achievement. Since individuals with low need for achievement were theorized to lack clear strategic preferences in many politically interesting situations, the identification of those variables is essential in order to determine the circumstances under which they are most likely to pursue the influence-maximizing mixed strategy. Furthermore, it is not clear what the exact relationship is between the strategic preferences, or the risk-taking preferences of individual decision-makers and the collective preferences of their political party. Without additional knowledge concerning these linkages, we are left with simplistic assumptions and the potential for embracing ecological fallacies.

The organizational capabilities of political parties, or of any participants in political coalitions, are important in converting their intended actions into real actions. Despite this important relationship, little is known about the behavior or attributes that are necessary to make a decision-maker believe another's threats. Although this relationship has been studied extensively with regard to international politics, where the literature on deterrence and arms races bears on this point, almost no research has been done on organizational interactions within political party politics. These questions have not been investigated in the past because prior research on political party coalitions assumes that allies always cooperate with each other in pursuit of shared goals. It is only when this assumption is rejected – as it must be when studying redistributive coalitions – that questions concerning the organizational implementation of intra-coalition competition become relevant. I have not studied these relationships so much as I have imposed simplifying assumptions that permit the observation of tendencies within these relationships. It is to be hoped that such theoretical developments will be undertaken as a first step toward the measurement of potential and implemented organizational capabilities.[2]

The most important failure of the theory rests in its inability to distinguish between potential political influence and actual political influence. To be sure, identifying the distribution of potential influence among political parties is an important first step. Potential influence is almost certainly highly correlated with the actual distribution of influence. Nevertheless, they are not the same thing. As the theory and the empirical results make clear, no party can hope to exert influence within the government unless

Conclusions

it has some base of legislative representation. What is more, larger parties within coalitions tend to receive more of the politically useful important benefits of their coalitions than do their smaller partners, even though they do not receive a disproportionately larger share of those benefits. Despite this evidence that size is related to political influence, the empirical evidence has also revealed that size does not govern disproportionalities in the allocation of redistributive benefits. It also demonstrates that larger parties are less desirable coalition partners than smaller parties and that larger parties are more likely to lose in subsequent elections than are smaller parties. Thus, while size is necessary for political influence, it is not sufficient. The theory has succeeded in explaining the distribution of size and, therefore, has explained changes in the potential influence of political parties. The theory has not explained why some parties benefit from their large size, while others suffer. While I suggest explanations in subsequent portions of this chapter, I have not developed a rigorous theory concerned with the conversion of potential influence into real influence. This remains a problem for future research. Despite these inadequacies, I believe the theory sheds some light on the processes of coalition formation, coalition maintenance, and coalition termination.

Implications for India

The reader primarily interested in Indian politics is probably left with a series of unanswered questions. Although I have explained a substantial portion of the variance in the outcomes of several Indian elections – both to the state assemblies and to the national parliament – I have not explained in depth the successes and failures of individual political parties or individual politicians. Instead, I have presented statistical patterns that describe trends, but ignore the ever present and always interesting exceptions. Thus, I have reported that a preference for a mixed strategy and a high degree of need for achievement lead to political success. This is generally true. On the other hand, the Jana Sangh in Uttar Pradesh had leaders with high need for achievement, and experienced a political disaster in the 1969 midterm elections. Why these leaders failed to succeed, and why they were inclined to behave cooperatively, has not been explained. Indeed, I cannot explain this exceptional case. Rather than attempt to do so, I have only provided broad brush strokes that outline the pattern of coalition politics in India. Others have and will continue to provide the finer strokes that are essential to complete the picture.

In addition to my zealous commitment to statistical reportage, I have, no doubt, left some readers disappointed by my lack of attentiveness to India-oriented variables. I have not, for example, explored the relationship between need for achievement and strategic orientations, on the one

Conclusions

hand, and caste, religion, language, region, or general culture, on the other hand. This is both a virtue and a vice of this study. It is a virtue in that I have shown the ability of a general theory of political coalition behavior to explain the often surprising and usually exotic flow of political outcomes in India since the end of the fourth general election. Thus, without focusing on the unique character of Indian politics, the theory has succeeded in accounting for almost all of the variation in the change in legislative strength of the All-India parties between 1967 and 1972.

At the same time that the theory provides an explanation of the outcome of several Indian elections, it does not explain why some parties recruit leaders with the 'right' strategic predispositions and risk-taking orientations, while other parties do not. Explanations of this sort may require an examination of the linkages between the variables included in my analyses and exogenous variables related to early socialization experiences. Factors such as caste, region, family income, occupational mobility and the like fall within the latter category of variables. That is, the traditional variables of the student of Indian politics may be the specific determinants of each individual's risk-taking propensities or strategic predispositions. In that sense, caste and other peculiarly Indian phenomena may be surrogate indicators of the variables included in this study. The advantage of such surrogate indicators is, of course, their relevance to the specific political system in which they manifest themselves. Their disadvantage is their inability to be generalized to other political systems. By avoiding surrogate indicators, I have enhanced the potential generalizability of the theory, while sacrificing a certain amount of relevance for the student of Indian politics.

Despite these caveats, this study does contain several important findings about Indian political party politics. Most important, it indicates the significance of elite recruitment policies in altering the potential influence of political parties. A party's level of need for achievement or its strategic predisposition depends exclusively on its recruitment and promotion policies. If a party's leaders are willing to consider an individual's motivational and strategic predispositions as an important criterion in their decision to promote that person to a position of responsibility, then the party can develop the kind of leadership that is likely to achieve political success. On the other hand, if a party's leaders become complacent and are satisfied with the status quo, they are likely to promote individuals who are unlikely to take risks in order to improve the party's position. Under such circumstances, the party's leaders are not only not likely to increase the party's political influence, they may actually cause an erosion in its position. Insofar as satisfaction with the status quo is more common among leaders of large parties than among leaders of small parties, one would expect large parties to decline in influence and be replaced by smaller, rising parties. Of course, to the extent that rising parties change their recruitment patterns in response to their increased political influence and become more status quo oriented, they, in turn, increase the likelihood of their own decline.[3]

Recruitment of risk-takers is not a simple procedure. In pursuing such a recruitment policy, caution must be exerted in order to avoid promoting leaders who are so risk-acceptant that they implement a very competitive strategy in their dealings with other political parties. To do so, as we have seen, may mean political disaster. Instead, care must be taken to recruit leaders who are able to negotiate, bargain, and compromise. Leaders who are tenaciously dedicated to making unreasonable demands can be even more of a liability than leaders who are tenaciously dedicated to cooperation with their allies.

Political coalitions and political development

Studies of political development focus on a wide variety of phenomena with which political systems are concerned. Among the foci that have been investigated are such processes as organization building, differentiation and specialization of roles, industrialization, participation, and integration. All of these processes are concerned with movement toward the fulfillment of a specific goal. Despite the theoretical focus on *movement* toward a goal, most investigations of development focus on a political system's *proximity* to the goal. For instance, studies concerned with industrialization assume that the most industrialized nations are the most developed nations, even though such an assumption is unwarranted by their theoretical arguments. It would be more accurate to assume that the nations with the fastest rate of industrial growth are the most developed, at least with respect to the goal of industrialization. This assumption focuses on the process of industrialization rather than on industrialization as an end-state. The assumption that the most industrialized nations are the most developed, on the other hand, implies that there is an ultimate level of industrialization beyond which no political system can go. Thus, such an assumption is concerned with industrialization as an attribute rather than a process.

If one focuses on processes in defining political development, then one is forced to examine the process of goal-attainment rather than the actual level of goal-attainment. That is, the appropriate focus of development studies is change or rates of change rather than specific attribute levels. By focusing on processes rather than attributes, one is able to speak of political development in terms of the political system's ability to maximize the probability of achieving certain specified goals, given the environmental constraints in which it must operate. Indeed, one might define

Conclusions

political development as the successful manipulation of the political environment to maximize the probability that one's goals are achieved.

This definition has several advantages. First, it does not impose a goal on political actors. It does not, for example, require us to consider all traditional elites as less developed, while forcing us to consider all non-traditional elites as developed. Quite the contrary, this definition permits us to define any political actor as being more or less developed strictly as a function of that actor's ability to manipulate the political environment in order to achieve its goals. For instance, we can examine the competition between a society's agricultural elite and its industrial elite in terms of their relative success at controlling the priorities of the political system. To the extent that the system's priorities favor the industrial elite (as a consequence of their efforts) we may say that the industrial elite are developing with respect to their goals. On the other hand, to the extent that the agricultural elite are able to control the priorities of the political system, we may say that they are the more politically developed group.

Second, by defining political development in terms of probability maximization, we are not forced to view development unidimensionally. A single political actor can be fairly developed with respect to one goal and be much less developed with respect to some other goal. For instance, a bureaucrat may be very developed in his ability to circumvent policy decisions that he does not favor, but not in his ability to influence which policies are legislated. A consequence of introducing multidimensionality into the definition is that our attention becomes increasingly focused on the appropriate strategic behavior, given particular goals. Less attention is given to the institutions or structures within which goals are pursued, while more attention is given to the manipulation of those structures or institutions.

The theory of coalition politics that I have presented is concerned primarily with the ability of political actors to manipulate their political environment. It is concerned with the ability actors have to implement the appropriate strategic behavior given such environmental constraints as their resource pool and the tolerance limits of their allies. These are exactly the concerns embodied in the definition of political development that I have suggested. Consequently, the theory can be generalized as a model of political development. Thus, for any postulated goal, the theory suggests the identification of the appropriate strategy and the appropriate risk-taking propensities required to maximize the probability that the goal will be attained. When the goal is the maximization of long-term influence, for example, the theory suggests the use of a mixed strategy. When the goal is the maximization of one's tenure in a decision-making body, the strategy suggested by the theory is cooperation. What the appropriate strategies are for other development goals remains a question for future research.

Appendix I: Election results

This appendix contains data on the number of seats won by the All-India parties in several Lok Sabha and several Vidhan Sabha elections. Blank cells in the tables indicate elections during which the specified party did not exist.

Prior to 1964 and after 1971, the Samyukta Socialist Party has been assigned the seats won by the Socialist Party. When a double figure, such as 51+1 accompanies the Congress Party, the first number refers to the ruling Congress (R), while the latter number refers to the Congress (O). Where a single number appears for the Congress, it refers to the Congress (R). When no figure is given for the Congress (O), after 1969, that party won no seats.

Number of Lok Sabha seats won

BIHAR

Party	1952	1957	1962	1967	1971
Congress	45	41	39	34	39+3
CPI	0	0	1	5	5
CPI (M)				0	0
Jana Sangh	0	0	0	1	2
PSP		2	2	1	0
SSP	3		7	0	2
Swatantra			7	0	0

KERALA

Party	1952	1957	1962	1967	1971
Congress	7	6	6	1	6
CPI	1	9	6	3	3
CPI (M)				9	2
Jana Sangh	0	0	0	0	0
PSP		1	0	0	
SSP	0		0	3	0
Swantantra			0	0	0

MADHYA PRADESH

Party	1952	1957	1962	1967	1971
Congress	32	35	24	24	21
CPI	0	0	0	0	0
CPI (M)				0	0
Jana Sangh	0	0	3	10	11
PSP	0		3	0	0
SSP	1		1	1	1
Swatantra			0	1	0

ORISSA

Party	1952	1957	1962	1967	1971
Congress	11	7	14	6	15

Appendix I: Election results

CPI	1	1	0	0	1
CPI (M)				0	0
Jana Sangh	0	0	0	0	0
PSP	2		1	4	0
SSP	1		1	1	0
Swatantra			0	8	3

PUNJAB

Party	1952	1957	1962	1967	1971
Congress	9	13	10	9	10
CPI	0	0	0	0	2
CPI (M)				0	0
Jana Sangh	0	0	0	1	0
PSP		0	0	0	0
SSP	0		0	0	0
Swatantra			0	0	0

UTTAR PRADESH

Party	1952	1957	1962	1967	1971
Congress	81	70	62	47	73+1
CPI	0	1	2	5	4
CPI (M)				1	0
Jana Sangh	0	2	7	12	4
PSP		4	2	2	0
SSP	2		1	8	0
Swatantra			3	1	0

WEST BENGAL

Party	1952	1957	1962	1967	1971
Congress	24	23	22	14	13
CPI	5	6	9	5	3
CPI (M)				5	20
Jana Sangh	2	0	0	0	0
PSP	2		0	1	1
SSP	0		0	1	0
Swatantra			0	0	0

Number of Vidhan Sabha seats won

BIHAR

Party	1952	1957	1962	1967	1969	1972
Congress	235	210	185	128	118	167
CPI	0	7	12	24	25	35
CPI (M)				4	3	0
Jana Sangh	0	0	3	26	34	25
PSP		31	29	18	18	
SSP	23		7	68	52	33
Swatantra			50	3	3	2

Appendix I: Election results

KERALA

Party	1952	1954	1957	1960
Congress	49	45	44	63
CPI	32	23	60	29
CPI (M)				
Jana Sangh	0	0	0	0
PSP		18	9	20
SSP	13			0
Swatantra			0	0

KERALA

Party	1965	1967	1970
Congress	36	9	32
CPI	3	19	16
CPI (M)	40	52	28
Jana Sangh	0	0	0
PSP	0	0	3
SSP	13	19	6
Swatantra	1	0	0

MADHYA PRADESH

Party	1952	1957	1962	1967	1972
Congress	258	232	142	167	220
CPI	0	2	1	1	3
CPI (M)				0	0
Jana Sangh	6	10	41	78	48
PSP		12	33	9	
SSP	16	6	14	10	7
Swatantra			2	7	0

ORISSA

Party	1952	1957	1961	1967	1971
Congress	67	56	83	31	51+1
CPI	7	9	4	7	3
CPI (M)				1	2
Jana Sangh	0	0	0	0	1
PSP		11	10	21	4
SSP	10		1	2	0
Swatantra			0	49	36

PUNJAB

Party	1952	1954	1957	1962
Congress	60	22	71	49
CPI	6	4	3	9
CPI (M)				
Jana Sangh	0	0	5	4

Appendix I: Election results

PSP	0	0	0	0
SSP	0		0	
Swatantra			0	

PUNJAB

Party	1967	1969	1972
Congress	48	38	66
CPI	5	4	10
CPI (M)	3	2	1
Jana Sangh	9	8	0
PSP	0	1	
SSP	1	2	0
Swatantra	0	1	0

UTTAR PRADESH

Party	1952	1957	1962	1967	1969
Congress	390	286	249	199	211
CPI	0	9	14	13	4
CPI (M)				1	1
Jana Sangh	2	17	49	98	49
PSP	1	44	38	11	2
SSP	19	25	24	44	33
Swatantra			15	12	5

WEST BENGAL

Party	1952	1957	1962	1967
Congress	154	152	157	127
CPI	28	46	50	16
CPI (M)				43
Jana Sangh	9	0	0	1
PSP	15	21	5	7
SSP	0		0	7
Swatantra			1	1

WEST BENGAL

Party	1969	1971	1972
Congress	55	105+2	216
CPI	30	13	35
CPI (M)	80	111	14
Jana Sangh	0	1	0
PSP	5	3	
SSP	9	1	0
Swatantra	0		0

Appendix II: Research design

Eighty-eight political elites, representing the leadership of twenty-one state branches of six All-India parties, were interviewed for this study. They were drawn from a population of 119 individuals. The breakdown of interviews by state and party is as follows:

Party	State	Number of subjects	Per cent of total
Jana Sangh	National	2	67
Jana Sangh	Punjab	5	100
Jana Sangh	Uttar Pradesh	6	100
Jana Sangh	Bihar	5	100
Jana Sangh	Madhya Pradesh	6	85
Jana Sangh	Total	24	92
Swatantra	National	3	100
Swatantra	Uttar Pradesh	2	67
Swatantra	Orissa	6	85
Swatantra	Total	11	85
PSP	National	4	100
PSP	Uttar Pradesh	2	67
PSP	Bihar	4	80
PSP	West Bengal	1	50
PSP	Total	11	79
SSP	National	3	75
SSP	Uttar Pradesh	6	100
SSP	Bihar	6	75
SSP	West Bengal	2	50
SSP	Madhya Pradesh	2	50
SSP	Kerala	1	25
SSP	Total	20	67
CPI	National	0	0
CPI	Punjab	2	67
CPI	Uttar Pradesh	3	100
CPI	Bihar	4	100
CPI	West Bengal	2	40
CPI	Kerala	4	67
CPI	Total	15	65
CPI (M)	National	0	0
CPI (M)	West Bengal	5	63
CPI (M)	Kerala	2	50
CPI (M)	Total	7	54
Grand total		88	74

As can be seen from this breakdown, the more right wing a leader's party, the more likely I was to interview the leader. This slight bias was not, of course, by

Appendix II: Research design

design. Neither was it a consequence of any particular animosity on the part of the leftists for an American researcher. Instead, the relatively lower frequency with which the leftists were interviewed can be explained in terms of differences in their life styles and the consequent complexity involved in contacting some of them. Several of these individuals were engaged in hunger strikes against their state government at the time it would have been possible for me to interview them. One was in jail. Several of the leaders in Kerala could not be reached because, unfortunately, I arrived in Kerala just a few days before a crisis erupted in that state's government. The remaining subjects who were not interviewed lived in areas which were too difficult to reach within a reasonable period of time.

Among the individuals who were interviewed, all but five were either cabinet ministers in a coalition government or held the position of President, Vice President, or Secretary (or their equivalent) within a state unit or the national unit of their party. The five exceptions were identified as important party leaders by a majority of their colleagues despite their failure to hold an official position of importance.

THE INTERVIEWS

Ten pre-test interviews were conducted to facilitate the development of the interview instrument. These practice sessions with the interview instrument revealed that questions regarding caste added little information and created much discomfort for many subjects. Since the focus of the study was not on sociological determinants of coalition behavior, I decided to eliminate questions dealing with caste. Unfortunately, this does preclude an examination of the relationship between caste, on the one hand, and risk-taking and strategic predispositions on the other hand.

The instrument, which may be found in appendix III, was organized to begin with general questions regarding the overall outlook and coalition experiences of the respondents' parties. Questions then followed regarding specific events, interactions and experiences in the coalitions. Following these questions a series of speculative questions were asked which attempted to assess the problem-solving techniques of the subjects under specified hypothetical conditions. These were followed, finally, by questions about the background of the respondents.

It was possible to conduct most of the interviews in English. However, one was conducted in Malayalam (with the assistance of an interpreter), and four were held in Hindi. I used interpreters for three of these, and performed the fourth on my own. Of course, the intervention of an interpreter raises important questions regarding the accuracy of the interpretation of both the questions and the answers. In the case of the Hindi interviews, I was sufficiently experienced to be able to assess the dependability and reliability of the interpreter, and to make any necessary adjustments in the phraseology of the questions. Nevertheless, some reliability has, no doubt, been sacrificed in the interviews that involved an interpreter. In the case of the Malayalam interview, I can do no more than assume from the content of the responses that the questions were asked accurately and were interpreted reasonably.

Although much has been said about the difficulties to be encountered by an American interviewing Indian political elites, it was my experience that with very few exceptions the respondents were accessible, friendly, and eager to respond. This may have been the case because they were aware that their opponents were also being interviewed, creating a situation in which they felt obliged to

Appendix II: Research design

present 'their side of the story'. Whatever the reason, the elites were generally quite willing to cooperate. Only twice did a potential subject refuse to be interviewed, and only once was an interview terminated midstream because the subject was no longer willing to cooperate. Other incomplete interviews (and there were three others) resulted from scheduling difficulties.

Appendix III: The questionnaire

Questions preceded by an asterisk (*) were used in the coding of need for achievement. Questions preceded by a number sign (#) were used in the coding of strategic predispositions.

I would like to ask you a few questions about your party, and particularly about its strategy in coalitions. I hope you will answer them in terms of both pre-election alliances and post-election coalitions. Your answers will, of course, be completely confidential.

*1. Would you please tell me what are the most important objectives that your party has for 1970? Any others?
*2. How do you think coalitions affect the public image and political influence of your party?
3. How do you think they have affected the public image and political influence of your coalition partners?
4. What criteria do you use in deciding on the party or legislators with whom you coalesce?
5. Are there any parties with which your party would not even consider a coalition? Why?
6. Of these parties, which would you least want to coalesce with? Which next? ... Finally?
7. Does your party usually wait to be offered a coalition, or does it sometimes initiate the negotiations itself? Why? Could you give me some examples?
*8. Do you think that there is any advantage to initiating negotiations? What are the advantages?
9. In negotiating a coalition, what are you most likely to discuss first? Then what? Any other things?
10. What factors have most commonly caused coalition negotiations with your party to fail? Why?
#11. In the give and take of forming a coalition, what are the things your party is most willing to make concessions on? Why?
#12. What other things has your party conceded?
#13. In which areas is the party least willing to make concessions? Why?
#14. What other things has your party refused to concede?
#15. If in the midst of a coalition, some party or group of parties offered your party a more accommodating alliance, would you accept it? Why?
#*16. Would you rather win a legislative victory that would lead to the breakup of a coalition your party was in, or would you rather have the coalition remain intact and not win the victory? Why?
*17. Of course being in the government gives you the opportunity to distribute patronage. What effect has this had on the relations between the party's leaders and its rank and file membership?
*18. Do you feel that the distribution of patronage can be an effective tool for improving the party's electoral appeal? How?

Appendix III: The questionnaire

*19. Can patronage improve the party's legislative effectiveness? How?
20. Which of the following aspects of coalitions do you think contributes most to your party's electoral appeal: (a) publicity gained from being in the government; (b) the psychological boost gained by being part of the government; (c) the opportunity to distribute patronage; or (d) the opportunity to implement a program? Which is next most important? Which is third?
21. Why do you think that (a, b, c, or d) is most effective?
*22. In what ways do coalitions affect the organization and cohesion of your party? Its discipline?
23. Does your party's state or national leadership generally make coalition decisions? Why?
24. Are decisions about pre-election alliances made first at the district, state, or national level? Why?
*25. What has your party gained from joining coalitions?
26. What has it lost?
27. Would your party have gained more by not joining? Why?
28. In your experience, did the bigger or the smaller parties in the coalition gain more? Why?
*29. What did you originally expect to gain from the coalitions?
30. How do you think your original expectations compare with your actual experience? Why?
*31. Do you think you have gained more or less than the parties you coalesced with? In what ways?
32. (If appropriate) Then how do you account for the the results of the midterm election?
33. What have you learned about the other parties from your coalition experience. Anything else?
#*34. Does your party have a coalition strategy? What is it?
*35. Compared to coalitions, what are the advantages and disadvantages of pre-election alliances? Any others?
36. Do you think that coalitions that are based on pre-election alliances are more successful? Why?
*37. Do they cost more in the sense of limiting the spread of your party's organization? Why?
38. Please list the following choices from best to worst:
   (a) a coalition with two parties and 55 per cent of the legislature;
   (b) a coalition with five parties and 55 per cent of the legislature;
   (c) a coalition with two parties and 75 per cent of the legislature; or
   (d) a coalition with five parties and 75 per cent of the legislature.
39. Why have you chosen them in that order?
40. How large should a coalition be in terms of the size of the council of ministers? Why?
41. What should be the criteria for distributing ministries? Any others? Why?
*42. This is a very hypothetical question. I realize that this situation shall never arise in India. Nevertheless, I am interested in your general attitude toward the problem. Let's say there were a legislature with one dominant party, several parties of approximately equal strength, and one or two weaker parties. If in that legislature your party had 18 per cent and the other parties had 30 per cent, 20 per cent, 15 per cent, 11 per cent, and 6

Appendix III: The questionnaire

per cent respectively, which of the following do you think would be the best coalition for your party: (Show cards in random order.)

(a) 30, 20, 18=68% (b) 30, 18, 15=63% (c) 30, 18, 11=59%
(d) 30, 18, 6=54% (e) 20, 18, 15=53% (f) 20, 18, 11, 6=55%

Why would you prefer that one?

43. If you could not form that coalition, which would you prefer next? Why?
44. Would you please list, in the order of importance, with the most important first, the ministerial posts that your party most hopes to capture when it forms a coalition government? Are there any others? Why do you most prefer these?
45. What do you think about expanding the size of the ministry in order to accommodate new members of the coalition? Why?
46. What other ways of accommodating newcomers are there?
47. In negotiating toward a merger with another party, is it important that your party maintains its identity after the merger? Why?
48. Would your party object to having the identity of its merger partner maintained if its identity were not maintained? Why?
49. When did you first become interested in politics? Why?
50. Have any other members of your family ever been active in politics?
51. What organizations, other than your party, do you belong to? Are you especially active in any of them? Which ones?
52. What offices have you held in your party? When? What office do you hold now?
53. Besides politics, what is your occupation?
54. How much formal education have you had?
55. Have you ever belonged to any other political party? When? Any others?
56. What was your father's occupation?
57. For most of your childhood, would you say your family had a poor, moderate, or high income?
58. (If an MLA or an MP) Are you from an urban, semi-urban, semi-rural, or rural constituency?
59. How old are you?

Notes

2. A THEORY OF COALITION BEHAVIOR

1. The long-term is defined as some nth iteration in a series of decision-making situations such that it represents the last iteration during which an actor can convert any resources it obtained from the political environment into subsequent political influence. The period immediately prior to an election, or immediately prior to a constitutional convention would be examples of the long-term. The short-term is defined as the periods of normal interaction within a given political environment. An example of the short-term is from the end of an election to the period prior to the initiation of campaigns (either for a party's nomination, or for election to a political office) for a subsequent election.

2. Typically, one either infers goals from the observed behavior of decision-makers or one infers behavior from the goals that are assumed to be preferred by the decision-makers. The latter strategy is what Riker and Ordeshook call posited preference, while the former strategy is what they call revealed preference. Posited preference allows one to examine behavior from the perspective of an assumed goal and from the assumption of rationality. Revealed preference is used to discover the goals pursued by decision-makers, given their known actions and the assumption of rationality. I have chosen to postulate, or posit goal preferences, rather than attempt to discover, or reveal the 'true' goals sought by political parties. More detailed discussions of the advantages and disadvantages of these approaches may be found in William Riker and Peter Ordeshook, *An Introduction to Positive Political Theory* (Englewood Cliffs, NJ: Prentice-Hall, 1973), pp. 14–15 and in Steven Brams, 'Positive Coalition Theory: The Relationship Between Postulated Goals and Derived Behavior', in *Political Science Annual*, IV, ed. Cornelius Cotter (Indianapolis: Bobbs-Merrill, 1973), pp. 3–40.

3. Additional definitions of the coalition concept can be found in Brams, 'Positive Coalition Theory' and in Bruce Bueno de Mesquita and J. David Singer, 'Alliances, Capabilities, and War: A Review and Synthesis', *Political Science Annual*, IV, ed. Cornelius Cotter (Indianapolis: Bobbs-Merrill Company, 1973), pp. 237–41.

4. It is common to distinguish between winning, losing, and blocking coalitions. I prefer to distinguish only between winning coalitions and losing coalitions. Since a blocking coalition does not permit its members to achieve their goals, it is a losing coalition with respect to their shared objectives. If a coalition has enough resources to block another coalition's efforts to achieve a particular goal, then with respect to the blocking coalition's desire to prevent another group's success, it is a winning coalition. In this way, a coalition's status always depends upon the particular goal in question. This makes the resources that a coalition holds subject to varying degrees of importance, depending on their relationship to the particular goal being pursued at the moment. An interesting discussion of the uses, and limitations, of blocking coalitions can be found in William Riker, *The Theory of Political Coalitions* (New Haven: Yale University Press, 1962), pp. 40, 103–4, 255–6.

5. Collective goods are indivisible goods available to all members of a collectivity. Private goods are divisible and need not be available to all members of a collectivity. Thus, one must purchase private goods, while membership in the

Notes

appropriate collectivity is sufficient for one to obtain collective goods. Several interesting questions are related to the behavior of decision-makers in groups that provide collective goods. For a discussion of these questions see Mancur Olson, *The Logic of Collective Action: Public Goods and the Theory of Groups* (New York: Schocken Books, 1968); Mancur Olson and Richard Zeckhauser, 'An Economic Theory of Alliances', *Review of Economics and Statistics*, XLVIII (1966), pp. 266–79; Norman Frohlich and Joe A. Oppenheimer, 'I Get By with a Little Help from My Friends', *World Politics*, XXIII (1970), pp. 104–20; Norman Frohlich, Joe A. Oppenheimer, and Oran Young, *Political Leadership and Collective Goods* (Princeton: Princeton University Press, 1971); and Riker and Ordeshook, *An Introduction*, pp. 69–77.

6. An example should make this clear. Let us say a group of people pool their time, money and talents to search for a cure for cancer. Unfortunately, their pooled resources are inadequate and their search fails. Their coalition has lost, but there is no winner. Had they succeeded, there would not have been a loser, at least in the normal sense of the term. That is, when a coalition competes against 'nature', rather than against people, there can be winners or losers; there need not be both.

7. In large groups, actors have incentives to provide less than their 'fair share' of the resources required to secure a collective good. In such situations, members of a coalition are commonly encouraged to contribute more resources by the threat of punishment or the opportunity for additional rewards. Both the offer of additional rewards, and the threat of punishment are side payments. Because of the central role played by side payments in coalitions formed for the purpose of providing a collective good, very few coalitions are actually excluded from the theory to be presented because of their primary concern with the provision of collective goods.

8. For the sake of variety, I use contestant, actor, participant, group, and player interchangeably throughout the text. If I intend them to mean different things, I specify the difference in the text.

9. Size is used to refer to the quantity of rule-relevant resources controlled by a political actor. Thus, the largest political party in a legislature is the one controlling the most seats. If one were to measure a party's popularity, the percentage of votes it secures would be a better measure of size than the number of legislative seats it secures.

10. This assumption simply recognizes the fact that any political participant has the option of withdrawing from a coalition if it is better off on its own. Further discussion of this assumption is found in Riker, *The Theory*, pp. 39, 254.

11. This point is reinforced by an examination of the studies contained in Sven Groennings, E. W. Kelley, and Michael Leiserson, eds.,*The Study of Coalition Behavior: Theoretical Perspectives and Cases from Four Continents* (New York: Holt, Rinehart and Winston, 1970).

12. Various formulations of this assumption may be found in Riker, *The Theory*, William Gamson, 'A Theory of Coalition Formation', *American Sociological Review*, XXVI (1961), pp. 373–82; Steven Brams and William Riker, 'Models of Coalition Formation in Voting Bodies', *Mathematical Applications in Political Science*, VI (Charlottesville: University Press of Virginia, 1972), pp. 79–124; Theodore Caplow, 'A Theory of Coalitions in the Triad', *American Sociological Review*, XXI (1956), pp. 488–92; Theodore Caplow, 'Further Development of a Theory of Coalitions in the Triad', *American Journal of Sociology*, LXIV (1959), pp. 488–93; and John Von Neumann and Oscar Morgenstern, *The*

Theory of Games and Economic Behavior (Princeton: Princeton University Press, 1944).

13. In a system with n members, let the payoff to each member in a particular situation equal $v(1), v(2), \ldots, v(n)$. The situation is zero sum if the sum of $v(1)+v(2)+ \ldots +v(n)$ equals zero. Put somewhat differently, let i refer to winners and j refer to losers, then a zero-sum situation exists if

$$\sum_{i=1}^{m-x} v(i) = -\sum_{j=m-x+1}^{x} v(j)$$

14. Riker, for example, assumes that the value of the total payoff varies as a function of the winning coalition. Gamson, on the other hand, assumes that the value of the payoff is constant. See Riker, *The Theory*, and Gamson, 'A Theory', William Gamson, 'An Experimental Test of a Theory of Coalition Formation', *American Sociological Review*, XXVI (1961), pp. 565–73; William Gamson, 'Coalition Formation at Presidential Nominating Conventions', *American Journal of Sociology*, LXVIII (1962), pp. 151–71.

15. Among those who have made interesting uses of ideology in their discussions of coalition behavior are Michael Leiserson, 'Factions and Coalitions in One-Party Japan: An Interpretation Based on the Theory of Games', *American Political Science Review*, LXII (1968), pp. 770–87; Michael Leiserson, 'Power and Ideology in Coalition Behavior: An Experimental Study', in Groennings *et al.*, *The Study of Coalition Behavior*, pp. 323–35; William Gamson, 'Experimental Studies of Coalition Formation', in *Advances in Experimental Social Psychology*, ed. Leonard Berkowitz (New York: Academic Press, 1964), pp. 82–110; Bruce Russett, 'Components of an Operational Theory of International Alliance Formation', *Journal of Conflict Resolution*, XII (1968), pp. 285–301; Robert Axelrod, *Conflict of Interest: A Theory of Divergent Goals with Applications to Politics* (Chicago: Markham, 1970), pp. 165–87.

16. See the discussion in Brams, 'Positive Coalition Theory', pp. 16–24.

17. A much lengthier discussion of this observation is contained in Riker's elaboration of the disequilibrium principle. This discussion is found, primarily, in *The Theory*, chapter 9.

18. Incompatibility is a necessary condition in political systems that include more than one group. This follows from the assumption that groups form to pursue particular preference orderings with respect to the options available to the society. If two sets of people had identical preference orderings with respect to desired ends and desired means of achieving those ends, they would have no reason to form separate groups (barring ignorance of each other's preferences). Consequently, the existence of more than one group is *prima facie* evidence of incompatibilities with respect to at least some goals or some preferred strategies.

19. Gamson, 'A Theory', p. 374.

20. This is a restatement of the conditions required for a mixed motive game. That is, the episodic condition, or any other condition that provides a basis for coalition formation in the face of incompatibilities, suggests that some participants can do better by coordinating their behavior than they can do by acting alone. It also suggests, of course, that there is no outcome which maximizes the payoff to everybody. In other words, there must be losers as well as winners. There are, of course, an enormous number of discussions of mixed motive, pure coordination, and pure competition games. One particularly clear explanation of the differences among these games is Thomas C. Schelling, 'The Strategy of

Notes

Conflict: Prospectus for the Reorientation of Game Theory', *Journal of Conflict Resolution*, II (1958), pp. 203–64.

21. That is, for all members of a winning coalition, it is assumed that

$$\sum_{a=1}^{r} p_i(O_a)_{t+n} \geqslant \sum_{a=1}^{r} p_i(O_a)_t$$

where O_a refers to outcome a, p_i refers to the probability of some actor i in the winning coalition achieving the outcomes 1 through r in set a. The variable t refers to the present and $t+n$ refers to some future situation. It is assumed that the set of outcomes 1 through r exclude the shared goal for which the specific winning coalition was formed. This equation simply posits that every member of a winning coalition can either maintain or improve its probability of achieving its unshared goals relative to all the other members of the winning coalition. Of course, this must be false. If the members of the coalition are assumed to have incompatible goals, then if one increases its probability of achieving goal r, the probability of not r must have been diminished. Since the presence of incompatibilities requires that for some goal r there is at least one member who prefers r and one who prefers not r, the episodic condition can not actually permit any actor to enhance its future prospects of achieving r. If it did, then some coalition member's probability of achieving not r would have to be decreased, thereby violating the episodic condition. Consequently, the best actors can hope for under the episodic condition is that they maintain their likelihood of achieving their unshared goals relative to their coalition partners, while increasing their likelihood relative to those outside the winning coalition.

22. That is, assume actors B and C comprise a winning coalition against actor A. Let B have b capabilities, C have c capabilities, and A have a capabilities. The payoff received by the coalition is equal to $a-e$. The portion of that payoff which can be converted into future political influence is equal to v, where $a-e \geqslant v$. B's fair share of the convertible portion of the payoff is $v(b/b+c)$. C's fair share is $v(c/b+c)$. With side payments equal to s, C's actual share of the payoff is $v(c+s/b+c)$, while B's actual share is $v(b-s/b+c)$. As a result of this distribution of the payoff, B's capabilities at $t+n$ equal $b+v(b-s/b+c)$ and C's equal $c+v(c+s/b+c)$. A's political influence is diminished to $a-v$. Although B and C may still have fewer total capabilities than A, the magnitude of the inequality is reduced. It is also possible that they now have as much as or more than A. Consequently, both have increased their political influence relative to A. This is, of course, one expected consequence of joining a coalition. B's capabilities may still be greater than C's, but the magnitude of this inequality has been reduced by $v(2s)$. That is, C has increased its political influence at a greater rate than B. Since political influence is assumed to be required to achieve goals, this indicates that C's future influence has increased at the expense of A and, to the extent of $v(2s)$, at the expense of its partner B. The increase in C's influence which is due to the side payment is, by definition, a violation of the episodic condition.

23. The fair share payoff described in note 22 is an example of the parity norm. The parity norm can be measured in terms of the proportion of absolute resources that an actor contributes to the total resource pool of a coalition. Alternatively, the parity norm can be measured in terms of the pivotal power an actor contributes to a winning coalition. That is, it can be measured in terms of the share of essential resources that an actor contributes. This approach to the distribution of payoffs is discussed in Lloyd S. Shapley, 'A Value for N-Person Games', in *Contributions to the Theory of Games*, eds. H. W. Kuhn and A. W.

Tucker, *Annals of Mathematical Studies*, no. 28 (Princeton: Princeton University Press, 1953), pp. 307–17; William Riker and Lloyd S. Shapley, 'Weighted Voting: A Mathematical Analysis for Instrumental Judgements', in *Nomos X: Representation*, eds. Roland Pennock and John W. Chapman (New York: Atherton Press, 1968), pp. 199–216; and Riker and Ordeshook, *An Introduction*, pp. 163–75.

24. An assumption underlying this study is that most interesting coalitions permit actors to acquire benefits which can alter their probability of achieving their unshared goals in the future. Some examples of this type of coalition include electoral coalitions where incumbency, as a payoff, increases one's likelihood of being elected in the future; governmental coalitions where holding certain cabinet positions increases one's access to the mass media, to patronage, and to other resources which can enhance one's future electoral appeal; wartime alliances where the acquisition of additional territory or other natural resources can increase a nation's political influence; peacetime alliances where economies of scale, or protective umbrellas can conserve one's own resources and thereby free them for application to other sectors besides defense. Such applications can, of course, increase the government's ability to mobilize support among a broader set of constituents within the nation.

25. The side payments that a coalition member offers a partner must come from the member's share of the payoff. That is, the value of a coalition cannot be negative, in an absolute sense, for any member. If it were, that member would have an incentive to withdraw. It will be recalled that no actor can do worse than in a coalition by itself. This is, in fact, the basis of Riker's rejoinder to Richard Butterworth's 'A Research Note on the Size of Winning Coalitions', *American Political Science Review*, LXV (1971), pp. 741–45. Riker's rejoinder is found in the same issue of the *Review*, pp. 745–50.

26. There are several proofs of the size principle. The initial proof is in Riker, *The Theory*, pp. 32–46 and 247–78. Subsequent proofs include William Riker, 'A New Proof of the Size Principle,' in *Mathematical Applications in Political Science*, ed. Joseph Bernd, II (Dallas: Southern Methodist University Press, 1967), pp. 167–74; and Riker and Ordeshook, *An Introduction*, pp. 176–201.

27. Gamson's derivation of the cheapest winning coalition hypothesis may be found in 'A Theory'. Gamson includes the parity norm primarily because it is the most frequently observed decision-rule governing the distribution of payoffs. It is not a requirement of the theory in a formal sense, so much as it is an acknowledgment of a sociological observation. A recent test of the parity norm in real political coalitions can be found in Eric Browne and Mark Franklin, 'Aspects of Coalition Payoffs in Parliamentary Democracies', *American Political Science Review*, LXVII (June 1973), pp. 453–69.

28. Assume three actors A, B, and C, with the following distribution of resources $A > B > C$, but $A < B + C$. B's parity payoff in $B \cup C$ is $B/B \cup C$, while B's parity payoff in $A \cup B$ is $B/A \cup B$. $B/A \cup B < B/B \cup C$. Consequently B prefers $B \cup C$ to $A \cup B$. C's expected payoff in $B \cup C$ is $C/B \cup C$, while it is $C/A \cup C$ in coalition $A \cup C$. $C/A \cup C < C/B \cup C$. Consequently C prefers coalition $B \cup C$ to $A \cup C$. Since both B and C have fewer capabilities than A it follows that $B \cup C$ is a smaller winning coalition than either $A \cup B$ or $A \cup C$. That is, the cheapest winning coalition is preferred when the payoff is constant for all coalitions and when the parity norm is applied.

29. Riker hypothesizes that $A \cup C$ might form instead of $B \cup C$ under special circumstances. This occurs when actor A, taking a zero payoff for itself, offers

Notes

its expected benefits to C who benefits more from this arrangement than from $B \cup C$. Of course, B may make a counter-offer, in which case the outcome is uncertain between $A \cup C$ and $B \cup C$. A fuller discussion of this case is found in Riker, *The Theory*, pp. 286–8.

30. Axelrod, *Conflict of Interest*; Gamson, 'Experimental Studies', and several studies in Groennings *et al.*, *The Study of Coalition Behavior*, deal with the question of ideology in coalitions.

31. The question of bargaining steps and ideological preferences is dealt with by Gamson, 'Experimental Studies'; and by J. C. Burris and R. Frye, 'The Effects of Initial Resources of Individuals upon their Selection of a Partner in the Formation of Coalitions', paper presented to the Southeastern Psychological Association Convention, 1966.

32. In addition to the studies that apply pivotal power to which I have already referred, one might wish to read W. Vinacke and A. Arkoff, 'Experimental Study of Coalitions in the Triad', *American Sociological Review*, XXII (1957), pp. 406–14; H. Kelley and A. J. Arrowood, 'Coalitions in the Triad: Critique and Experiment', *Sociometry*, XXIII (1960), pp. 231–44; R. Willis, 'Coalitions in the Tetrad', *Sociometry*, XXV (1962), pp. 358–76.

33. Caplow 'A Theory of Coalitions'; and Caplow, 'Further Development'.

34. J. Chertkoff, 'A Revision of Caplow's Coalition Theory', *Journal of Experimental Social Psychology*, III (1967), pp. 172–7; J. Chertkoff, 'The Effects of Probability of Future Success on Coalition Formation', *Journal of Experimental Social Psychology*, II (1966), pp. 265–77; J. Chertkoff, 'Sociopsychological Theories and Research on Coalition Formation', in Groennings *et al.*, *The Study of Coalition Behavior*, pp. 297–322.

35. By discrete I mean that coalition behavior at t_n is independent of coalition behavior at t_{n-1}. That is, earlier coalition experiences do not have a systematic impact on subsequent coalition behavior.

36. J. Chertkoff, 'A Revision'.

37. Among the coalition studies that include feedback effects concerning prior coalition behavior are Richard Ofshe and Lynne Ofshe, 'Choice Behavior in Coalition Games', *Behavioral Science*, XV (1970), pp. 337–49; Richard Ofshe and Lynne Ofshe, 'Social Choice and Utility in Coalition Formation', *Sociometry*, XXXII (1969), pp. 330–47; Lynne Ofshe and Richard Ofshe, *Utility and Choice in Social Interaction* (Englewood Cliffs, NJ: Prentice-Hall, 1970); B. Lieberman, 'Experimental Studies of Conflict in Some Two-Person and Three-Person Games', *Mathematical Methods in Small Group Processes*, eds. J. Criswell, H. Solomon, and P. Suppes (Palo Alto: Stanford University Press, 1962), pp. 203–20.

38. Lieberman, 'Experimental Studies'.

39. The anti-competitive approach is reviewed in Gamson, 'Experimental Studies'. Among the more interesting applications of this approach are J. Bond and W. Vinacke, 'Coalitions in Mixed-Sex Triads', *Sociometry*, XXIV (1961), pp. 61–75; P. Hoffman, L. Festinger, and D. H. Lawrence, 'Tendencies Toward Group Comparability in Competitive Bargaining', *Human Relations*, VII (1954), pp. 141–60; T. Uesugi and W. Vinacke, 'Strategy in a Feminine Game', *Sociometry*, XXVI (1963), pp. 75–88; B. Lieberman, 'i-Trust: A Notion of Trust in Three-Person Games and International Affairs', *Journal of Conflict Resolution*, VIII (1964), pp. 271–80; and R. C. Gates, 'Armchair, Board Room, Cabinet: The Province of Economics', Inaugural Lecture, University of Queensland (1967).

40. H. Wolff, *The Sociology of George Simmel* (New York: The Free Press, 1950) especially pp. 165–6.

41. An example of this lumpiness problem is found in Browne and Franklin, 'Aspects of Coalition Payoffs in Parliamentary Democracies', *American Political Science Review*, LXVII (June 1973), pp. 453–9.

42. The literature referred to in note 39 contains many empirical observations of this phenomenon.

43. Caplow, 'Further Development'.

44. Gamson, 'Experimental Studies', pp. 100–1.

45. Hoffman *et al.*, 'Tendencies Toward Group Comparability'.

46. Bond and Vinacke, 'Coalitions'. Considerably more discussion of this important point is provided later in this chapter.

47. Once again I want to stress the sociological aspects of the parity norm in addition to its theoretical characteristics. It is, as noted in the studies of Ofshe and Ofshe, by Lieberman, by Gamson, and by others to whom I have referred, the most commonly observed decision-rule applied to the distribution of coalition payoffs – provided the payoffs are not redistributive.

48. This condition is intended to reflect the possibility that a member of a winning coalition can increase its resource base at a rate which is dangerously slower than the rate of a relevant challenger within the coalition. A relevant challenger is one who is likely to oppose one's interests in future coalitions. The situation referred to in note 22 where side payments resulted in differential rates of growth in influence might be an example of a situation where a winner has incentives to terminate its winning coalition.

49. Of course, if a mixed strategist is in a coalition only with competitors, the probability that the coalition will be terminated as soon as any competitive demand is made by anyone is very high. As I demonstrate shortly, it is rational to make a competitive demand during the first iteration of a coalition situation that includes at least one cooperator. In a coalition where competitive demands can be directed only at competitors, the presence of a demand in the initial choice-situation almost inevitably leads to the surpassing of some participants' tolerance limits. Such a coalition is doomed to rapid extinction. I assume, therefore, that empirically observable coalitions include at least one member who is willing to accept competitive demands.

50. Melvin Guyer, 'A Review of the Literature on Zero-Sum Games in the Social Sciences' report, Mental Health Research Institute, University of Michigan (n.d.).

51. In the earliest iterations of the game all players tended toward the competitive strategy. This is, of course, the minimax solution in episodic prisoners' dilemma games.

52. To be somewhat more precise, it is not possible to distinguish between a competitive strategy and a mixed strategy when only one episode in a series of iterations has occurred. In fact, under the episodic condition there is no such thing as a mixed strategy (at least as that term is used here). This follows from the fact that in a single, discrete episode one can either make demands or not make demands. If no demands are made one is cooperative and if some demands are made one is competitive. Thus, even when there are several iterations under the episodic condition, the discreteness of episodes precludes the use of a mixed strategy. The fact that a competive demand is most likely to be rewarded in the first iteration of a redistributive situation follows from the observation that the initial iteration is a discrete event, at least in the sense that there were no prior iterations in the situation, and therefore K_j was equal to zero

53. A particularly clear presentation of the derivation and implications of the

Notes

preference equation can be found in Riker and Ordeshook, *An Introduction*, pp. 45–62.

54. An example should help clarify any confusion between the utility of an outcome, the probability of achieving the outcome, given different strategies, and the utility of the strategies. One might desire to be a millionaire. Such an individual might have saved some money in order to invest it. Two strategies confront the individual. The money could be invested in playing roulette or in securing a medical degree. Although one is unlikely to become a millionaire as a doctor, one is almost certain not to become a millionaire playing roulette. A hard working, exceptionally able doctor in the appropriate location might succeed in becoming a millionaire. A roulette player, on the other hand, is almost certain to lose his money in the long run. This follows from an examination of the payoffs associated with different bets and the probability of such bets being successful. Still, one might value the enjoyment associated with playing roulette more than the hard work involved in studying and practicing medicine. Consequently, if the fun of roulette is valued more than the desire to be a millionaire (adjusted to reflect the inequality in the probability of this outcome given the two available strategies), then the higher risk strategy of playing roulette would be pursued by a rational decision-maker. If the utility for becoming a millionaire were great enough, then the individual would study medicine even though he associated a greater utility with playing roulette than with studying medicine.

55. If the actor is an essential member of the winning coalition, then its ouster means the termination of the entire coalition. If the actor can be replaced, or if the coalition is still winning after the actor is ousted, then the other members have all the more incentive to oust such an exploitative partner.

56. Need for achievement is defined in greater detail in John Atkinson, ed., *Motives in Fantasy, Action and Society* (Princeton: D. Van Nostrand Company, 1958), pp. 179–204.

57. It should be noted that need for achievement is hypothesized to lead to a preference for the mixed strategy. I am not, however, hypothesizing that a preference for a mixed strategy is necessarily associated with high need for achievement. That is, need for achievement is a sufficient, but not a necessary condition for some forms of the mixed strategy. This distinction will be clearer once table 2.3 and the attendant discussion have been presented.

58. Among the many studies that underscore the relationship between risk-taking behavior and need for achievement are John Atkinson, *An Introduction to Motivation* (Princeton: D. Van Nostrand, 1964); Atkinson, *Motives*, David McClelland, *The Achieving Society* (New York: The Free Press, 1961); and J. Brown, *The Motivation of Behavior* (New York: McGraw Hill, 1961).

59. Conditions (*d*), (*e*), and (*f*) follow from the computations reported in table 2.2.

60. The cooperative strategy follows most closely the behavior of decision-makers who follow the anti-competitive approach in their coalition dealings. Such individuals are likely to have low need for achievement and high need for affiliation. Need for affiliation is 'a concern with establishing, maintaining, or restoring a positive affect relationship with another'. The desire of such individuals to maintain a favorable social atmosphere makes them particularly susceptible to the manipulations of demanding coalition partners. They are, therefore, desirable partners for individuals with high need for achievement. Additional discussion of need for affiliation is found in John Atkinson, J. Heyns, and J. Veroff, 'The Effect of Experimental Arousal of the Affiliation Motive on

The Indian context: 1967–1971

Thematic Apperception', in Atkinson, *Motives*, pp. 95–104. Additional discussion of the relationship between need for affiliation and coalition behavior can be found in Bruce Bueno de Mesquita, 'A Model of Coalition Behavior: The Case of India, 1967–1971' (Ph.D. dissertation, Department of Political Science, University of Michigan, 1971), especially pp. 126–40.

3. THE INDIAN CONTEXT: 1967–1971

1. Indian politics takes place in an ethnically, linguistically, religiously, culturally, and socially diverse environment. This diversity makes India an excellent laboratory from which to study coalition politics. As diversity increases, the randomization of variables exogenous to the theory presented here probably increases as well. This randomization facilitates statistical inferences by reducing the correlation of error terms. It is in this sense that I mean India is representative of the general pattern of coalition experiences.
2. Grand coalitions include all possible members.
3. There is a great deal of debate as to why the opposition, which controlled a majority of the seats in the legislature, failed to form a government. Whether this failure resulted from their inability to agree with each other, or from interference by the governor of the state would be an interesting study in its own right.
4. Deendayal Upadhyaya, Bharatiya Jana Sangh Report on Fourth General Elections (Bharatiya Pratinidhi Session, New Delhi, April 21–3, 1967), p. 4.
5. Jagdish Prasad Mathur, *Jana Deep Souvenir* (14th Annual Session of BJS, December 1967), pp. 32–3.
6. *Ibid.*, p. 33.
7. *Ibid.*, p. 35.
8. Resolutions Passed by the All-India Working Committee (BJS, June 14–16, 1968), pp. 33–4.
9. Ram Prakash Gupta, *Jana Deep Souvenir*, (BJS) p. 72.
10. There are several interesting discussions of the development of the Jana Sangh's organization. Among the more interesting ones are: Motilal A. Jhangiani, *Jana Sangh and Swatantra: A Profile of the Rightist Parties in India* (Bombay: Manaktalas, 1967); Jean A. Curran, *Militant Hinduism in Indian Politics: A Study of the RSS* (New York: Institute of Pacific Relations, 1951); Craig Baxter, *The Jana Sangh: A Biography of an Indian Political Party* (Philadelphia: University of Pennsylvania Press, 1969).
11. There are several party documents that express this strategic orientation rather clearly. Among them are: *Jana Deep Souvenir*, p. 36; *AIWC Assessment of Mid-Term Polls*, February 1969; Atal Bihari Vajpayee, Presidential Address, April 25, 1969.
12. For a thorough study of the Swatantra Party, especially with respect to its history, and its base of support, see Howard Erdman, *The Swatantra Party and Indian Conservatism* (Cambridge: Cambridge University Press, 1967).
13. Angela S. Burger, *Opposition in a Dominant-Party System* (Berkeley: University of California Press, 1969); also interviews with Jana Sangh and Swatantra elites conducted between November 1969 and June 1970.
14. Swatantra Party, *Third National Convention* (Bangalore, February 1–2, 1964), pp. 52–3.
15. *Ibid.*
16. 49.1 per cent of the Indian political elites interviewed in connection with

Notes

this study agreed that pre-election alliances were harmful to the organizational development of their parties ($N=69$). This may, incidentally, account for their failure to forge many pre-election alliances in 1970 and 1971. Of course, following the fifth general election, many of these same opposition parties were severely defeated by the Indira Gandhi branch of the Congress Party, i.e., the Congress (R).

17. Francis A. Meckery, 'The Politics of Coalitions', *Swarajya* (February 21, 1970), p. 9.
18. Interview with a member of the Orissa cabinet, January 1970.
19. Sunil Das, *West Bengal Polity Today* (PSP, June 15, 1968), p. 4.
20. Resolution on Political Situation (PSP National Conference, Baroda, 1970).
21. Prem Bhasin, *The Fateful Period* (Praja Socialist Party, n.d.), pp. 5–6.
22. SSP, *Statement of Principles, Programme and Political Line* (April 3–6, 1966), p. 34.
23. The SSP placed considerable emphasis on the need for a time-bound program. By imposing such a restriction on non-Congress coalitions, the SSP leadership hoped to reduce the extent to which the opposition parties would use the coalitions to further their own political ends. At the same time, it provided the SSP leadership with a mechanism to withdraw from any coalition with which they were not satisfied. For details on the SSP's position with respect to pre-election alliances see the party's *Election Manifesto* (1967), especially pp. 1–2.
24. This view was most clearly expressed by S. M. Joshi in *Choice Before Socialists* (SSP, November 15, 1969), p. 5. Joshi's views, however, represented the objectives of only one wing of the SSP. While he and his supporters were eager to advance the position of all socialist parties, other leaders in the SSP were eager to improve disproportionately the role of the SSP and, of course, their own position as well. This particular distinction became somewhat academic after the SSP and the PSP merged into a single socialist party.
25. Om Prakash Deepak and Roma Mitra, 'The Elections and After', *Mankind* (April 1967), p. 27.
26. CPI, *Review of Fourth, General Election* (April 23–30, 1967), pp. 50–1.
27. *Ibid.*, p. 25.
28. Since the fifth general election, the CPI has participated in a coalition government in Kerala and in West Bengal. Both of these coalitions are with the Indira Gandhi branch of the Congress Party. There can be little doubt that these coalitions are benefiting the CPI, particularly since participation in the governments is giving the CPI an opportunity to 'catch up' with its major rival – the CPI(M) – in both of these states. The benefit derived from the Kerala coalition is probably heightened by the fact that the CPI leads the government in that state.
29. CPI(M), *Election Review and Party's Tasks* (April 10–16, 1967), p. 12.
30. CPI(M), Political Resolutions (December 23–9, 1968), p. 41.
31. Some important leaders in the SSP differed with the party's general attitude toward anti-Congressism after the Congress Party split into the Congress (R) and the Congress (O). Among those leaders who preferred to give greater support to the Congress (R) were S. M. Joshi, Karpuri Thakur, and Ramanand Tiwari.
32. Burger, *Opposition*; Donald Zagoria, 'The Ecology of Peasant Communism in India', *American Political Science Review*, LXV (1971), pp. 144–60.
33. The data for this discussion were provided by Bashiruddin Ahmad of the Centre for the Study of Developing Societies, Delhi.
34. H. Erdman, *The Swatantra Party*, and Ahmad (see note 33).

The Indian context: 1967–1971

35. 95.1 per cent reportedly are either illiterate or have only a minimal amount of education, compared to 84.2 per cent of Congress voters in these two categories.

36. Only 74.9 per cent of Jana Sangh voters were either illiterate or only slightly educated. Compared to most other parties in India, this is a rather good showing.

37. The data on income, religious minorities, scheduled castes and scheduled tribes, literacy, urbanization, and radio receivers are from Myron Weiner, ed., *State Politics in India* (Princeton: Princeton University Press, 1968), pp. 11, 28, and 33. Election data are from Craig Baxter, *District Voting Trends in India* (New York: Southern Asian Institute of Columbia University, 1969); R. Chandidas, L. Clark, R. Fontera, and W. Morehouse, eds., *India Votes* (New York: Humanities Press, 1968).

38. Paul Brass, *Factional Politics in an Indian State: The Congress Party in Uttar Pradesh* (Berkeley: University of California Press, 1965); Burger, *Opposition*; Rajni Kothari, *Politics in India* (Boston: Little, Brown, 1970).

39. The three states were Uttar Pradesh, Madhya Pradesh, and Haryana.

40. These states include West Bengal, Kerala, Orissa, and Madras.

41. Burger, *Opposition*.

42. Lloyd Rudolph and Susanne Rudolph, *The Modernity of Tradition* (Chicago: University of Chicago Press, 1967); Lloyd Rudolph and Susanne Rudolph, 'Political Role of India's Caste Associations', *Pacific Affairs*, XXXIII (1960), pp. 5–22.

43. For a detailed account of the events in Haryana see Subhash Kashyap, *The Politics of Defection* (New Delhi: Associated Publishing House, 1969).

44. Supporting evidence for this interpretation can be found in the *Times of India*, January 16, 1968.

45. Kashyap, *The Politics of Defection*, p. 430.

46. A lengthy discussion of Charan Singh's strategy can be found in Subrata Kumar Mitra, 'Role of the Bharatiya Kranti Dal in the Politics of Uttar Pradesh, 1967–70', unpublished M.A. thesis, Delhi University, 1971.

47. Charan Singh, Speech, March 4, 1967.

48. Charan Singh's willingness to lose supporters who were not crucial to the survival of his coalition is an excellent example of what William Riker has called the disequilibrium principle in *The Theory*.

49. Kashyap, *The Politics of Defection*, p. 169.

50. The Raja of Ramgarh left the Janata Party in 1962 to join the Swatantra Party. With his support, Swatantra became the leading opposition party in Bihar. When the Raja of Ramgarh was unable to resolve a dispute he had with the national leadership of the Swatantra Party, and Minoo Masani in particular, he simply withdrew his support, thereby destroying the Swatantra Party in Bihar. The Raja then reformed the Janata Party, but later abandoned it in favor of the Congress Party. As I have already noted, he defected from the Congress to join the JKD. Later, he rejoined the Congress and participated in the Congress–Shoshit Dal alliance. When this no longer served the Raja's interests, he defected to the Bharatiya Kranti Dal, only to abandon it and reform the Janata Party when he entered the Paswan ministry.

51. A fuller text of the PSP's statement can be found in the *Patriot*, May 4, 1968.

52. See the *Times of India*, *Hindustan Times*, *Statesman*, and the *Patriot*, for June 1968.

Notes

53. A fuller text of the chief minister's remarks can be found in the *Times of India*, June 26, 1968.
54. *Patriot*, June 26, 1968.
55. For more details, see the *National Herald*, May 12, 1969.
56. Kashyap, *The Politics of Defection*, pp. 347–9.
57. Interview with a member of the Orissa cabinet, January 1970.
58. Interview with a member of the Orissa cabinet, January 1970.
59. For a fuller discussion of G. N. Singh's outlook, see the *Indian Express*, August 3, 1967.
60. As noted in the *Hindustan Times*, August 8, 1967, such speculation was widespread and came from reliable sources.
61. Agitation against the national government for accepting an international settlement concerning the Rann of Kutch.
62. *Hindustan Times*, April 25, 1968.
63. See the coverage of this issue in the *Indian Express,* July 15, 1968.
64. *Indian Express*, July 15, 1968.
65. An interesting discussion of this viewpoint is found in the *Hindustan Times*, March 7, 1969.
66. This extraordinary statement by a member of the government is reported in the *Statesman*, September 14, 1967.

4. SIZE AND COALITION POLITICS

1. An interesting discussion of the role of vote banks in Indian politics may be found in F. G. Bailey, *Politics and Social Change: Orissa in 1959* (Berkeley: University of California Press 1970), pp. 109ff.
2. This correlation coefficient, like all the other correlation coefficients related to legislative size presented in this chapter, refers to the performance of the parties in the Vidhan Sabha (i.e. state legislative assembly) elections.
3. As noted earlier, largeness does not necessarily insure increased influence. Parties that became large too quickly or too soon find themselves excluded from winning coalitions. Such parties experience a decline in their political influence as a result of their largeness.
4. The purpose of pre-election alliances is to facilitate an increase in the number of seats that are secured for a given percentage of the vote. Thus, it is the desire to increase influence, both by dividing votes among fewer competitors and by converting more votes into seats, that prompts political parties to enter pre-election alliances.
5. The frequency with which minor shifts in size occurred is documented in Kashyap, *The Politics of Defection*. The problem of political defections became so severe that the Indian government established a commission to investigate defector politics. Among its recommendations was the suggestion that coalition ministries be limited to no more than 10 per cent of the membership of the state's legislative assembly. The commission also recommended that coalition leaders show restraint in using cabinet appointments as lures to attract defectors. Despite the instabilities created by defector politics, little heed was given to the commission's recommendations.
6. In 1969, midterm elections were conducted in the Punjab, Uttar Pradesh, West Bengal, and Bihar. A midterm poll was conducted in Kerala in 1970. Orissa and West Bengal had midterm elections in 1971. Of the seven states included in this study only Madhya Pradesh did not have a midterm election.

Size and coalition politics

7. There are several interesting discussions of single-party dominant systems. The most relevant ones for this study are Rajni Kothari, 'The Congress "System" in India', *Asian Survey*, IV (December, 1964), pp. 1161–73; Burger, *Opposition*; Riker, *The Theory*, pp. 72–6.

8. Ramanohar Lohia, untitled article in *Mankind* (January, 1970), pp. 43ff.

9. When individuals aggregate themselves into non-winning groups, and when there is no winning coalition in the competitive system, then the individuals have formed protocoalitions. An extensive discussion of the significance of protocoalitions is found in Riker, *The Theory*.

10. Michael Leiserson, 'Power and Ideology in Coalition Behavior: An Experimental Study', in Groenning et al., *The Study of Coalition Behavior*, p. 330.

11. It is, of course, difficult to measure intensity without making an interpersonal comparison of utilities. By the same token, without a common scale, interpersonal comparisons of utility are meaningless at best and misleading at worst. One measure of intensity which does not require interpersonal comparisons is presented by Alvin Rabushka and Kenneth Shepsle, *Politics in Plural Societies* (Columbus, Ohio: Charles E. Merrill, 1972), pp. 43–53.

12. Lohia, p. 43 (reference in note 8 above).

13. The specific question from which the important portfolio measures were derived was 'Would you please list, in order of importance, with the most important first, the ministerial posts that your party most hopes to capture when it forms a coalition government? Are there any others? Why do you most prefer these?' The respondents were instructed not to include the chief ministership or the deputy chief ministership in their list. This was done because I assumed that there would be virtually no variance in first and second preferences if these most important positions were included. Of course, in calculating the number of important ministries controlled by each party, these positions were included. Two procedures were used to measure the relative importance of each cabinet position. First, a simple count of the number of times that each portfolio was mentioned as one of the first four responses of the subjects was used to rank order them. Second, I weighted the responses on the basis of the position in which they were named. Thus, a first choice was multiplied by four, the second choice by three, the third choice by two, the fourth choice by one, and all subsequent choices by zero. The Spearman rank order correlation between the data generated by the two ranking systems is 0.95, indicating that they are almost identical. The former ranking system was adopted for the analyses since it requires fewer assumptions about the ordinality of the data and about differences in the intensity with which the preference orderings were held by the respondents.

In addition to Home, Agriculture, Land and Land Revenue, Education, Finance, Irrigation and Power, Industries, and Labour, some respondents named Health, Cooperatives, Food, and Public Works. These portfolios, however, were named far less frequently than the first eight.

It should be noted that all of the interview subjects were leaders in All-India parties. I assume that their preferences with respect to cabinet positions are not appreciably different from the preferences of leaders from other political parties. Although the evidence presented in this chapter indicates similarities in the patterns of behavior between regional parties and All-India parties, I do not have data that permit an evaluation of this assumption.

14. The first difference is slightly biased in favor of small parties. This follows from the fact that large parties, by definition, can lose many seats, but can only win a few. Small parties, on the other hand, can win many seats, but can only

Notes

lose a few. Later in this chapter, I report the correlations between party size in the coalitions and the change in seats and votes won between 1967 and the midterm elections. That these coefficients prove to be nearly equal to zero is especially significant given the slight bias in the measures in favor of the small parties.

15. All-India parties are, by the definition of the Indian government, broad based parties that secure at least 4 per cent of the vote or 3.33 per cent of the seats in elections in four state legislative assemblies; or 4 per cent of the vote or 4 per cent of the Lok Sabha seats from four states. All-India party leaders are, therefore, more involved with and more concerned about national politics than are regional party leaders. Regional parties generally are restricted to one state. They are less torn by conflictual cues from disparate leaders within their own organization than are All-India parties. If a group of leaders in a regional party differ markedly with another group of leaders in the same party, they can, with relatively little cost, break away and form a new party. This has happened on many occasions in the Punjab, Bihar, and West Bengal, among other places. When a faction of leaders in an All-India party make a similar decision, they incur a far greater cost. They sacrifice a substantial amount of organizational capabilities, a nationally recognized political symbol and so on. Where such attempts have been made – as in the split in the Congress Party into the Congress and the Congress (O) in 1969 – one of the factions generally emerges as being much weaker than the other. Indeed, it is quite uncommon for both factions to maintain their All-India status.

There are additional reasons for the special attention I give to the All-India parties. The theory is concerned with parties that are primarily interested in the maximization of their long-term political influence. The All-India parties, without exception, have expressed some desire to increase their influence and to secure monopoly control over decision-making in the states and, eventually, in New Delhi. The regional parties, on the other hand, are much more concerned with maximizing policy goals than political goals. Consequently, they are less interesting from the perspective of the theory being tested here.

16. Strictly speaking, significance tests are not applicable here since the data are not drawn from a random sample. On the other hand, the parties being studied are, from the perspective of the generalizability of the theory, a sample of all the parties that could have been used to test the theory. In any event, I use significance tests primarily as a means to distinguish, in an ordinal sense, between large and small coefficients, given different sample sizes. As a general rule, I will report significance levels for all of the most essential analyses, regardless of the level achieved. Thus, I encourage the reader to establish his own criteria for judging the goodness of fit, rather than arbitrarily ignoring all relationships with a random probability greater than 0.05.

17. Mitra, 'Role of the Bharatiya Kranti Dal' provides an interesting account of how Charan Singh used the pivotal position of the BKD to enhance the party's electoral prospects. Mitra draws the link between the principles of strategic behavior and their specific application to politics in Uttar Pradesh. He is particularly helpful in giving theoretical meaning to the use of casteism by Charan Singh. It is in the light of these strategic principles that casteism becomes important, rather than in terms of a simple appeal to tradition.

5. STRATEGIC BEHAVIOR AND POLITICAL INFLUENCE

1. Marcus Franda, 'The CPI (Marxist) and Partial Political Power', unpublished manuscript.

2. This would be somewhat akin to events data analysis as it is most commonly applied in the study of international relations. For a discussion of this approach, see the June 1972 issue of the *Journal of Conflict Resolution*, XVI, no 2.

3. An alternative procedure was also considered. This procedure is based on the assumption that each state party branch had a single key leader whose preferences were responsible for the strategic orientation of the entire party within the state. I tested this approach by assuming that such a key leader would hold the highest office within his party during the tenure of the coalitions. The individual holding that position (i.e. state party president, or its equivalent) was named by all respondents from his party in his state when they were asked to name the most important members of their party.

The major drawback of this approach to the data is that it requires a tremendous oversimplification of Indian politics. Indeed, one of the interesting characteristics of Indian politics is the widespread factionalization which exists within most parties. These factions have manifested their very different political orientations on several occasions within the Congress Party, Swatantra, the communist parties, the socialist parties, and even in the generally well integrated Jana Sangh. Several coalition governments have been terminated in part as a result of intraparty disputes. The key decision-maker approach suffers from another serious flaw. It requires that we assume that individual cabinet ministers did not have a major impact on the strategic behavior manifested in their own ministries. Instead, we are required to assume that a single leader guided strategic decisions in all the ministries controlled by his party.

The procedure I have adopted avoids almost all of the difficulties inherent in the key leader approach. On the other hand, it is not without its own problems. Assuming collective leadership requires that I assume that each individual leader had an equal impact on the strategic orientation of his party. This is an over-simplification, especially when we focus on important decisions that are likely to effect the longevity of a coalition or the distribution of benefits within the coalition. Nevertheless, averaging the predispositions of each leader at least allows all of them to have an impact on the party's strategic predisposition. Since there is no *a priori* basis on which to establish a weighting scheme, I follow this simple averaging procedure.

The appropriateness of the collective leadership approach is underscored by the empirical investigations. In every case, this method explains more of the variance in the distribution and conversion of coalition benefits than does the key leader approach.

The reader interested in the importance of individual leaders within each of the major Indian parties might examine some of the following studies: Brass; *Factional Politics*; M. M. Rahman, *The Congress Crisis* (New Delhi: Associated Publishing House, 1970); Myron Weiner, *Party Building in a New Nation: The Indian National Congress* (Chicago: University of Chicago Press, 1967); Stanley Kochanek, *The Congress Party of India* (Princeton: Princeton University Press, 1968); Erdman, *The Swatantra Party*; Moham Ram, *Indian Communism: Split Within a Split* (New Delhi: Vikas Publishing, 1969); E. M. S. Namboodiripad, *What Really Happened in Kerala: The Story of the Disruptive Game Played by Rightwing Communists* (CPI(Marxist), January 1966); Bhowani Sen, *CPM's Fight Against United Front in West Bengal* (Communist Party of India, no date); Hari Kishore Singh, *A History of the Praja Socialist Party* (Lucknow: Narendra Prakashan, 1959); Burger, *Opposition*; Baxter, *The Jana Sangh*.

Notes

6. NEED FOR ACHIEVEMENT, RISK AND SUCCESS

1. Many of the most important studies of need for achievement can be found in Atkinson, *Motives*. Another very important study of need for achievement is McClelland, *The Achieving Society*.

2. Achievement imagery is defined as competition with a standard of excellence, pursuit of a unique accomplishment, or a long-term involvement with an achievement goal. A detailed definition is given in Atkinson, *Motives*, pp. 180–8.

3. There have been several studies of the relationship between need for achievement and economic development. The best known is McClelland's *The Achieving Society*. Another study in this vein is J. B. Cortes, 'The Achievement Motive in the Spanish Economy Between the 13th and 18th Centuries', *Economic Development and Cultural Change*, IX, no. 2 (1961), pp. 144–63.

4. Some other indicators that McClelland has identified include doodling patterns, color preferences, and literary works. While literary works can be used to code all of the usual aspects of need for achievement, the other measures can only tap in indirect ways the usual indicators of n-achievement.

5. An interesting study that makes use of presidential inaugural addresses is Richard Donley and David Winter, 'Measuring the Motives of Public Officials at a Distance: An Exploratory Study of American Presidents', *Behavioral Science*, XV (1970), pp. 227–36.

6. Joel Raynor, 'Preliminary Notes on the Coding of the Professor's Interview on Job and Job Pressures for n Achievement, n Affiliation, and n Power' (Mimeo, Department of Psychology, University of Buffalo, March 28, 1967). The conventional scheme for coding need for achievement is described in Atkinson, *Motives*, pp. 179–204.

7. To my knowledge, the only other attempt to measure need for achievement from interview data was conducted by Joel Raynor in conjunction with the preparation of his coding manual.

8. Alvin Zander and John Forward, 'Position in a Group, Achievement Motivation and Group Aspirations', *Journal of Personality and Social Psychology*, VIII (March, 1968), pp. 282–8.

9. A party is counted only once per state no matter how many of the state's coalitions it participated in.

10. This observation is repeatedly underscored in the studies contained in Atkinson, *Motives*.

11. That need for achievement is not necessarily linked with success is particularly well explained in an educational film entitled *Need to Achieve*, produced by the National Educational Television network.

12. Ordinarily, homogeneity of variance is assumed in a one-way analysis of variance. This could have presented a problem for this study in that I am interested both in a difference in group means and a difference in within group variance. Fortunately, the homogeneity of variance assumption may be relaxed provided the groups are of equal size. This is one reason for selecting the median as the cutting point in grouping the achievement data, rather than selecting the mean. Using a dichotomous scheme, and testing the achievement hypotheses through the use of analysis of variance has several advantages over correlational techniques. First, it does not require that the data are continuous. Second, it does not require linear effects within groups. This is especially desirable since the n-achievement data are, as noted, probably error prone. By dichotomizing,

I am likely to minimize some of the measurement error since I no longer require a precise breakdown of values.

13. Other studies that focus on related aspects of political style are Joseph A. Schlesinger, *Ambition and Politics: Political Careers in the United States* (Chicago: Rand McNally, 1966); Gordon S. Black, 'A Theory of Political Ambition: Career Choices and the Role of Structural Incentives', *American Political Science Review*, LXVI (March, 1972), pp. 144–9; Robert Putnam, 'Studying Elite Political Culture: The Case of "Ideology"', *American Political Science Review*, LXV (September, 1971), pp. 651–81.

14. Phillips Cutright and Peter Rossi, 'Grass Roots Politicians and the Vote', in *Politics and Social Life*, Nelson Polsby, Robert Dentler, and Paul Smith, eds. (Boston: Houghton Mifflin, 1963), pp. 771–80; and J. David Greenstone, 'Party Pressure on Organized Labor in Three Cities', in *The Electoral Process*, M. Kent Jennings and Harmon Ziegler, eds. (Englewood Cliffs, NJ: Prentice-Hall, 1966), pp. 55–80.

15. Burger, *Opposition*; Bailey, *Politics and Social Change*; Rudolph and Rudolph, *Modernity of Tradition*; Rudolph and Rudolph, 'The Political Role', Marcus Franda, 'The Organizational Development of India's Congress Party', *Pacific Affairs*, XXXV (1962), pp. 249–60.

16. Burger, *Opposition*; Baxter, *The Jana Sangh*.

17. Although results using log (n-achievement) are not reported in the text, they were computed. In order to transform the n-achievement index to its natural logarithm, it was necessary to add 1.0 to all n-achievement scores. This was done to eliminate negative values for which, of course, logarithms are not defined.

18. Without the Jana Sangh from Uttar Pradesh included in the analysis, the equation for the change in Vidhan Sabha seats is $-9.73 + 37.27 \log (\text{Mix}) + 22.04 \log (\text{Vote}) - 0.85$ (1967 VS seats). $R^2 = 0.71$, $N = 18$. This equation is virtually identical to the equation which includes the Jana Sangh. The robustness of these results highlights the stability of the function.

7. CONCLUSIONS

1. The correlation between the mixed strategy and party size in the coalitions is -0.24 ($N = 21$). The correlation between each party's average strategy and its size in the coalitions is -0.01 ($N = 21$).

2. One study that makes a tentative attempt to evaluate the interaction between resources and organizational skills is 'The Effective Population in International Politics', by A. F. K. Organski, Bruce Bueno de Mesquita, and Alan Lamborn, in Richard Clinton, William Flash, and R. Kenneth Godwin, eds., *Political Science in Population Studies* (Lexington, Massachusetts: D. C. Heath, 1972), pp. 79–100.

3. An excellent study of elite recruitment within the Indian political party context is Burger, *Opposition*.

Bibliography

BOOKS

Airan, J. W., ed. *The Nature of Leadership: A Practical Approach.* Bombay: Lalvani Publishing House, 1969.
Atkinson, John. *An Introduction to Motivation.* Princeton: D. Van Nostrand Company, 1964.
  (ed.) *Motives in Fantasy, Action, and Society.* Princeton: D. Van Nostrand Company, 1958.
Axelrod, Robert. *Conflict of Interest: A Theory of Divergent Goals with Applications to Politics.* Chicago: Markham, 1970.
Bailey, F. G. *Politics and Social Change: Orissa in 1959.* Berkeley: University of California Press, 1970.
Balaram, N. E. *A Short History of the Communist Party of India.* Trivandrum: Prabhatham Printing and Publishing Company, 1967.
Baxter, Craig. *The Jana Sangh: A Biography of an Indian Political Party.* Philadelphia: University of Pennsylvania Press, 1969.
  District Voting Trends in India: A Research Tool. New York: Southern Asian Institute of Columbia University, 1969.
Bhatkal, R. G., ed. *Political Alternatives in India.* Bombay: Popular Prakashan, 1967.
Brass, Paul. *Factional Politics in an Indian State: The Congress Party in Uttar Pradesh.* Berkeley: University of California Press, 1965.
Brecher, Michael. *Political Leadership in India: An Analysis of Elite Attitudes.* Delhi: Vikas Publications, 1969.
Brown, J. S. *The Motivation of Behavior.* New York: McGraw-Hill, 1961.
Burger, Angela. *Opposition in a Dominant-Party System: A Study of the Jana Sangh, the Praja Socialist Party, and the Socialist Party in Uttar Pradesh, India.* Berkeley: The University of California Press, 1969.
Center for the Study of Developing Societies. *Party System and Election Studies.* New Delhi, 1967.
Chandidas, R.; Clark, L.; Fontera, R.; and Morehouse, W., eds. *India Votes: A Source Book on Indian Elections.* New York: Humanities Press, 1968.
Coser, Lewis. *The Functions of Social Conflict.* New York: Free Press, 1956.
Curran, Jean A. *Militant Hinduism in Indian Politics: A Study of the RSS.* New York: Institute of Pacific Relations, 1951.
Dhooria, R. L. *I Was a Swayamsewak.* New Delhi: Sampradayikta Virodhi Committee. n.d.
Duverger, Maurice. *Political Parties.* Translated by Robert and Barbara North. London: Methuen, 1954.
Erdman, Howard L. *The Swatantra Party and Indian Conservatism.* Cambridge: Cambridge University Press, 1967.
Frohlich, Norman; Oppenheimer, J. A.; and Young, Oran. *Political Leadership and Collective Goods.* Princeton: Princeton University Press, 1971.
Groennings, Sven; Kelly, E. W.; and Leiserson, Michael, eds. *The Study of Coalition Behavior: Theoretical Perspectives and Cases from Four Continents.* New York: Holt, Rinehart and Winston, 1970.
Jena, B. B. *Parliamentary Committee in India.* Calcutta: Scientific Book Agency, 1966.

Jhangiani, Motilal A. *Jana Sangh and Swatantra: A Profile of the Rightist Parties in India.* Bombay: Manaktalas, 1967.
Kashyap, Subash. *The Politics of Defection: A Study of State Politics in India.* Delhi: National Publishing House, 1969.
Kishore, M. A. *Jana Sangh and India's Foreign Policy.* New Delhi: Associated Publishing House, 1969.
Kochanek, Stanley A. *The Congress Party of India: The Dynamics of One-Party Democracy.* Princeton: Princeton University Press, 1968.
Kothari, Rajni. *Politics in India.* Boston: Little Brown and Company, 1970.
Lerner, Daniel. *Passing of Traditional Society.* Glencoe: The Free Press, 1958.
Limaye, Madhu. *Politics of Transition.* Bombay: Vasant Helekar, 1969.
Lipset, Seymour M. *Political Man: The Social Bases of Politics.* Garden City: Anchor Books, 1963.
Luce, R. Duncan, and Raiffa, Howard. *Games and Decisions: Introduction and Critical Survey.* New York: John Wiley and Sons, 1957.
Masani, Minoo. *The Communist Party of India: A Short History.* London: Derek Verschoyle, 1954.
Congress Misrule and the Swatantra Altenative. Bombay: Manaktalas, 1966.
McClelland, David. *The Achieving Society.* New York: The Free Press, 1961.
Nayar, Balraj. *Minority Politics in the Punjab.* Princeton: Princeton University Press, 1966.
Ofshe, Lynne and Ofshe, Richard. *Utility and Choice in Social Interaction.* Englewood Cliffs, NJ: Prentice-Hall, 1970.
Olson, Mancur. *The Logic of Collective Action: Public Goods and the Theory of Groups.* New York: Schocken Books, 1968.
Organski, A. F. K. *Stages of Political Development.* New York: A. Knopf, 1965.
Overstreet, Gene, and Windmiller, Marshall. *Communism in India.* Bombay: The Perennial Press, 1960.
Park, Richard L. *India's Political System.* Englewood Cliffs, NJ: Prentice-Hall, 1967.
Park, Richard L., and Tinker, Irene, eds. *Leadership and Political Institutions in India.* Princeton: Princeton University Press, 1959.
Rabushka, Alvin and Shepsle, Kenneth. *Politics in Plural Societies.* Columbus, Ohio: Charles E. Merrill, 1972.
Rahman, M. M. *The Congress Crisis.* New Delhi: Associated Publishing House, 1970.
Ram, Mohan. *Indian Communism: Split Within a Split.* New Delhi: Vikas Publishing, 1969.
Rapoport, Anatol, and Chammah, A. M. *Prisoner's Dilemma: A Study in Conflict and Cooperation.* Ann Arbor: University of Michigan Press, 1965.
Riker, William. *The Theory of Political Coalitions.* New Haven: Yale University Press, 1962.
Riker, William and Ordeshook, Peter. *An Introduction to Positive Political Theory.* Englewood Cliffs, NJ: Prentice-Hall, 1973.
Rudolph, Lloyd and Rudolph Susanne. *Modernity of Tradition.* Chicago: University of Chicago Press, 1967.
Schlesinger, Joseph A. *Ambition and Politics: Political Careers in the United States.* Chicago: Rand McNally, 1966.
Singh, Hari Kishore. *A History of the Praja Socialist Party.* Lucknow: Narendra Prakashan, 1959.

Bibliography

Thibaut, J. W., and Kelley, H. H. *The Social Psychology of Groups.* New York: John Wiley and Sons, 1959.
Thrall, R. M.; Coombs, C. H.; and Davis, R. L., eds. *Decision Processes.* New York: John Wiley and Sons, 1954.
Verma, R. K. *Lohia.* Allahabad: Rashmi Prakashan, 1969.
Von Neumann, John, and Morgenstern, Oscar. *The Theory of Games and Economic Behavior.* Princeton: Princeton University Press, 1944.
Weiner, Myron. *Party Building in a New Nation: The Indian National Congress.* Chicago: The University of Chicago Press, 1967.
    ed. *State Politics in India.* Princeton: Princeton University Press, 1968.
Wolff, H. H. *The Sociology of George Simmel.* New York: The Free Press, 1950.

ARTICLES AND UNPUBLISHED MATERIALS

Banerjee, D. N. 'The Political Situation in West Bengal'. *Swarajya.* February 14, 1970.
Bixenstine, V. E.; Chambers, N.; and Wilson, K. 'Effect of Asymmetry in Payoff on Behavior in a Two-Person Non-Zero-Sum Game'. *Journal of Conflict Resolution.* VIII, 1964, pp. 151–9.
Black, Gordon S. 'A Theory of Political Ambition: Career Choices and the Role of Structural Incentives'. *American Political Science Review.* LXVI, March 1972, pp. 144–59.
Bond, J. R., and Vinacke, W. E. 'Coalitions in Mixed-Sex Triads'. *Sociometry.* XXIV, 1961, pp. 61–75.
Brams, Steven, 'Positive Coalition Theory: The Relationship Between Postulated Goals and Derived Behavior'. *Political Science Annual.* IV, Cornelius Cotter, ed. Indianapolis: Bobbs-Merill, 1973, pp. 3–40.
Brams, Steven and Riker, William. 'Models of Coalition Formation in Voting Bodies'. *Mathematical Application in Political Science.* VI, Charlottesville: University Press of Virginia, 1972, pp. 79–124.
Brass, Paul. 'Coalition Politics in North India'. *American Political Science Review.* LXII, 1968, pp. 1174–91.
Browne, Eric and Franklin, Mark. 'Aspects of Coalition Payoffs in Parliamentary Democracies', *American Political Science Review.* LXVII, June 1973, pp. 453–69.
Bueno de Mesquita, Bruce. 'A Model of Coalition Behavior: The Case of India, 1967–1971'. Ph.D. dissertation, Department of Political Science, University of Michigan, 1971.
Bueno de Mesquita, Bruce and Singer, J. David. 'Alliances, Capabilities, and War: A Review and Synthesis'. *Political Science Annual.* IV, Cornelius Cotter, ed. Indianapolis: Bobbs-Merill, 1973, pp. 237–80.
Burris, J. C. and R. S. Frye. 'The Effects of Initial Resources of Individuals upon Their Selection of a Partner in the Formation of Coalitions'. Paper presented to the Southeastern Psychological Association Convention, 1966.
Butterworth, Richard. 'A Research Note on the Size of Winning Coalitions'. *American Political Science Review.* LXV, 1971, pp. 741–5.
Caplow, Theodore. 'A Theory of Coalitions in the Triad'. *American Sociological Review.* XXI, 1956, pp. 488–92.
    'Further Development of a Theory of Coalitions in the Triad'. *American Journal of Sociology.* LXIV, 1959, pp. 488–93.

Articles and unpublished materials

Chertkoff, Jerome. 'The Effects of Probability of Future Success on Coalition Formation'. *Journal of Experimental Social Psychology.* II, 1966, pp. 265–77.

'A Revision of Caplow's Coalition Theory'. *Journal of Experimental Social Psychology.* III, 1967, pp. 172–7.

Cortes, J. B. 'The Achievement Motive in the Spanish Economy Between the 13th and 18th Centuries'. *Economic Development and Cultural Change.* IX, no. 2, 1961, pp. 144–63.

Cutright, Phillips and Rossi, Peter. 'Grass Roots Politicians and the Vote'. *Politics and Social Life.* Nelson Polsby, Robert Dentler, and Paul Smith, eds. Boston: Houghton Mifflin, 1963, pp. 771–80.

Deepak, O. P. 'Tasks Before the SSP'. *Mankind.* July 1967.

Deepak, O. P. and Mitra, R. 'Elections and After'. *Mankind.* April 1967.

Donley, Richard and Winter, David. 'Measuring the Motives of Public Officials at a Distance: An Exploratory Study of American Presidents'. *Behavioral Science.* XV, 1970, pp. 227–36.

Editors. 'Not the End: An Editorial'. *Economic and Political Weekly.* January 8, 1969.

Economic and Political Weekly. Annual Number, 1971.

Franda, Marcus. 'The Organizational Development of India's Congress Party'. *Pacific Affairs.* XXXV, 1962, pp. 248–60.

'Electoral Politics in West Bengal: The Growth of the United Front'. *Pacific Affairs.* XLII, 1969, pp. 279–93.

'The CPI (Marxist) and Partial Political Power'. Chapter VII. Manuscript.

Frohlich, Norman and Oppenheimer, Joe A. 'I Get By with a Little Help from My Friends'. *World Politics.* XXIII, 1970, pp. 104–20.

Gamson, William. 'An Experimental Test of a Theory of Coalition Formation'. *American Sociological Review.* XXVI, 1961, pp. 565–73.

'A Theory of Coalition Formation'. *American Sociological Review.* XXVI, 1961, pp. 373–82.

'Coalition Formation at Presidential Nominating Conventions.' *American Journal of Sociology.* LXVIII, 1962, pp. 157–71.

'Experimental Studies of Coalition Formation'. *Advances in Experimental Social Psychology.* Leonard Berkowitz, ed. New York: Academic Press, 1964, pp. 82–110.

Gates, R. C. 'Armchair, Board Room, Cabinet: The Province of Economics.' Inaugural Lecture. University of Queensland, 1967.

Goyal, D. R. 'Double Posture in Jana Sangh'. *The Citizen.* November 22, 1969.

Greenstone, J. David. 'Party Pressure on Organized Labor in Three Cities'. *The Electoral Process.* M. Kent Jennings and Harmon Ziegler, eds. Englewood Cliffs, NJ: Prentice-Hall, 1966, pp. 55–80.

Gupta, B. 'Leftist Bengal'. *Mankind.* December 1967.

Guyer, Melvin. 'A Review of the Literature on Zero-Sum and Non-Zero-Sum Games in the Social Sciences'. Mental Health Research Institute. University of Michigan, n.d.

Hoffman, P. J.; Festinger, L.; and Lawrence, D. H. 'Tendencies Toward Group Comparability in Competitive Bargaining'. *Human Relations.* VII, 1954, pp. 141–60.

Jha, U. 'The State of the SSP Organization'. *Mankind.* September 1968.

Karanth, K. S. 'Anti-National Role of Indian Communists: A Theoretical Analysis'. *Mankind.* September 1968.

Kelley, H. H. 'Techniques of Studying Coalition Formation'. *Midwest Journal of*

Bibliography

Political Science. XII, 1968, pp. 62–84.
Kelley, H. H. and Arrowood, A. J. 'Coalitions in the Triad: Critique and Experiment'. *Sociometry.* XXIII, 1960, pp. 231–44.
Kothari, Rajni. 'The Congress "System" in India'. *Asian Survey.* IV, 1964, pp. 1161–73.
— 'India's Political Take-Off'. *The Economic and Political Weekly.* July 1962.
— 'India's Political Transition'. *The Economic and Political Weekly.* August 1967.
— 'Political Consensus in India: Decline and Reconstruction'. *The Economic and Political Weekly.* October 1969.
Krishnanath, and Chatterji, P. 'Governors, Spoils, Non-Congress States'. *Mankind.* February 1968.
Lave, L. B. 'Factors Affecting Cooperation in the Prisoner's Dilemma'. *Behavioral Science.* X, 1965, pp. 26–38.
Leiserson, Michael. 'Factions and Coalitions in One-Party Japan: An Interpretation Based on the Theory of Games'. *American Political Science Review.* LXII, 1968, pp. 770–87.
Lieberman, B. 'Experimental Studies of Conflict in Some Two-Person and Three-Person Games'. *Mathematical Methods in Small Group Processes.* J. Criswell, H. Solomon, and P. Suppes, eds. Palo Alto: Stanford University Press, 1962, pp. 203–20.
— 'i-Trust: A Notion of Trust in Three-Person Games and International Affairs'. *Journal of Conflict Resolution.* VIII, 1964, pp. 271–80.
Limaye, Madhu. 'Parties of the Right'. *Mankind.* September 1969.
Lohia, R. 'History of the Socialist Movement'. *Mankind.* October 1969.
Luce, R. Duncan. 'A Definition of Stability for N-Person Games'. *Annals of Mathematics.* 1954.
Marlowe, D.; Gergen, K. J.; and Doob, A. N. 'Opponent's Personality, Expectation of Social Interaction, and Interpersonal Bargaining'. *Journal of Personality and Social Psychology.* III, 1966, pp. 206–13.
Meckery, F. A. 'The Politics of Coalitions'. *Swarajya.* February 21, 1970.
Morris-Jones, W. 'Dominance and Dissent'. *Government and Opposition.* August 1966.
Misra, P. 'Three-Way Split in Samyukt Socialists'. *The Citizen.* November 22, 1969.
Mitra, Subrata Kumar. 'Role of the Bharatiya Kranti Dal in the Politics of Uttar Pradesh, 1967–1970.' Masters Thesis, Political Science. Delhi University. March 1971.
Nath, K. 'Non-Congress Coalitions'. *Mankind.* May 1967.
Ofshe, Richard and Ofshe, Lynne. 'Choice Behavior in Coalition Games'. *Behavioral Science.* XV, 1970, pp. 337–49.
— 'Social Choice and Utility in Coalition Formation'. *Sociometry.* XXXII, 1969, pp. 330–47.
Olson, Mancur and Zeckhauser, Richard. 'An Economic Theory of Alliances'. *Review of Economics and Statistics.* XLVIII, 1966, pp. 266–79.
Organski, A. F. K.; Bueno de Mesquita, Bruce; and Lamborn, Alan. 'The Effective Population in International Politics', in *Political Science in Population Studies.* Richard Clinton, William Flash, and R. Kenneth Godwin, eds. Lexington, Massachusetts: D. C. Heath, 1972, pp. 79–100.
Park, Richard L. ' "Angularities" and the Secular State: An Interview with India's R.S.S.'. Mimeo, 1951.
Pattnayak, K. 'February Elections'. *Mankind.* February 1969.

Articles and unpublished materials

'Strategy and Philosophy of Non-Congressism'. *Mankind.* June 1968.
Poddar, D. 'Sixty Days of Bihar Non-Congressism'. *Mankind.* July 1967.
Porat, A. and Haas, J. 'Information Effects on Decision-Making'. *Behavioral Science.* XIV, 1969, pp. 98–104.
Putnam, Robert. 'Studying Elite Political Culture: The Case of "Ideology" '. *American Political Science Review.* LXV, September 1971, pp. 651–81.
Rapoport, Anatol and Guyer, Melvin. 'A Taxonomy of 2×2 Games.' *General Systems.* XI, 1966, pp. 203–14.
— 'The Psychology of Conflict Involving Mixed-Motive Decisions'. Mental Health Research Institute Preprint. University of Michigan, March, 1969.
Raynor, Joel. 'Future Orientation and Motivation of Immediate Activity: An Elaboration of the Theory of Achievement Motivation'. *Psychological Review.* LXXVI, 1969, pp. 606–10.
— 'Preliminary Notes on the Coding of the Professor's *Interview on Job and Job Pressures* for *n*-Achievement, *n*-Affiliation, and *n*-Power'. Mimeo, Department of Psychology, University of Michigan, March 28, 1967.
Raynor, Joel and Ruskin, J. 'Effects of Achievement Motivation and Future Orientation on Level of Performance'. *Psychological Review.* LXXVIII, 1971, pp. 36–41.
Riker, William. 'A New Proof of the Size Principle'. *Mathematical Applications in Political Science.* II, Joseph Bernd, ed. Dallas: Southern Methodist University Press, 1967, pp. 167–74.
Riker, William and Shapley, Lloyd S. 'Weighted Voting: A Mathematical Analysis for Instrumental Judgments', in *Nomos X: Representation.* Roland Pennock and John W. Chapman, eds. New York: Atherton Press, 1968, pp. 199–216.
Riker, William and Zavoina, W. 'Rational Behavior in Politics: Evidence from a Three-Person Game'. *American Political Science Review.* LXIV, 1970, pp. 48–60.
Rudolph, Lloyd and Rudolph, Susanne. 'The Political Role of India's Caste Associations'. *Pacific Affairs.* XXXIII, 1960, pp. 5–22.
Russett, Bruce. 'Components of an Operational Theory of International Alliance Formation'. *Journal of Conflict Resolution.* XXII, 1968, pp. 285–301.
Ruthnaswamy, M. 'A Credible Opposition'. *Swarajya.* February 28, 1970.
Sangal, O. P. 'The Unsplit View of Divided Communists'. *The Citizen.* November 22, 1969.
Schelling, Thomas C. 'The Strategy of Conflict: Prospectus for the Reorientation of Game Theory'. *Journal of Conflict Resolution.* II, 1958, pp. 203–64.
Scodel, A. 'Induced Collaboration in Some Non-Zero-Sum Games'. *Journal of Conflict Resolution.* VI, 1962, pp. 335–40.
Seminar Contributors. 'Our Political Parties'. *Seminar.* 124, December 1969.
— 'India's Left'. *Seminar.* 127, March 1970.
Shapley, Lloyd S. 'A Value for N-Person Games', in *Contributions to the Theory of Games.* H. W. Kuhn and A. W. Tucker, eds. Annals of Mathematical Studies, no. 28. Princeton: Princeton University Press, 1953, pp. 163–75.
Srivastava, V. 'For the Survival of Democracy'. *Swarajya.* February 7, 1970.
Stryker, S. and Psathas, G. 'Research on Coalitions in the Triad: Findings, Problems, and Strategy'. *Sociometry.* XXIII, 1960, pp. 217–30.
Taylor, M. and Herman, V. M. 'Party Systems and Government Stability'. *American Political Science Review.* LXV, 1971, pp. 28–37.

Bibliography

Uesugi, T. T. and Vinacke, W. E. 'Strategy in a Feminine Game'. *Sociometry.* XXVI, 1963, pp. 75–88.

Vinacke, W. E. and Arkoff, A. 'Experimental Study of Coalitions in the Triad'. *American Sociological Review.* XXII, 1957, pp. 406–14.

Vinacke, W. E. and Chaney, M. 'Achievement and Nurturance in Triads Varying in Power Distribution'. *Journal of Abnormal and Social Psychology.* LX, 1960, pp. 175–81.

Weiner, B. 'The Effects of Unsatisfied Achievement Motivation on Persistence and Subsequent Performance'. *Journal of Personality.* XXXIII, 1965, pp. 428–42.

Willis, R. H. 'Coalitions in the Tetrad'. *Sociometry.* XXV, 1962, pp. 358–76.

Winham, G. 'Political Development and Lerner's Theory: Further Test of a Causal Model'. *American Political Science Review.* LXIV, 1970, pp. 810–19.

Zagoria, Donald. 'The Ecology of Peasant Communism in India'. *American Political Science Review.* LXV, 1971, pp. 144–60.

Zander, Alvin and Forward, John. 'Position in a Group, Achievement Motivation and Group Aspirations'. *Journal of Personality and Social Psychology.* III, 1968, pp. 282–8.

DOCUMENTS

BJS

Bharatiya Jana Sangh, *Assessment of Mid-Term Polls*, 1969.
Election Manifesto, 1967.
Resolutions, December 28–30, 1967.
Resolutions, June 14–16, 1968.
Resolutions, December 7–8, 1968.
Resolutions, February 15–16, 1969.
Resolutions, April 25–7, 1969.
Resolutions, July 1–4, 1969.
Resolutions, August 30–September 1, 1969.
Resolutions, December 28–30, 1969.
Jana Deep Souvenir, December 1967.
Jana Deep Souvenir, April 25–7, 1969.
Organiser. Inclusive of issues from January 3, 1970 to February 28, 1970.

Upadhyaya, D. *Report on the Fourth General Election.* Bharatiya Jana Sangh, 1967.
Presidential Address. Bharatiya Jana Sangh, 1967.

Vajpayee, A. B. *Presidential Address.* Bharatiya Jana Sangh, 1969.

CPI

Achutha, Menon, C. *What Happened in Kerala?* Communist Party of India, n.d.

Bihar State Council. *Resolution on the Political Situation in Bihar.* Communist Party of India (Bihar). Mimeo, December 7, 1969.

Bose, P. *Need for a Third Force.* Communist Party of India. n.d.

Communist Party of India. *Programme of CPI.* October 31–November 7, 1964.
Programme of the CPI. February 7–15, 1968.
Review of the Fourth General Election. April 23–30, 1967.
Review of the Mid-Term Elections and Our Tasks and Resolutions. April 5–12, 1969.

Documents

New Age. Inclusive of issues from December 28, 1969 to February 22, 1970.
Sen, B. *CPM's Fight Against the United Front in West Bengal.* Communist Party of India. n.d.

CPI(M)

Communist Party of India (Marxist). *Election Review.* 1967.
Election Review and Party's Tasks. 1967.
Political Organisational Report. December 23–9, 1968.
Political Resolutions. December 23–29, 1968.
Resolutions. August 7–11, 1968.
Rightwing CPI Betrayal of Kerala. 1969.
Namboodiripad, E. M. S. *What Really Happened in Kerala?* CPI(M), 1966.

PSP

Bhasin, P. *The Fateful Period.* Praja Socialist Party. n.d.
Das, S. *West Bengal Polity Today*, PSP. 1968.
Praja Socialist Party. *Election Manifesto.* 1967.
General Secretary's Report. February 3–6, 1970.
Message to All Provincial and District Secretaries. Mimeo, February 11, 1970.
Resolution on Political Situation. Mimeo. 1970.

SSP

Joshi, S. M. *A Split at Varanasi.* Samyukta Socialist Party.
'Choice Before Socialists'. *Mainstream.* November 22, 1969.
Milal-e-Sherif Memorial College, Brochure including biography of P. K. Kunju, Kayamkulam, Kerala. undated.
Samyukta Socialist Party. *Bulletin.* Inclusive of the period September 1969 to December 1969.
Election Manifesto. 1967.
Political Resolutions. January 1970.
Statement of Principles. 1966.

Swatantra

Swatantra Party. *Swatantra in Parliament.* Inclusive of issues number 18–20, and number 2.
Swatantra Newsletter. Inclusive of issues from April 1969 to March 1970.
Third National Convention. February 1–2, 1964.

Miscellaneous Documents

Bharatiya Kranti Dal. *Aims and Principles.* n.d.
Constitution. n.d.
Government of India. *Fourth General Election: An Analysis.* n.d.
Report on the Mid-Term General Election: 1968–1969. Vol. II, 1970.
List of Members of the Lok Sabha. Fifth Edition, June 1969.
Government of West Bengal. *United Front in West Bengal: The First Year.* 1968.
Programme of the United Front. n.d.

Newspapers

The Hindu. January 1, 1967 – May 15, 1970.

Bibliography

The Hindustan Times. January 1, 1967 – May 15, 1970; September 15 – October 1, 1970; March 15 – March 30, 1971.
Indian Express. January 1, 1967 – May 15, 1970.
National Herald. January 1, 1967 – May 15, 1970.
Patriot. January 1, 1967 – May 15, 1970.
The Statesman. January 1, 1967 – May 15, 1970.
Sunday Standard. March 1967 – May 1970.
The Times of India. January 1, 1967 – May 15, 1970; September 15 – October 1, 1970; March 15 – March 30, 1971.

Index

achievement motive, *see* need for achievement
actors, *see* decision-makers
Ahmad, Bashiruddin, 176
Akali Dal, viii, 51, 52, 97
Akali Dal (Master), viii, 66, 67, 68
Akali Dal (Sant), viii, x, 66, 67, 68, 100
Akhtar Ali Khan, 70
All-India parties
  defined, 180
  see also individual party entries
Alvares, Peter, 74
Ambedkar, B. R., x
Andhra Pradesh, 62
anti-competitive coalitions, 17–18, 99, 172
anti-Congressism, *see* non-Congressism
Arkoff, H., 172
Arrowood, A. J., 172
Assam, 62
Atkinson, John, 174, 175, 182
average strategy, 118–19, 120, 122–4
Axelrod, Robert, 169, 172

BKD, *see* Bharatiya Kranti Dal
Bailey, F. G., 178, 183
Bangla Congress, viii, 76, 78, 80
Basu, Jyoti, 80, 116
Baxter, Craig, 175, 177, 181
benefits, *see* payoffs
Berkowitz, Leonard, 169
Bharatiya Jana Sangh, *see* Jana Sangh
Bharatiya Kranti Dal
  in coalitions, 59, 71–2, 73, 82, 98, 108, 125–6
  defections to, x, 71, 74, 177
  in elections, 72, 77
  see also Charan Singh
Bhasin, Prem, 55, 176
Bihar, 64, 72–6, 148–50
  coalitions in, ix, x, 49, 54, 57, 62, 72–6, 98, 124, 126–8
  government crisis in, 73, 75, 76
  President's Rule in, 72, 74, 75, 76
Black, Gordon S., 183
Bond, J., 172, 173
Brams, Steven, 167, 168, 169
Brass, Paul, 177, 181
Brown, J., 174
Browne, Eric, 171, 173
Bueno de Mesquita, Bruce, 167, 175, 183
Burger, Angela, 175, 176, 177, 179, 181, 183

Burris, J. C., 172
Butterworth, Richard, 171

CPI, *see* Communist Party of India
CPI (M), *see* Communist Party of India (Marxist)
cabinet portfolios, distribution of, 66, 67, 68, 93, 103–11, 125, 138, 191
Caplow, Theodore, 14–16, 18–19, 99, 168, 172, 173
caste, 64, 65, 78, 110, 144, 154, 180
central government, ix, 63, 77, 79
Chandidas, R., 177
Charan Singh, 68–72, 108–11, 125, 177, 180
cheapest winning coalition, *see* coalitions, size of
Chertkoff, Jerome, 15–16, 17, 99, 110, 172
China, viii
choice variability, 17
Clark, L., 177
cleavages, by state, 64–5
close constituencies, 134–7
coalition formation, 4–7, 11–18
  assumptions, 7, 8, 10
  and control, 14–16
  and ideology, *see* ideology
  in iterative situations, *see* coalitions, iterative
  under the redistributive condition, 22–6
  strategy in, 7, 23–6, 46, 103
coalition maintenance, 5, 6, 7, 11, 21, 25–7
coalition termination, 5, 7, 11, 21–2, 28–9, 31, 45–7, 126, 173
coalition theory
  assumptions, 1, 3, 4, 5, 7, 10–15, 20–48, 151–3
  incompatible preferences in, 5, 8, 27, 54, 169, 170
coalitions
  anti-competitive, 17–18, 99, 172
  collective goods in, 4, 167–8
  defined, 3
  episodic, *see* episodic condition
  governments, *see individual state entries*
  iterative, 15, 16, 18–19, 22–4, 98–9, 173
  payoffs, *see* payoffs
  private goods in, 3, 167–8
  redistributive, *see* redistributive condition
  size of, 3, 4, 12, 13, 49, 98, 100, 110, 167, 171
collective goods, 4, 167–8

193

Index

Communist Party of India, 57-8, 59
 base of support, viii, 57, 61
 in coalitions, 51, 54, 57, 58, 66, 68, 69, 70, 72, 73, 76, 85-7, 96, 109, 176
 in elections, 68, 72, 77, 80, 82
 leadership in, viii, 66
 policies of, 2, 56, 70, 78, 97
 strategy of, viii, 57, 76, 97, 113-15, 119
Communist Party of India (Marxist), 58-9
 base of support, viii, 58, 59, 61, 78, 143
 in coalitions, viii, 55, 59, 66, 68, 73, 76-81, 85-7, 109, 116, 126
 in elections, ix, 68, 72, 77, 80
 and the Naxalite Revolt, 77-8
 policies, 58, 97
 strategy, 55, 58, 59, 76, 97, 113-15, 119
competitive strategy, 1, 27-9, 33, 34-5, 37-41, 116-28, 133-4, 151, 173
 defined, 30-1, 117-19
 and the joint outcome, see joint outcome
 and longevity, 30, 37, 38, 42
 and payoffs, see payoffs
Congress Party
 base of support, 50, 61, 66, 68, 177
 in coalitions, 58, 67, 73, 75, 78, 87, 98-9
 defections from, x, 50, 62, 64, 66-8, 73, 76, 81, 84
 in elections, ix, 50, 56, 61-5, 68, 72, 77, 80, 81, 82, 90, 92
 leadership in, viii, ix, 68, 69, 81
 as national government, ix, 63, 77, 79
 and non-Congressism, see non-Congressism
 split in, ix, 52, 54, 57, 58, 59, 96, 180
 as state government, 68, 69, 72, 79, 81, 85
Congress (O), ix, 72
 coalitions with, 52, 54, 57, 59, 60, 72, 98, 149
Congress (R), see Congress Party
constituency contests, 134-7
content analysis, 130-3
cooperative strategy, 1, 18, 29, 33, 34-5, 37-41, 116-28, 133-4, 139, 151, 174
 defined, 30, 117-19
 and the joint outcome, see joint outcome
 and longevity, 30, 37, 38, 42
 and payoffs, see payoffs
Cortes, J. B., 182
credible threats, 44, 45, 144, 151
Curran, Jean, 175
Cutright, Phillips, 183

DMK, 62

Dalmianagar, 73
Dang, Satya Pal, 66
Das, Sunil, 55, 176
decision-makers, 5, 6, 152, 181
 incompatabilities among, 7, 27, 169
 and risk-taking, 41-4
 and size, see size of political actors
decision-making process, monopoly control of, 5, 10, 21, 27, 29, 36, 46, 90, 102-3, 112, 180
Deepak, Om Prakash, 56, 176
defectors
 obligations of, 127
 payoffs for, 64, 66-8, 69, 73, 75, 82, 83, 178
demands, 32-3
 credibility of, 44, 45, 144, 151
 frequency, 33, 34
 sequence, 33, 35, 40-1, 137
 severity, 35, 125-8
development, see economic development and political development
disequilibrium principle, 177
Donley, Richard, 182
Dravida Munnetra Kazhagam, 62

economic development, 61-3, 65, 182
elections in India
 midterm (1969-71), viii, x, xi, 52, 53, 57, 59, 67, 68, 71, 75, 79-80, 92, 109-10, 121-4, 138-40, 178
 1967, viii, xi, 50, 51, 56, 57, 61-5, 68, 76, 81, 91-2, 138-40
 1972, 54, 81, 91, 92, 121-4, 138-40
electoral adjustments, see pre-election alliances
episodic condition, 6-18, 169, 170, 173
 limitations of, 8, 9, 10, 21-2
Erdman, Howard, 175, 176, 181
essential members of winning coalitions, 174

fair constituency, 136
Festinger, L., 172
Fontera, R., 177
forward bloc, ix, 59, 77, 78, 80
forward bloc (Marxist), ix, 80
Forward, John, 182
Franda, Marcus, vii, 180, 183
Franklin, Mark, 171, 173
Frohlich, Norman, 168
Frye, R., 172

Gamson, William, 12-13, 168, 169, 171, 172, 173
 predictions for triad, 13-14, 99
 quoted, 7, 19

Index

Gandhi, Indira, ix, 57, 59
Gandhi, Mohandas K., ix
Gates, R. C., 172
Gill, Lachman Singh, 67
Ghosh, Ashutosh, ix, 79
Ghosh, Atulya, 79
Ghosh, P. C., 79
Gorkha League, ix, 80, 95
Govindan Nair, M. N., 86
Greenstone, J. David, 183
Groennings, Sven, 168, 172
Gujarat, 62
Gupta, C. B., 68, 69, 72
Gupta, Ram Prakash, 175
Guyer, Melvin, 34, 173
Gwalior, Rajmata of, 81, 83, 84

Haryana, 49, 56, 62, 64, 66
Heyns, J., 174
Hindu Maha Sabha, ix, 72, 97
Hindustan Times, 83, 116, 177, 178
Hoffman, P. J., 19, 172, 173
Hul Jharkhand, ix, 73, 76, 77
hypotheses, 26, 35, 42, 44, 45

ideology, 2, 5, 43, 96, 124
  and coalition formation, 7, 13, 93-4, 100-3, 169, 172
  important portfolios, 103-11, 120, 123-4, 125, 127, 137-8, 144, 179
income, by state, 61-3
incompatible preferences, 5, 8, 27, 54, 169, 170
Indian Election Commission, 136
Indian Express, 178
Indian National Congress, *see* Congress Party
Indian National Democratic Front, ix, 79, 80
Indian Socialist Party, ix, 86, 87
iterative coalitions, *see* coalitions, iterative
iterative games, 34

Jammu, 62
Jan Congress (Madhya Pradesh), x, 82
Jan Congress (Orissa), x, 53, 59, 81
Jana Congress, 68, 69
Jana Kranti Dal, x, 72, 73, 74, 77, 177
Jana Sangh, 50-3
  base of support, viii, ix, x, 61, 127, 143, 177
  in coalitions, x, 51, 54, 57, 59, 66, 68, 69, 70, 71, 72, 73, 76, 82-5, 109, 124-8, 148-50
  in elections, viii, 53, 68, 72, 77, 80, 82, 100

  leadership, 50, 83, 139, 148
  organization of, 52, 148-9, 175
  policies of, viii, 2, 50, 51, 54, 56, 70, 73, 76, 83, 97, 100, 125-7
  strategy of, 50-3, 113-15, 119, 124-8, 139
Janata Party (Bihar), x, 59, 74, 75, 77, 177
Janata Party (Punjab), x, 67, 68
Jhangiani, Motilal A., 175
Jharkhand, ix, x, 73, 74, 75, 77
joint outcome, 31, 37, 38, 39, 40, 42
Joshi, S. M., 176

Kamath, H. V., 74
Karshaka Thozhilali Party, 85
Kashmir, 62
Kashyap, Subhash C., 177, 178
Kelley, E. W., 168
Kelley, H., 172
Kerala, 85-7
  coalitions in, 49, 59, 62, 85-7
  elections in,, 56, 64
  government crisis in, 86-7
  united front, 85, 97, 100
Kerala Congress, 87
Kerala Socialist Party, 85
Khan, Akhtar Ali, 70
Kissan Mazdoor Party, x, 72
Kochanek, Stanley, 181
Kothari, Rajni, vii, 177, 179
Kunju, P. K., 85-6, 87
Kurup, P. R., 86
Kutch Satyagraha, 83, 86, 178

Lamborn, Alan, vii, 183
Lawrence, D. H., 172
Leiserson, Michael, 101, 168, 169, 179
Lieberman, B., 17, 172, 173
literacy, 65
local parties, *see* regional parties
Lohia, Rammanohar, 56, 57, 60, 94-5, 102, 179
Lok Sevak Dal, x, 82, 83
Loktantric Congress Dal, x, 73, 77
longevity, 30, 37, 38, 42

Madhya Pradesh, 81-5
  coalitions in, x, 49, 81-5, 98
  defections in, 62, 81, 82-3, 85
  elections in, 56, 62, 64
  government crisis in, 83-4
Madras, *see* Tamilnad
Maharashtra, 62
Maitra Kashi Kanya, 78
Mandal, B. P., 73
Masani, Minoo, 177
Master Akali Dal, *see* Akali Dal (Master)

195

Index

Master Tara Singh, viii
Mathur, Jagdish Prasad, 175
McClelland, David, 129–30, 174, 182
Meckery, Francis, 54, 176
Mehendiratta, P., vii
memory, 33
minimal winning coalition, *see* coalitions, size of
minimum programs, 54, 56, 66, 71, 77, 78, 81, 85, 125–6, 176
ministries, distribution of, *see* cabinet portfolios
minority groups, 64–5
Mishra, D. P., 81, 85
Mitra, Roma, 56, 176
Mitra, Subrata Kumar, vii, 177, 180
mixed strategy, 29–41, 116–28, 133–7, 139, 141–8, 151–2, 173, 174
 defined, 31, 117–19
monopoly control, *see* decision-making process, monopoly control of
Morehouse, Ward, 177
Morgenstern, Oscar, 168
motivation, 41–4, 107, 129–50, 154
Mukherjee, Ajoy, viii, 76, 77, 78–9, 80, 116
multi-cornered contests, 63–4, 100
Muslim League, x, 51, 59, 85, 87, 97
Mysore, 62

n-achievement, *see* need for achievement
naive actors, 20–1, 26–7
Namboodiripad, E. M. S., 86–7, 181
Narain, Raj, 60
national government, ix, 63, 77, 79
National Herald, 75, 178
national parties, 180
 see also individual party entries
Naxalite revolt, 77–8
need for achievement, 45–6, 129–50
 defined, 41, 129–33, 182
 and redistributive payoffs, 137–40
 and risk-taking, 2, 41–4, 134–7
 and strategic preferences, 133–7, 151, 174
need for affiliation, 130, 174
need for power, 130
Nijiliagappa, ix
non-Congressism, 2, 50, 53, 54, 55, 56–7, 60, 93–5, 101–3, 176
*n*th iteration, 25–8, 29, 46, 167
number of candidates, 63–4, 100

Ofshe, Lynne, 172, 173
Ofshe, Richard, 172, 173
Olson, Mancur, 168
Oppenheimer, Joe, 168

Ordeshook, Peter, 36, 167, 168, 171, 174
organizational capabilities, 44–5, 52, 53, 89, 110, 114–15, 134, 140–7, 151–2
Organski, A. F. K., vii, 183
Orissa, x, 49, 53, 55, 62, 64, 81

PDA, 70, 126
PSP, *see* Praja Socialist Party
Pakistan, 66
parity norm, 8, 10, 12, 23–4, 25–7, 31, 103–8, 109, 170, 171, 173
 defined, 9, 12–13
Park, Richard, vii
Paswan, Bhola, *see* Shastri, Bhola Paswan
Patriot, 74–5, 177, 178
patronage, 103–4, 138, 149, 171
payoffs, 1, 6–7, 10, 18, 20
 disproportionalities in, 8–10, 17, 32–3, 34–5, 104–6, 107, 123–4, 151
 non-redistributive, 8, 16, 26, 92–3, 105
 redistributive, 20–1, 27–30, 31, 33, 37, 38, 45–6, 92–3, 103–11, 116–28, 137–50, 151, 173
 and strategy, 34–5, 37, 38–9, 112–28
People's Republic of China, viii
personality, 41–4
pivotal power, 8, 13–14, 69, 99, 108, 109, 170, 172, 180
policy goals, 30, 31, 125–7, 149, 180
political development, 151, 155–6
political influence, 1, 3, 8, 10, 20, 25, 26–8, 29, 30–1, 45, 90, 107, 112–28, 139–48, 151–3, 170, 180
political parties
 success of, 6, 49, 104–5, 113–15, 120–4, 134–7, 139–48, 180
 see also individual political parties and size of political actors
political recruitment, 141, 154–5, 183
portfolios, *see* cabinet portfolios *and* important portfolios
Praja Socialist Party, x, 54–5, 61, 74
 in coalitions, 54, 55, 69, 71, 72, 73, 81, 82, 96, 109, 127
 in elections, 68, 72, 77, 80, 82
 policies, 54, 55, 73, 74, 78, 97
 strategy of, 54, 55, 113–15, 119, 127
Prasad, Mahamaya, 73, 74, 75
predispositions, 39, 41, 107
 risk-taking, 132–3, 134, 154–5
 strategic, 116–19, 140–1, 147, 154
pre-election alliances, 56, 63–4, 76, 81, 94, 95, 97–8, 100, 178
preference equation, 36–7, 42–4, 134, 174
President's Rule, uses of, 50, 67, 68, 71, 72, 74, 75, 76, 79, 81
Preventive Detention Act, 70, 126

196

Index

prisoner's dilemma, 34
private goods, 3, 167-8
protocoalitions, 95-100, 179
Punjab, viii, x, 51, 66-8
   coalitions in, x, 49, 51, 62, 66-8, 72, 98
   elections in, 52, 64, 68
Putnam, Robert, 183

Rabushka, Alvin, 179
radios per thousand population, 65
Rahman, M. M., 181
Raj Narain, 60
Raja Naresh Chandra Singh, 85
Raja of Ramgarh, x, 72, 73, 74, 75, 77
Rajagopalachari, C., 54
Rajasthan, 50, 56
Rajmata of Gwalior, 81, 83, 84
Ram, Mohan, 181
Ramgarh, Raja of, *see* Raja of Ramgarh
Rann of Kutch, 83, 86, 178
Raynor, Joel, 130, 182
recruitment, 141, 154-5, 183
redistributive condition, 11, 19-30, 151-3
   coalition formation under, 22-6
   strategy under, 7, 18, 23-6, 27-30, 46, 103
   see also payoff, redistributive
redistributive equation, 32-6, 37, 38
regional parties, 49, 72, 107, 180
religious minorities, 64-5
remote constituencies, 134-7
Republican Party of India, x, 59, 66, 67, 68, 69, 72, 73, 77, 80, 109
Revolutionary Socialist Party of India, xi, 59, 77, 78, 85, 87
Riker, William, 12-13, 36, 99, 167, 168, 169, 171, 172, 174, 177, 179
risk-taking, 2, 36-44, 132, 134-7, 141, 149, 174
Rohtos industries, 73, 127
Rossi, Peter, 183
Rudolph, Lloyd, 177, 183
Rudolph, Susanne, 177, 183
Russett, Bruce, 169
Russia, *see* Soviet Union

SSP, *see* Samyukta Socialist Party
SUC, xi, 80
SVD, *see individual state entries*, coalitions in *and* pre-election alliances
Saklecha, Virenda, 83
Samyukta Socialist Party, ix, x, xi, 60, 61, 86, 117
   in coalitions, 66, 68, 69, 70, 72, 73, 78, 82, 85-6, 109, 148-50
   in elections, xi, 68, 72, 77, 80, 82, 110
   land revenue policy, 69-70, 83, 125-6

leadership, 56, 57, 78, 148, 149
policies, 56, 78, 83, 97, 127, 176
strategy, 56-7, 113-15, 119
Samyukta Vidhayak Dal, *see* pre-election alliances *and individual state entries*, coalitions in
Sant Akali Dal, *see* Akali Dal (Sant)
Satyagraha, 83, 86, 178
scheduled castes, *see* caste
Schelling, Thomas, 169
Schlesinger, Joseph A., 183
Sen, Bhowani, 181
Shapley, Lloyd S., 170, 171
Shastri, Bhola Paswan, 73, 74, 75, 76, 177
Shepsle, Kenneth, vii, 179
Shoshit Dal, 73, 75, 76, 77, 177
Shukla, Shyama Charan, 85
side-payments, 8, 34, 168, 171, 173
Singer, J. David, 167
Singh, Baswan, 74
Singh, Charan, *see* Charan Singh
Singh, G. N., 81-5
Singh, Gurnam, 67
Singh, Hari Kishore, 181
Singh, Harihar, 75, 76
Singh, Raja Naresh Chandra, 85
Singh, Suraj Narain, 74
single-party dominance, 63, 179
Sinha, Mahamaya Prasad, 73, 74, 75
Sino-Indian War, 58
size of political actors, 5, 6, 9-10, 19, 22-6, 29, 95-100, 102-8, 113-15, 140, 151, 152-3, 154
   defined, 89-91, 168
   see also coalitions, size of
size principle, *see* coalitions, size of
Socialist Unity Conference, xi, 80
Soviet Union, viii, 101
Statesman, 84, 116, 177, 178
Stokes, Donald E., vii
strategy in coalitions, 7, 23-6, 46,103
   see also competitive strategy, cooperative strategy, mixed strategy, payoffs, *individual political party entries and individual state entries*
subjectively minimal winning coalition, 13
Supreme Court, 75
Swarajya, 54
Swatantra Party, 53-4
   base of support, xi, 54, 61, 70, 175
   in coalitions, x, 52, 53, 54, 57, 59, 68, 69, 70, 75, 81, 109
   in elections, xi, 53, 68, 72, 77, 80, 81, 82
   leadership, 53, 70, 139, 177
   policies, 53, 54, 70, 97, 125
   strategy, 53, 54, 113-15, 119, 139
Syndicate, *see* Congress (O)

Index

TAT, see Thematic Appperception Test
Tamilnad, 50, 56, 62, 64
Thakur, Karpuri, 176
Thematic Apperception Test, 129, 130, 132
Thomas, Gouri, 85
Thomas, T. V., 86
Times of India, 67, 74, 116, 177, 178
Tiwari, Ramanand, 176
tolerance limits, 29, 30, 31, 32–3, 34, 37, 40, 44, 45, 46, 151
trade unions, 55, 59, 70, 126
tribals, 64, 65

Uesugi, T., 172
uncertainty, 39–40, 41, 45, 133–7
United Front, see pre-election alliances, *and individual state entries*, coalitions in *and* united fronts in
United Punjab Janta Party, x, 67, 68
United States of America, 143–4
Upadhyaya, Deendayal, 50–1, 175
urbanization, 65
Urdu, 127
utility, 36, 37, 42, 101, 174, 179
Uttar Pradesh, 68–72
  coalitions in, 49, 54, 68–72, 98, 108–10, 124–8

defections in, 62, 70, 71
elections in, 52, 62, 64

Vajpayee, Atal Bihari, 175
Veroff, J., 174
Vinacke, W., 172, 173
Von Neumann, John, 168
vote banks, 144, 178

Weiner, Myron, 177, 181
West Bengal, 76–81
  coalitions in, ix, xi, 49, 54, 55, 62, 76–81, 98, 116–17
  defections in, ix, 79
  united fronts in, ix, 54, 64, 76, 97, 100
Willis, R., 172
Winter, David, 182
Wolff, H., 172
Worker's Party, 80

Young, Oran, 168

Zagoria, Donald, 176
Zander, Alvin, 182
Zeckhauser, Richard, 168
zero-sum assumption, 6, 10, 169